13 Acts of Academic Journalism and Historical Commentary
on Human Rights

POLITICAL AND SOCIAL CHANGE

Edited by Martin Bak Jørgensen and Óscar García Agustín

VOLUME 6

Zu Qualitätssicherung und Peer Review der vorliegenden Publikation

Die Qualität der in dieser Reihe erscheinenden Arbeiten wird vor der Publikation durch einen Herausgeber der Reihe sowie durch einen externen, von der Herausgeberschaft ernannten Gutachter im Blind-Verfahren geprüft. Dabei ist der Autor der Arbeit dem Gutachter während der Prüfung namentlich nicht bekannt.

Notes on the quality assurance and peer review of this publication

Prior to publication, the quality of the work published in this series is reviewed by one of the editors of the series and blind reviewed by an external referee appointed by the editorship. The referee is not aware of the author's name when performing the review.

Ben Dorfman

13 Acts of Academic Journalism and Historical Commentary on Human Rights

Opinions, Interventions and the Torsions of Politics

Bibliographic Information published by the Deutsche Nationalbibliothek
The Deutsche Nationalbibliothek lists this publication in the Deutsche Nationalbibliografie; detailed bibliographic data is available in the internet at http://dnb.d-nb.de.

Library of Congress Cataloging-in-Publication Data
Names: Dorfman, Ben, author.
Title: 13 acts of academic journalism and historical commentary on human rights opinions, interventions and the torsions of politics / Ben Dorfman.
Other titles: Thirteen acts of academic journalism and historical commentary on human rights
Description: Frankfurt am Main ; New York : Peter Lang GmbH, Internationaler Verlag der Wissenschaften, [2017] | Series: Political and social change, ISSN 2198-8595 ; Vol. 6
Identifiers: LCCN 2017011606| ISBN 9783631722336 (print) | ISBN 9783631723357 (e-pdf) | ISBN 9783631723364 (epub) | ISBN 9783631723371 (mobi)
Subjects: LCSH: Human rights. | Press and politics.
Classification: LCC JC571 .D758 2017 | DDC 323—dc23 LC record available at https://lccn.loc.gov/2017011606

Cover Image: © ThamKC / Fotolia.com

Printed by CPI books GmbH, Leck

ISSN 2198-8595
ISBN 978-3-631-72233-6 (Print)
E-ISBN 978-3-631-72335-7 (E-PDF)
E-ISBN 978-3-631-72336-4 (EPUB)
E-ISBN 978-3-631-72337-1 (MOBI)
DOI 10.3726/b11280

© Peter Lang GmbH
Internationaler Verlag der Wissenschaften
Frankfurt am Main 2017
All rights reserved.
Peter Lang Edition is an Imprint of Peter Lang GmbH.

Peter Lang – Frankfurt am Main · Bern · Bruxelles · New York ·
Oxford · Warszawa · Wien

This publication has been peer reviewed.

www.peterlang.com

To my students and children. Thank you.

Acknowledgements

This book is a result of the two and a half years of reflections on global affairs, historical issues and human rights. It wouldn't exist without my students, reflections on my children and the many extraordinary people I've met through my now not-short career who have suggested that I should handle the issues I'd like to address my own way, and compose what amounts to an activist book. Our work as academics, intellectuals and, indeed, civic-minded members of the public at-large *must* concern the realization of people's basic dignity and essential human equality. Come the twenty-first century, the road to such things has become too long. It's time to begin to find an end to certain of our social and political journeys and to let the freedom and dignity of all human beings shine through.

Among those progressively-minded individuals encouraging the work behind this book are most certainly Óscar Garcia Agustín and Martin Bak Jørgensen, the editors of this worthwhile series. Their own work on issues concerned with problems of social injustice and political right has been inspiring and, with the current series, they've created a home for those who not only want to address such problems at-large, but do so creatively and in a different voice. Their work and collegiality have been decisive for this book.

In addition to the series editors, I'd like to express my thanks to Barbara J. Falk, Peter Hervik, Kalle Pihlainen, Peter Hervik, Kirsten Jæger and Sandro Nickel, all of whom provided valuable commentary on earlier versions of the work. I would also like to thank the Department of Culture and Global Studies and the Faculty of Humanities at Aalborg University as both provided invaluable support for this project. Department Chair Marianne Rostgaard deserves particular thanks for her interest. Thanks also go to Patrick Thomas Casey, the project's copyeditor and style commentator. His attention to detail greatly helped the final product to emerge.

Of course, no investigative or expressive act can be arrived at without the influence of others. For the many friends, family and loved ones contributing to my intellectual development and providing atmospheres in which I could finish this project, I'm grateful. I offer special thanks to my parents, Eve Kenyon and Bruce Dorfman, for imbuing me, each in their own way, with a spirit of humanity and universal justice.

Ben Dorfman
Portland, Oregon
November 2016

Contents

Introduction: The Torsions of Politics

Human Rights and Where We Are (And a Discussion of "Historical Commentary" and "Academic Journalism") (November 21, 2016)

It's been two years – perhaps two and a half by the time this finally shows up in print – like few others. The war that was announced to have ended all the way back in 2003 most decidedly has not (the Iraq War – now partly morphed into civil war in Syria), the world's supposedly most reliable source of rights-based politics (Europe) has become awash in oft-shocking levels of xenophobia as it's dealt with a flood of migrants from precisely the locales where war *doesn't* seem to stop, the United States, supposedly the world's *other* great example of democratic practice, has elected a what might be a pseudo-demagogue to be its next President (the controversial Donald Trump), and we've seen so many fluctuations in the supposedly good-for-everyone liberal global financial system that what are supposed to be First World countries like Greece have needed to be bailed out – that to say nothing of the bailout of the American auto industry some years before. In certain ways, all is fine. Democracy still functions in places like Europe and the U.S., people – at least many of them – maintain access to their bank accounts, and for every civil rights crackdown in countries like Turkey or Egypt, there seem to be demonstrations reminding us that such things aren't ok. Those are the good signs. The bad signs are wars that *don't* seem to stop (what *will* bring the fighting in Syria to an end?), intercultural conflicts of which many in the world's dominant political geographies seem to be barely aware (religious conflict on the Indian subcontinent, e.g.) and the fact that ranges of countries either continue to support dictators or have taken newly authoritarian turns (are you a part of that trend, America?). Humanitarians can take comfort in their victories – the legalization of gay marriage in the United States, say, or UN attention to dire rights situations in locales from North Korea to South Sudan. Humanitarians stand agog, however, as bombs explode in European capitals, Western politicians invoke vocabularies of force and poverty continues to plague large parts of the world. For all the activism out there, the mountain of difficulties we face on the global stage can challenge the fortitude of one's convictions, making it hard, at least sometimes, to find the spirit to get out and fight.

The current project is an imperfect – perhaps deeply imperfect – attempt to address at least *some* of these issues as well as a few more, largely of a historical nature. I can't explain *all* the dimensions of the work here except to say that I've felt compelled to respond to a variety of problems confronting our world and reflect on others related to milieus of social and political justice from not particularly distant pasts. I've been interested to enter into general conversation – conversation from the positions in which I stand – as well as to latch such conversation into discussions about and concrete regimes of human rights; that with rights standing as perhaps the preeminent socio-political discourse of our times. The issues to which I've responded to are simply those which entered my view over a particular period of time: roughly the end of 2014 to the first half of 2016. The notion of "general conversation" emerges from my sense of the role of the academic: that some need to be generalists and broader-scale, more subjective communicators over and above dedicated specialists whose call sign is the deepest levels of science. The focus on rights again derives from notions that they're the present day's ultimate socio-political concept – the idea or ideal by which many of us register how things "ought" to be and which represent mile-markers regarding successful approaches to international affairs and domestic politics. This book's pieces are "scholarly;" they rely extensively, perhaps decisively, on academic convention and debate. Still, I prefer notions of "academic journalism" and "historical commentary" – that as I've attempted to speak in a *somewhat* different voice and with a different purpose and style. If I could classify this book as *The New Yorker* with footnotes, I would. Unfortunately, such characterizations don't fully work as the writing isn't up to that kind of snuff and the articles can get a little caught in the academic muck and mire. Still, I have attempted to work subjectively and based on opinion wherein, though invoking a particular set of academic knowledges and skills, I've sought to paint with a broader brush and work via a slightly more "public intellectual" approach.

I'd like to say something about the latter concept first. Modern academics is a mixed bag. It's filled with dedicated teachers, supporters of general education projects, individuals invested in civic enlightenment ideals as well as more than a few activists. The increase in disciplinary specialization since the end of the Second World War is a well-known trend. With the expansion in both the size and number of global universities, detailed work that's beyond the reach of most members of the general public has become much of what modern academic life is about.[1] Still, academics descend the stairs of the ivory tower frequently enough. I.e., regardless of demands that they often write primarily for those in their field,

---

1   See, e.g., Jerry A. Jacobs, *In Defense of Disciplines: Interdisciplinarity and Specialization in the Research University* (Chicago: University of Chicago Press, 2013); Russel Jacoby, *The Last Intellectuals: American Culture in the Age of Academe* (New York: Basic Books, 1987).

many in the humanities and social sciences – those *I* know anyway – would characterize their work as concerned with a higher purpose: amelioratory projects of one kind or another, or general attempts to do good.[2] That means critical thought. It means investigations of how things "are." It means breaking down cultural assumptions and getting audiences – us – to think about the socio-political issues by which we find ourselves confronted. Indeed, some even line themselves up with *specific* sets of causes or the work of one or the other political *party*. There is an active and in fact *quite* public element to contemporary academic life.[3]

Still, the ivory tower *can* be high – how many from the general public in fact *could* read the works written by most in the contemporary liberal arts? – and the demand that academics carve out niches for themselves often means that while many university and college professors have opinions about the goings-on of their times, those opinions have to be expressed obliquely and with discomfort, sometimes *great* discomfort, about stepping outside the zones in which they are technically "expert." One critic has discussed "myopia" – that whereas college faculty were once automatically figures with public roles, today's professorial class is boxed into modes of expression so narrow that senses of the at-large intellectual have gone into retreat.[4] "Myopia" feels harsh. Again, at least among those *I* know, more than a few keep an eye on the larger picture and have concerns about *ranges* of socio-political issues. Still, the nature of scholarship *qua* business is that it *can* from time to time be difficult to speak out of one's values first and that it's less than easy to find ways to bridge the kind of writing one finds, say, in *feuilletons*, with something also leading readers to the depth and maze of closer scholarly

---

2   See David Croteau, William Hoynes, and Charlotte Ryan, eds., *Rhyming Hope and History: Activists, Academics, and Social Movement Scholarship* (Minneapolis: University of Minnesota Press, 2005).

3   The "post-Marxism" of figures like Ernesto Laclau or Chantal Mouffe, or the "return" to Marx by a figure like Slavoj Žižek, would be examples. Though I'm personally less supportive of it, so would the attempt to "renew" social democracy by figures like Anthony Giddens. See Philip Goldstein, *Post-Marxist Theory: An Introduction* (Albany: SUNY Press, 2005); Ernesto Laclau and Chantal Mouffe, *Hegemony and Socialist Strategy: Towards a Radical Democratic Politics* (London: Verso, 1985): Aijaz Ahmad, "Three 'Returns' to Marx: Derrida, Zizek, Baidou," *Social Scientist* 40, nos. 7/8 (2012): 43–59; Anthony Giddens, *The Third Way: The Renewal of Social Democracy* (Cambridge: Polity, 1998).

4   See Jacoby, *The End of Utopia: Politics and Culture in an Age of Apathy* (New York: Basic Books, 1999).

debate. Simply put, it's not easy being a commentator and at-large essayist at the same time that one tries to be an academic technician too.[5]

I haven't combined those things perfectly here – far from it. Indeed, I've perhaps attempted to do something one can't – write at the interstices of newspaper reporting, the personal essay and articles of a peer-reviewed kind. I've perhaps tried to make an impossible landing at the crossroads of the academic monograph and the casual observer's blog – the "me" and something more substantive. Indeed, reflecting on some of the essays in this book, one finds some funny elements. Explanatory footnotes sometimes take up more than half the page, and there's a good deal of material to be mined in those notes (ironic when "academic rigidity" is something I've tried to avoid). The "straight" scholarship sometimes happens *in* those notes while the main text stands as something more mannered. The "artistic" parts of the writing – the "essayistic" dimensions of the pieces – sometimes work and sometimes don't. Writing in a more subjective, impressionistic and "activist" style is new to me, and the smoothness of the prose hits rather more bumps (sometimes many more) than I'd like. This book's essays *can* be back-loaded – there's a lot of historical scene-setting, and it sometimes takes some substantial introductions before the central points set in. The language occasionally gets caught up in its own momentum as there can be a lot (a *lot*) of ideas at play at once. The impetus, however – the *goal* – has been attempting to offer at least *some* plain statements and a more "natural" approach to discussing particular issues at the same time as allowing non-academics to hold at least *some* of the ropes that those in universities and think-tanks use to repel down every day. I.e., I've sought to stand as *some* kind of example of the spirit of commentary while tipping my cap to the fact that scientific researchers have complex perspectives on points many *assume* to be particular ways – wherein we should learn from those who live up close with topics for extended periods of time. This book constitutes *my* reactions to social and political scenes – scenes in which I sometimes also step well outside my comfort zone to put in my own two cents. Non-academics or students who pick up this volume may well say "ok, there's an academic at work" – that while there's some in the academic world who may ask "what precisely *is* this?" If there's any way in which I've combined both – a spirit of art and adventure with a modicum of scholarly knowledge – I'll count the project as a win.

A word about that on which about I've chosen to write. This project moved forward in fits and starts. It began as an attempt to write a traditional monograph

---

5   See Jonathan D. Culler and Kevin Lamb, eds., *Just Being Difficult?: Academic Writing in the Public Arena* (Stanford: Stanford University Press, 2003).

about human rights' nature, arguing that while rights are perceived as an "absolute" (they're understood as near-metaphysical, or simply "there"), they are, in fact, historically-based. Rights didn't exist once, and they may well not exist again.[6] That's at the same time that, though rights might not be something towards which all human history has pointed – a "necessary" end to our historical experiences – we have the right to believe in them nonetheless (i.e., rights man-made nature doesn't detract from their value). Now, I can hear some readers asking "how come he didn't write *that* book; that sounds interesting to me?" My problem was that, in what seems to be an era when reference to rights has become especially rife, so *many* issues came across my television set, into my online space, were featured in the newspapers that I read and entered my personal domains – issues revolving around rights – that I felt compelled to discuss *those* problems as well. There were simply so *many* problems and goings-on about which I felt I had something to say. As any writer knows, time is always a problem. One can't do everything one wants. I thus choose the latter path: commentary on contemporary and historical events with a view towards how *I* reacted to issues given an interest in speaking broadly and deploying the particular knowledge bases that I have. That work began in October 2014. Over the end of 2014 and the start of 2015, it generated a range of essays that gained critique, and then had to be rethought and sometimes reset (framed in relation to different topics and events). Practical issues of teaching and administration generated a pause in the writing. The project took off again from the beginning of 2016 on. Therein, in terms of the dates of the essays, there's an early piece before a temporal gap, after which the other twelve pieces are noted as composed. I've simply decided to present the essays based on their compositional chronology – that as opposed to thematic arrangements suggesting a more monographical focus than there actually is.

Now, *if* the dates we're talking about roughly *are* October 2014 to May 2016 (a little over a year and a half), there are *massive* numbers of issues about which I could have written. One issue that fell out of this book, e.g. – an area on which there originally *was* a piece – is the problem of the right to health, development and a clean environment; something I packaged in an earlier essay on the Ebola

---

6   Rights scholar Jack Donnelly, e.g., has written that "no society, civilization, or culture prior to the seventeenth century…had a widely-endorsed practice, or even vision, of equal and inalienable human rights." The reference to the seventeenth century is to a post-Renaissance/Enlightenment start date for rights. The larger point, however, is rights' historicity. See Donnelly, "The Relative Universality of Human Rights," *Human Rights Quarterly* 29, no. 2 (2007), 284–5. See also Lynn Hunt, *Inventing Human Rights: A History* (New York: W.W. Norton & Co., 2007).

crisis. That was left out in deference playing to my strengths – social, political and historical issues. That was again in view of the amount of time I had. To write about events as they unfold, including in a manner picking-up on at least *some* degree of scholarly literature and debate, is no easy task. The choices here reflect one man in his lifeworld – a bit like a game show contestant grabbing whatever dollar bills he or she can as they stand in one of those booths that blow them around.

I don't want to overdo issues of process – the ultimate question being *what* one has said as opposed to how one has said it. The "grabbing dollar bills" idea, however, *has* importance to this work as one of its goals, including the choice of a chronological, diary-esque presentation, has been to reflect *how* we operate – the ways in which we relate to flows of information, *how* we come into contact with socio-political issues and the ways in which we see the unfolding of history's "concatenations" from the perspectives that we do. Throughout this book, I try to avoid much name-checking or extensive references to academic schools or philosophical movements (at least I largely attempt to leave such things to the footnotes). Still, I *have* always been attracted to notions advanced by a group of philosophers towards the start of the twentieth century which claim that there's an inevitability to one standing where one does, and that one *must* and only *can* speak from the perspectives and locations that one has (that movement being Phenomenology, an early twentieth century forerunner to existential philosophy).[7] That's a large – extremely large – component of the writing here: me speaking from where *I* am in relation to what has caught *my* eye. I.e., the "process" or "genre" issue suggests two things. First, people have the right to be interested in what they want. Ideas that everyone "must" take notice of something may be true in a way; many activists want attention paid to their causes, and justly so. Still, we need to tune-in to the fact that people *will* take interest in

---

7   Specifically, Edmund Husserl, phenomenology's founding father, made the observation that above all, one finds oneself in a "world" – an environment, or space, in which one is surrounded by things "literal" and "figurative" (both physical things and concepts). His point was very much the "finding oneself" – that there's simply no way around *that* one is experiencing what one is and that one sees what one does (we approach the world in a "natural attitude," he maintained). Now, Husserl proposed that we could get behind our "natural" condition – that it was possible to discover how objects were "constituted." In terms of how culture functions, however, and how those of us simply living in the world relate to our lives, the point was that we see things as we see them and discuss what we see in the ways that we do (i.e., relating to our naive existence). See Husserl, *Ideas Pertaining to a Pure Phenomenology and to a Phenomenological Philosophy, First Book*, trans. F. Kersten (The Hague: Martinus Nijhoff, 1983), 56. See also Dermot Moran, *Introduction to Phenomenology* (London: Routledge, 2002).

the things that they do, and that approaching the world from our perspectives – those that we have for whatever reasons we have them – is humanity's basic work. Second, my sense is that what professional humanists and social scientists *might* do is *magnify* such tasks – i.e., the liberal arts academic might do what everyone does *anyway*, just with more detail, or perhaps a bit more provocation or aplomb. I've thus written in the way that I have – again, in a style I would call "academic journalism" and "historical commentary" – to signal that I am who I am and that we have to accept the ways that each one of us is. That becomes an invitation for others to be who *they* are, explaining what *they* might see – that so dialogue can begin.[8] This book represents a *quite* subjective enterprise based on the suggestion that we all muddle through the situations we have as best as we can.

Now, that being said, it *is* appropriate to say something about the themes of this book – to exceed the formal discussion, as such. Again, human rights *are* this book's unqualified focus – a point to which I'll get in a moment. In the context of discussing rights, however, I often engage themes of historical evolution and cultural identity – issues stemming from the domains of historical and cultural studies in which I in fact have some modicum of background. I.e., there's a tendency among this book's essays to dodge in and out of simply asserting that things "are" a particular way, and to lean heavily on qualification. There's a lot of looking at different *angles* of identity and historical evolution, and speculating on how things *might* be considered or thought about were they to be a particular way. That's derived from my sense of how history tends to be written – the fact that historians do little if not take multiple positions on issues that are one and the same. It also concerns problems of pinning down identities in any concrete, or "final," sense – a cultural studies concern. E.g., was the Holocaust a "unique" event, or did it involve trends present in *every* genocide? Are histories of global conflict tied primarily to the role of great powers, or are they generated mainly at levels of region and locality? *Must* oppression be the lens through which we view the pasts of women and ethnic minorities, or have disenfranchised groups often exercised what might be surprising – indeed, decisive – levels of agency while *appearing* to be pushed to history's margins? There are advantages and disadvantages to multiple sides of various arguments. In any case, such questions are the bread and butter of historical and culturological investigation. They involve basic analytical sensibilities regarding historical, social and cultural issues. Providing a feeling for those sensibilities plays into the background of nearly all this book's

---

8   See, e.g., Calvin O. Schrag, *Radical Reflection and the Origin of the Human Sciences* (West Lafayette: Purdue University Press, 1980).

essays. It doesn't always help lighten the writing. Intellectually, however, they felt important to engage.[9]

In this vein, however, *another* problem that emerges in this book is some of the presumptions I use regarding relations between the "West" and the "non-West" – or, as I prefer, the world to which the West expanded and colonized in more than one sense, and those who did the bulk of the expanding and the colonizing. I.e., though attempting to introduce a degree of historiographical finesse and sensitivity to cultural identity, I often argue that what's been characterized as the world's political, economic and cultural "core" has historically retained and *currently* retains essentially oppressive relations with much of the world around it. Now, that's not indefensible. As eminent historian Eric Hobsbawm once phrased it, it's hard to discuss the difference between the "developed" and develop*ing* worlds without feeling "frustrated" – that as there's an industrialized world with European roots that has done well for itself over the past two or three hundred years while the destiny of so many others has been so often thrown into doubt.[10] I.e., many lead precarious existences, and the reality of exploitation, not only in economic senses, but in social, cultural and political senses, means that arguments about global "peripheries" may not be so far-fetched.[11] That's while we need take care. There *are* questions about what "exploitation" means, and one *has to* recognize that intense levels of independence have been fought for and won, sometimes at considerable cost.[12] When one advocates for basic justice – something at the heart of each of this book's essays – there *can* be a risk that one sees so *much* oppression that one disenfranchises those who have in fact worked tirelessly to throw off imperialism's yolk. One can sometimes minimize those who have shed significant blood, sweat and tears to become free.[13]

---

9   See Georg Iggers, *Historiography in the Twentieth Century: From Scientific Objectivity to the Postmodern Challenge* (Middletown: Wesleyan University Press, 1997); Simon Gunn, *History and Cultural Theory* (Harlow: Pearson Longman, 2006).

10 Eric Hobsbawm, *The Age of Empire: 1875–1914* (New York: Vintage, 1989), 25.

11 On the dynamics of "core" "periphery," see Immanuel Wallerstein, *World-Systems Analysis: An Introduction* (Durham, NC: Duke University Press, 2004).

12 See, e.g., Martin Thomas, *Fight or Flight: Britain, France, and Their Roads from Empire* (Oxford: Oxford University Press, 2014).

13 It's worth noting that the entire issue of imperialism is both a theoretically and historically massive topic. On one hand, there are claims by serious commentators asserting that, be it "capitalism, nationalism…secularism, liberalism, populism, socialism, communism, Marxism, modernism…evolutionism, the idea of progress, scientific knowledge, applied technology and the idea of the nation-state," the forces shaping life outside the West have been "European [in] origin and provenance." Indeed, figures like

No doubt. Using the vocabularies of one scholar of cultural imperialism – though in some ways reversing the meaning from what she intended – the "subaltern," or those on the margins, may *well* "speak."[14] I.e., pop the lid off our presumptions about the past and one can see "whole world[s] of struggle and resistance," to say nothing of decided wins.[15] *Massive* regions *have* been decolonized, and oppressed peoples have found liberation of a kind that's more than just chimera. Still, it's not just that important historians may have taken the view that locales like Europe and North America have often used the rest of the world as their personal playgrounds. It's also not only that *historically*, a small number of players once retained significant control over large portions of the globe. It's that one has to explain distributions of global cultural power and economic wealth as well as questions of who holds what amounts of the world's military might and why *today*. One has to clarify how we've ended up in situations where global privilege *continues* to unevenly play out, and that certain global regions appear to sit more in the driver's seat than others. Of the twenty wealthiest countries in the world by per capita GDP, e.g., seventeen lie in North America and Europe. Extend the list ten more spaces, and one adds another three or four more Western states

---

the intellectual Edward Said have portrayed virtually the entire developing world as the object of a colonizing "gaze" from the West. Again, though, there are dangers in such unidirectional senses of power, and, as new research is bringing to light, levels of resistance to colonial and imperial structures may have been yet more intense than thought – that already acknowledging that anti-colonialism is a well-recognized historical trend and that it's dangerous to simply assume *anything* about historical agency. See Sadik J. Al-Azm, "Western Historical Thinking from an Arabian Perspective," in *Western Historical Thinking: An Intercultural Debate*, ed. Jörn Rüsen (New York: Berghahn, 2002), 121; Edward Said, *Orientalism* (New York: Vintage, 1978); Said, *Culture and Imperialism* (New York: Vintage, 1993); Richard Gott, *Britain's Empire: Resistance, Repression, Revolt* (London: Verso, 2011). See also Bill Ashcroft, Gareth Griffiths and Helen Tiffin, eds., *The Post-Colonial Studies Reader* (London: Routledge, 1995).

14 See Gayatri Chakravorty Spivak, "Can the Subaltern Speak?" in *Marxism and the Interpretation of Culture*, ed. Cary Nelson and Lawrence Grossberg (Urbana: University of Illinois Press, 1988), 217–314. Spivak's point was actually skepticism towards the potential of independent "speech" on the part of either the post-colonial critic or the colonized themselves – a concept intended as a liberating observation by opening the eyes of those critical towards colonialism to their sometimes-unintentional reinforcement of colonialism's thoughtways. My sense is to take a less circuitous route. People have agency and may speak – that though sometimes against mountainously high odds.

15 Donald M. MacRaild and Avram Taylor, *Social Theory and Social History* (New York: Palgrave, 2004), 127.

(perhaps five, if one somehow includes Israel in that count).[16] Obviously, NATO stands as the world's largest military alliance (a Euro-American concoction), and be it Coca-Cola, Hollywood or global standards for fashion and style, intense arguments can be made that the preponderance of influence regarding the form and function of consumer items, media artifacts and the aesthetics of public space are *also* dominated by European and North American ideas. There are always exceptions. One has to be careful with blanket statements. However, politically, economically and culturally, one may need to fight to be seen. That's especially if one *isn't* from the privileged locales of North America or Western Europe.[17]

Again, fair enough. Power is complex, and it's not out of bounds to stake-out baseline positions and leave the rest to debate. Still, the *most* central theme of this book – the question on which every essay turns – *is* human rights. The focus of this book ultimately *is* what one scholar has termed our "highest moral precepts and political ideals" – a phrase one reads several times over the several essays that constitute this work.[18] I.e., though historical power relations and detailed sensibilities concerning cultural identity figure into large portions of the pieces here, my primary concern *is* discussing such issues and their scenery in relation to the standards to which all politics should theoretically be held – the standards that many people in many parts of the world, anyway, use as an- if not

---

16 See World Bank, "GDP Per Capita" (2016), available at http://data.worldbank.org/indicator/NY.GDP.PCAP.PP.CD?order=wbapi_data_value_2014+wbapi_data_value+wbapi_data_value-last&sort=desc.

17 Sten Rynning, *NATO Renewed: The Power and Purpose of Transatlantic Cooperation* (New York: Palgrave Macmillan, 2005); John Tomlinson, *Globalization and Culture* (Cambridge: Polity, 1999). On notions of the "West" and "non-West," see Jacinta O'Hagan, *Conceptualizing the West in International Relations: From Spengler to Said* (New York: Palgrave Macmillan, 2002). Obviously, Western Europe and North America aren't the only locales of global privilege, Westerners are not the only members of globally-privileged classes, and societies *not* located in locales like Western Europe or North America can also be dominated by classes of European descent (take locales like Australia, New Zealand or the larger part of Latin American states). Still, it's hard to ignore the European origins of modern privilege – that, as Wallerstein has noted, because the "core" of the modern world system is grounded in the historical emergence of European capitalism and exploration and that a Euro-derived world continues to hold disproportionate levels of especially wealth. See Wallerstein, *World-Systems Analysis*, 23. See also Gary Teeple and Stephen McBride, eds., *Relations of Global Power: Neoliberal Order and Disorder* (Toronto: University of Toronto Press, 2011).

18 Samuel Moyn, *The Last Utopia: Human Rights in History* (Cambridge, MA: Harvard Belknap, 2010), 1.

the- ultimate point of appeal. I refer here to ideas that are supposed to constitute humanity's "Magna Carta," as humanitarian activist and former American First Lady Eleanor Roosevelt once put it.[19] I refer to concepts involved with the basic existences that *everyone* should have, and ideas that are supposed to have play in *all* the societies in which we live. I refer to concepts addressing our basic dignity, and the liberties and privileges that should be taken away from none.

Now, the reason for the rights theme is twofold. Firstly, I've again noticed – others have too (Harvard historian Samuel Moyn is the leading voice in this area) – that, especially since the end of the Cold War, something has happened to rights ideas. Whereas "human rights" was once a vocabulary spoken near-solely by activists and contingents within the UN (and, yes, of course, the occasional government official too), "rights" are today vocabularies on the lips of many: government functionaries, decided rights advocates, rights organizations, many in the news media and, indeed, citizens simply musing on events from the comfort of their own homes. It's hard to quantify, and it's a non-scientific statement. However, I challenge anyone to listen to a week's worth of broadcasts from any major international news outlet – take the BBC or Al-Jazeera – and count the number of time one hears the term "human rights" (I did in the fall of 2014 with BBC World Service; the number was sixty-six over probably two hours of listening each day). Indeed, some have even maintained that human rights have displaced ranges of *earlier* ideas, from socialism to communism to capitalism to perhaps even liberalism, as humanity's "last utopia" (Moyn's term). I.e., rights are often invoked as the concepts that if they already don't, *should* lead us to a new historical age and, while they might encompass ideas from earlier ideological spectrums (the main "-isms" and "-ologies" of the nineteenth and twentieth centuries), they both should and would now do so in a synthetic way intended to be "post-political" as opposed to invested in a particular ideological camp.[20]

---

19 In Micheline R. Ishay, *The History of Human Rights: From Ancient Times to the Globalization Era* (Berkeley: University of California Press, 2004), 218. See also Paul Gordon Lauren, *The Evolution of International Human Rights: Visions Seen* (Philadelphia: University of Pennsylvania Press, 2008). Michael Ignatieff has also spoken of the "rights revolution," or the determined growth is reference and use of the idea of human rights. See Ignatieff, *The Rights Revolution* (Toronto: House of Anansi Press, 2000).

20 There's an extensive discussion on "post-politics," or the "post-political." Largely, it means either attempting to work beyond the space of partisanship – the way I mean it here – or a kind of "malaise" one finds in a world where liberalism, or perhaps neoliberalism, *did* "win" the Cold War, making it difficult for us to imagine political alternatives. Again, I generally mean the idea of non-partisanship when I talk about

It's hard to know precisely *why* this is the case – *why* human rights have accumulated the level of appeal that they have. For the most insightful commentary on this, I'll turn readers to the work of Moyn and his circle.[21] For my money, though, issues concern the end of the Cold War and the world's simple turn towards a different *Zeitgeist*. The years of 1989–91 were monumental. Socialism and communism lost their cachet; *if* socialism *were* to proceed, it would have to be with a radically different face.[22] Indeed, though triumphant for a time, liberalism took its hits too – that as we supposedly moved *beyond* history as a contest of ideas and could now speak to humanity's "higher" truths without filtering our beliefs through "systems."[23] The virtue of the post-Cold War world, and rights specifically, was that they could offer a higher unity of political aspiration, transcending the hoopla in which we usually engaged about whose "side" one might be on.[24]

It's moreover the case that arguing for the dominance of rights isn't particularly hard. Indeed, the notion that "rights" are often invoked to frame multiple sides of

---

post-politics and human rights. However, in some essays, I veer towards the latter definition as I have concerns that we too easily feel we "know" our political answers in our times – wherein we might sometimes forget certain basic modes of justice. See Ali Riza Taşkale, *Post-Politics in Context* (London: Routledge, 2016); Japhy Wilson and Erik Swyngedouw, eds., *The Post-Political and its Discontents: Spaces of Depoliticisation, Spectres of Radical Politics* (Edinburgh: University of Edinburgh Press, 2014).

21 See again Moyn, *The Last Utopia*. See also Moyn and Jan Eckel, eds., *The Breakthrough: Human Rights in the 1970s* (Philadelphia: University of Pennsylvania Press, 2013). Indeed, Moyn and his colleagues tend to place the turning point in the '70s. In some ways, though, that helps to pave the way for the post-Cold War attitude towards rights I discuss here – a point of which Moyn is well-aware, and which has helped inspire the writing here.

22 This has been approached in difference ways – in fact by many of the figures noted in footnote 3. Some have sought a kind of "Third Way" socialism where, to my mind, even *social democracy* becomes watered down to a neo-liberal form. Others, however, seek the militancy and commitment of traditional socialist thought, yet combined with a wider sense of diversity, identity and a less determined sense of historical ends. See again, Giddens, *The Third Way*; Laclau and Mouffe, *Hegemony and Socialist Strategy*. See also Michael Hardt and Antonio Negri, *Commonwealth* (Cambridge, MA: Harvard Belknap, 2009).

23 See, e.g., Leslie Sklair, *Globalization: Capitalism and its Alternatives* (Oxford: Oxford University Press, 2002).

24 This has been well laid-out by Moyn in *The Last Utopia*. See also Stephen Hopgood, *The Endtimes of Human Rights* (Ithaca, NY: Cornell University Press, 2013): Costas Douzinas, *The End of Human Rights: Critical Thought at the Turn of the Century* (Portland: Hart, 2000).

arguments about the same issue might be taken as argument enough. Take an action like bombing Islamic State (addressed in this book's first essay). Human rights are used to *defend* such actions – that IS is involved in some brutal human rights violations, and those need to be stopped. I couldn't agree more – rights violations are rights violations and they should be brooked nowhere, from anyone at any time. On the *other* hand, human rights can and sometimes *are* used to make arguments that we need to take *care* with such actions and, potentially, we shouldn't do such things *at all* – that as such actions are nearly guaranteed to *degrade* rights, *à la* the right to life or people's freedom of movement (a point I *also* make [i.e., bombing someone rarely makes them freer]). Indeed, sensibilities like those discussed concerning imperialism and colonialism *also* come into play: what happens if there have been long-term practices that might have left people feeling as though they haven't been *allowed* their sovereignty and the right to express themselves? What happens when violent resistance might be a reaction to violence *itself*, and the world finds itself caught in cycles of finger pointing and ongoing claims that the other side is "wrong" or simply doesn't "understand," period, full stop? Do we tip our hats to the experiences of the historically oppressed and look closely at how such oppression plays into situations? Or do we start simply proclaiming particular perspectives as "wrong" – that groups are violating *other's* rights, so we've got to do what it takes to make that stop? These aren't easy questions. In some ways, the present essays represent a struggle with such questions as opposed to any final answer. Still, what shines through is that rights are present in the thoughtways of the twenty-first century. Rights are "there" to the extent that not only do we see many political problems through their lenses, but that ranges of even *contradictory* perspectives on particular issues are framed in relation to rights as well. It *does* appear as though rights are the ultimate measure, somehow.[25]

All well and good. I.e., making explicit what many of us *sense* (rights' popularity) is an important move. Given the diverse ways in which we invoke rights, it seems that those invocations deserve discussion. Still, what rights? I.e., though the vocabulary may be common enough, to what *particularly* might one refer when *speaks* about "human rights," and what sense of the idea might one make oneself – e.g., when one declares "that's a human rights violation!" or "in the name of human rights, stop!"? What's at play in reference to an idea that *is* often referred to by governments and major media outlets? What's the referent for ideas we often use offhand? Such questions touch on another goal of this book:

---

25 See Douzinas, *Human Rights and Empire: The Political Philosophy of Cosmopolitanism* (London: Routledge, 2007).

putting a bit more meat on the bone to cries of indignation that, while important, *can* be easy to make. I.e., I'm interested to help readers who are interested in human rights learn a bit more about them – that again in relation to the kinds of events and scenes which, for many of us, bring rights concepts to mind.

In this context, there are a few points of which one might take note. Firstly, it's largely within the domain of UN declarations, treaties, covenants, conventions and proclamations that I work. The granddaddy of all human rights documents is the Universal Declaration of Human Rights (1948), and I treat it as such. This has two sides to it. Firstly, I have no quantifiable data. However, refer to the literature on human rights and it takes five minutes to see that the Universal Declaration is the alpha and omega for rights scholars, rights organizations and anyone else who deals with rights on either a regular or professional basis. It was to *that* document, e.g., that Eleanor Roosevelt referred when she proposed human rights as humanity's "Magna Carta".[26] It's the *Universal Declaration* that informs near-all subsequent declarations of- and conventions on- universal rights on a global plane. Now, agreed: there are sophisticated debates to be had about the nature of justice in terms of who deserves what and where. I'm also clear on the idea that, using one scholar's vocabulary, human rights are a "church." Rights *do* have a history, and we have to recognize that they're not the *only* way of thinking about the "good."[27] Still, my argument – one point which *is* consistent throughout this book – is that every one of the rights listed in the thirty articles of the Universal Declaration deserves to be upheld. I.e., I hold up the UN's primary rights document and say "uphold these rights to the maximum extent." Now, I admit that I come defenseless to the battle of the question as to *why* human rights except via an appeal to readers themselves. I.e., I'm asking readers to choose. In the words of the Universal Declaration, is one interested "freedom, justice and peace" in the world? Does one favor the "right to freedom of opinion and expression"? Does one support our ability to "assembl[e]...peaceful[ly]" and "take part in the government of [one's] own country"? Do not all of us deserve to be treated equally under the law and not be "subject to arbitrary arrest, detention or exile"? Does not everyone deserve food, housing, shelter and access to a doctor if one either needs or wants? Should not all be kept alive, even if some are evil – that based on the idea that the "right to life" is inherent and, take it away from some, and one has started down a dangerous path? Does not everyone deserve an "international order" in which

---

26 See again Ishay, *The History*, 218.

27 See Hopgood, *The Endtimes*, x. On the issue of theories of justice, see Michael Sandel, ed., *Justice: A Reader* (Oxford: Oxford University Press, 2007). On rights in their historicity, see *Inventing Human Rights*.

one's rights may be *realized*?[28] If one answers "yes" to these questions, you're the audience for this book. You're a rights believer, and you have a pew in the church. Again, I can't quite say *why* that church specifically except to say that it's darn hard to say what justice looks like from the pew of a *different* church.

Now, there are dangers here. I.e., even if one *is* a human rights "disciple," faced with the conundrum of killing, say, a Hitler-like figure, or a beast like Ratko Mladić, would one really *not* – that out of a commitment to justice's equal application or ideas that one should *never* step outside of rights' bounds? Would even the human rights "maximalist" *really* say that groups like Islamic State deserve the same rights as everyone else – that we have to think *so* hard about what those who murder, rape and pillage deserve when they think so little about such issues in relation to everyone else? Would we *really* ask for justice to be done in relation to those who abscond it, respecting those who seem to disrespect the *idea* of respect?[29] Again, there are many arguments about such points. There are utilitarian positions arguing for the "greatest happiness for the greatest number" of society's members.[30] There are theories of how to *apply* justice, addressing rights' institutionalization and procedural aspects.[31] One can philosophize on whether rights have *any* reality, perhaps dancing in front of us like a fata morgana.[32] I'll thus attempt to be clear. Yes, we need to sometimes bend our principles in the name of larger causes. I would never suggest that it's wrong to intervene in, say, a genocide because one might harm or kill those involved in its perpetration (indeed, as I write, there are rumblings that we might be moving towards genocidal conditions in South Sudan).[33] I'd also never suggest that one shouldn't stand between the terrorized and the terrorist, allowing innocents to

---

28 United Nations, "The Universal Declaration of Human Rights" (1948), available at http://www.un.org/en/universal-declaration-human-rights/index.html. Hereafter UDHR.

29 Andrew Altman and Christopher Heath Wellman, e.g., have made some interesting points on the idea of political assassination in relation to human rights. See Altman and Wellman, "From Humanitarian Intervention to Assassination: Human Rights and Political Violence," *Ethics* 118, no. 2 (2008): 228–57.

30 See John Troyer, ed., *The Classical Utilitarians: Bentham and Mill* (Indianapolis: Hackett, 2003).

31 See, e.g., Suzanne Egan, *The United Nations Human Rights Treaty System: Law and Procedure* (London: Bloomsbury, 2011).

32 See, e.g., Alasdair MacIntyre, *Whose Justice? Which Rationality?* (South Bend: University of Notre Dame Press, 1988).

33 See Aaron Ross, "South Sudanese Flee as Country Edges Closer to 'Genocide,'" *Reuters*, December 1, 2016, available at http://www.reuters.com/article/us-southsudan-congo-refugees-idUSKBN13Q50M.

be killed because one won't kill oneself. No one deserves to live with a feeling of fundamental insecurity or lack of assuredness about what will come next.[34] At such points, however – at the moment of *defending* rights – my sense is that we need to claim responsibility for any likelihood of stepping outside rights' bounds in that context. Especially when rights defense involves armed intervention, we need to acknowledge that we're entertaining *violating* rights – that though it may be in human rights' name. Again: no dictator deserves to proceed unchecked and no one should make others' lives miserable. All deserve their privileges and freedoms, full stop. *If* we're to uphold our highest ideals, however, we need to not only insist on those ideals, but be clear on the moments at which we *don't* meet their standards. We shouldn't blame others as concerns *our* choices about rights behavior and any actions in their name. What's called "derogating" rights *can* be just. It seems an awfully good question, however, as to whether "derogated rights" are really rights themselves.[35]

---

34 E.g., Benjamin J. Goold and Liora Lazarus, eds., *Security and Human Rights* (Portland: Hart, 2007).

35 This point has some controversial elements. One is that some would see what some call the "state of exception," or the fact that one has to sometimes step outside of rights in order to enforce them, as making the "derogation" of rights central to rights as such. I.e., rights are *founded* on the idea that one might not observe them; otherwise, why articulate them (an interesting point)? That's beyond the fact that some rights documents – the International Covenant on Civil and Political Rights (1966), e.g. – *claim* a "right of derogation" wherein, in times of "public emergency," one *might* suspend rights.

Regarding point one, I'd simply phrase things another way. Stepping outside of rights' boundaries is stepping outside of rights' boundaries. If one *wants* to uphold rights without exception, one can at least *try* (that in keeping with rights' intended universality). That means, though, that if one doesn't succeed in upholding rights, one is in fact *not* upholding rights. That isn't necessarily unjust. It is, however, a matter of how one characterizes the situation.

Regarding point two, I recognize that there seems to be a right to step outside of rights – wherein, one hasn't stepped outside of rights (one has exercised the right to rights' "derogation"). To me, though, this undermines human rights' cause. Using the Civil and Political Covenant's wording, if "everyone has the right to liberty and security of person," everyone has the right to liberty and security of person (I'm in the dark about how everyone become "not everyone"). Herein, one need be *darn* careful with "derogation" as there *is* a question as to whether or not rights derogation really involves "rights behavior." It seems a dangerous situation when the equation between "derogated rights" and "rights" becomes made too often. See Giorgio Agamben, *State of Exception*, trans. Kevin Attell (Chicago: University of Chicago Press, 2005); Evan J. Criddle, *Human Rights in Emergencies* (Cambridge: Cambridge University Press, 2016): United Nations,

Now, certain further issues also emerge from such points. First, we should note that there's an entire *battery* of "core international [rights] instruments," as the UN calls them, and that rights *don't* end with the Universal Declaration. For the purpose of awareness, I attempt to bring *some* of those instruments into the picture. I.e., this book works beyond the boundaries of the Universal Declaration as much as the Declaration is its feature document.[36] I *don't* go much into "regional" human rights regimes and declarations – e.g., those maintained by the Council of Europe, the Organization of American States or the African Union (though some *do* make a cameo appearance or two).[37] I also leave out the human rights acts of specific *states* – though rights perspectives from national constitutions occasionally enter the conversation.[38] However, *that* touches on an important dimension of the view of human rights that I maintain: namely, that human rights are a *discreet* idea, and that while national or regional law might *conform* with human rights, *human* rights are *larger* than the laws of nations. Human rights are rights that should, if not supersede the peculiarities and borders of specific states, then at least provide *parameters* into which national law should fit. I.e., though I often use the word "rights" as a substitute for "human rights," the two should *not* be confused. This is another debt I owe to Moyn: that part of what makes *human* rights intriguing is that they're *not* just about national life – they're about *humanity*. Articulations such as those emerging from institutions like the UN and its central battery of rights documents should be taken at face value. When human rights are posited as universal, universal is how they're intended

---

"International Covenant on Civil and Political Rights" (1966, articles 4, 9), available at http://www.ohchr.org/en/professionalinterest/pages/ccpr.aspx. This issue also connects itself to *jus cogens* – "peremptory" forms of international law. See also Robert Kolb, *Peremptory International Law – Jus Cogens: An Inventory* (Portland: Hart, 2015).

36 See United Nations, "The Core International Instruments of Human Rights and Their Monitoring Bodies" (2016), available at http://www.ohchr.org/EN/ProfessionalInterest/Pages/CoreInstruments.aspx.

37 See Dinah L. Shelton, *Regional Protection of Human Rights* (Oxford: Oxford University Press, 2008).

38 Examples of national human rights acts are be items like the British Human Rights Act of 1998 or the Canadian Human Rights Act of 1985. See The National Archives, "Human Rights Act 1998," available at http://www.legislation.gov.uk/ukpga/1998/42/contents; Government of Canada, "Canadian Human Rights Act" (1985), available at http://laws-lois.justice.gc.ca/eng/acts/h-6/. See also David Erdos, *Delegating Rights Protection: The Rise of Bills of Rights in the Westminster World* (Oxford: Oxford University Press, 2010).

to be. One is doing rights a disservice if one suggests that there are limitations in terms of to whom fundamental rights might pertain.[39]

This does open up its own can of worms. I.e., I'm not a lawyer, and it's a feature of this book that its focus is on rights' intentions as much as anything else. It's tricky to demand that nations uphold certain rights when, once one gets *beyond* the Universal Declaration, one has to sign onto and ratify particular treaties in order for them to gain legal traction. I.e., there *is* a question as to what happens when one hasn't signed onto a piece of paper that says one is participating in rights' contracts – that above and beyond issues of what to do with pluralities or actors that either won't or don't *want* to play by universal rules, whether they've signed a contract or not. The fact is – and I can't ignore it – that rights' democratic nature *allows* peoples and social groups latitude to decide for themselves. Self-determination, including *national* self-determination, falls within rights' purview. While insisting on *internationality*, human rights still maintain certain visions of a world of nation-states.[40] That's a problem, representing a minefield I don't always elegantly traverse. What I *do* do, however, is recognize that such problems *exist*. Though they're not always fully solved, I tip my hat in the direction of such ideas and suggest they need be *considered*. That's while speaking clearly about what the international community *in fact* says rights are *supposed* to achieve – universal emancipation and broad guarantees for the intellectual and physical self. I.e., ranges of powerful actors and institutions have made heavy statements to the effect that one really *should* pursue rights to their maximal

---

39 In Moyn's vocabulary, the "rights of man," as he puts it – rights as they were developed in historical contexts before the UN – involved a "whole people incorporating itself in a state": the national polity, as such. It's the development of the *human* rights vocabulary that inculcates the notion of cross-border rights transcending nation. See Moyn, *The Last Utopia*, 21. It's also worth mentioning that I'm not criticizing national human rights acts. I'm absolutely supportive of them. There are distinctions to be made, however, between laws explicitly helping to inculcate *universal* applications of rights and those delimiting rights as for a particular group (namely, citizens). See, e.g., Monique Castermans-Holleman, Fried van Hoof and Jacqueline Smith, eds., *The Role of the Nation-State in the 21st Century: Human Rights, International Organisations and Foreign Policy* (The Hague: Kluwer, 1998).

40 See, e.g., Milena Sterio, *The Right to Self-Determination under International Law: "Selfistans," Secession, and the Rule of the Great Powers* (London: Routledge, 2013); Mortimer Sellers, ed., *The New World Order: Sovereignty, Human Rights and the Self-Determination of Peoples* (London: Bloomsbury, 1996).

extent and that "exceptions" shouldn't be the primary focus.[41] Indeed, to the extent that the question *is* law, more than one legal scholar has suggested that the point with rights is to gain their broadest possible inculcation.[42] This book simply picks up on that task – what it seems like is a seriously-taken notion of bringing rights projects home to their fullest and maximum extent.

That being said, however, there are then the essays that constitute this book. Those address the following issues: bombing Islamic state, the recent terror attacks in Brussels, the presidential candidacy of Bernie Sanders, reflections on the Cold War scenery of the city of Potsdam, crackdowns on journalism and free speech in Erdoğan's Turkey, the 2015 death of jazz trumpeter Clark Terry, considerations of a recent documentary on Saudi Arabia, the issue of nuclear saber-rattling in North Korea, questions of the realization of LGBT rights on the international stage, religious violence in India, Pakistan and Bangladesh, the presidential candidacy of Donald Trump, the response of the artist Ai Weiwei to Danish and, by association, European, rightist immigration politics and reflections on a recent visit to the Bergen-Belsen concentration camp. Despite what is now an extensive introduction, the essays of this book are in fact designed to be read on their own; they are self-contained universes. To that extent, certain arguments repeat across the essays, and the *specific* arguments of the individual pieces don't always work in concert with one another. Certain sources, phrases, and concepts are also oft-repeated – one will again find some quotes and assertions reiterated verbatim, and I've again sometimes stepped out of my comfort zone to write certain of the essays here; that in a spirit of inquisitive citizenry and an interest in broad socio-political dialogue. Rights experts may find certain of my arguments not particularly new – highlighting that socio-economic rights are as much a part of the human rights picture as rights like freedom of speech or participation in government, e.g. (that while I often describe free thought and expression as human rights' ultimate heart). Experts in the particular *topics* that serve as the background of some of the pieces, from Middle East history to Cold

---

41 See, e.g., Barend van der Heijden and Bahia Tahzib, eds., *Reflections on the Universal Declaration of Human Rights: A Fiftieth Anniversary Anthology* (The Hague: Martinus Nijhoff, 1998). See also Philip Alston and Ryan Goodman, eds., *International Human Rights* (Oxford: Oxford University Press, 2012).

42 See, e.g., William Paul Simmons, *Human Rights Law and the Marginalized Other* (Cambridge: Cambridge University Press, 2011); Allen Buchanan, *The Heart of Human Rights* (Oxford: Oxford University Press, 2013); Orna Ben-Naftali, ed., *International Humanitarian Law and International Human Rights Law* (Oxford: Oxford University Press, 2011).

War history to North Korean politics to the Holocaust, may also have their beefs. There's been a lot of facts to check in this book about many different topics, and any mistakes are purely my own. A criticism of some of the essays along the way has been that they pack in too much. I've tried to thin them out. Readers will nonetheless confront the occasional thorny thicket along the way.

Still, all of that circles back around to what this book is. This book is a collection of works of commentary – a characterization one might especially apply to the pieces on bombing Islamic State, the bombings in Brussels, the Bernie Sanders and Donald Trump pieces, the essay on press crackdowns in Turkey, the reflections on jazz and civil rights, the piece on Saudi Arabia, culture and human rights, the address to the issue of international liberties for the LGBT community, the piece on problems of immigration and the arts in Europe and Denmark and the essay on reemerging religious violence on the Indian sub-continent. There are again historical meditations – that especially in the essays on Potsdam and the Holocaust. The book seeks to provoke and observe as much as "end" conversations. It seeks to avoid setting knowledge bars so high that only experts can get in (hence some of the long introductions). Ultimately, though, this book seeks to *advocate* for rights. The pieces in this book *ask* governments, social groups, institutions, individuals and organizations to move *towards* rights standards – to move towards the goals that many feel we're not only *obliged* to try to achieve but which it would be good if we did. I've written this book to motivate us *further* down rights paths and to take us towards, if not a "last utopia," then at least something better than what we have now. Setting into motion all the balls needed to take us toward such objectives is no easy task. It took until modernity for *any* kind of rights concept to come widely into discourse and until about seventy years ago for thoroughgoing articulations of decided *human* rights to emerge. It's also only within the past few decades that human rights have become such a popular point of appeal. "Academic journalism" and "historical commentary" can only help the rights project by keeping us up-to-date on events and mobilizing ideas about where rights problems exist and how they might be thought about. Still, if this book, or any of the essays within it, inspire students, other scholars or members of the general public to proceed with their *own* activism or investigations into rights-based issues, I'll be satisfied. If anyone takes any part of the essays in this book and says, "I feel the need to react to that" or "I'd like to find out more about such things," I'll take it as a win. If one feels one has a range of rights issues one would like to *add* to those addressed here, and one's own "academic journalism" and "historical commentary" in which to engage, I hope one does. That's as human rights encourage nothing if not our engagement with each other. Human rights promote few things if not the unfolding our viewpoints and consideration of the different ways in which we might contribute to finding a way forward for *all* of us, at one time. As the Universal Declaration phrases it, humanity's ultimate destination should be the "inherent dignity and the equal and inalienable rights of all members of the human family."[43] We should look to arrive at a moment in which we have social and political atmospheres in which we feel assured of our personhood and have the sense that the fight for essential justice might be a touch less hard. That's as, while we can't do anything about the torsions surrounding justice in the past, we might do something about such issues now and in the future. That's to the end of making the torsion around our social and political lives noticeably less stressful than it up to now has been.

---

43 UDHR, preamble.

Bombing IS

The Battle for Kobani
(October 14, 2014)

Abstract: *What does action against Islamic State look like from a human rights perspective? Complex. On one hand, IS rights violations should not be brooked (whose should?). On the other hand, the violence of intervention may always mean rights violations – a point which rights advocates need to take seriously.*

The group now calling itself "Islamic State" has become serious business. Having removed the "Syria" and, most noticeably, the Western-originated "Levant" from the name, the militant organization has situated itself just outside the borders of NATO. *The New York Times*, e.g., recently published provocative pictures of Turkish Kurds watching their Syrian brethren on the verge of being overrun – that in the town of Kobani, just miles from Turkey's southern edge.[1] *The Guardian*, via the United Nations, is claiming over 5500 civilian dead in the wake of IS offensives in Iraq. The numbers are unclear in Syria – as a whole, the UN estimates that as of August, the country's vastly complex civil war had killed more than 191,000 combatants and civilians alike.

"Location Syria. Green Pin on the Map."
© Zerophoto / Fotolia.com 79754658

If the numbers are correct, and the dead are all Syrian, the civil war has cost the country roughly 1% of its population. That's based on a 2014 count of

---

1   See Mark Landler and Eric Schmitt. "As Islamic State Nears Conquest of Syrian Town, U.S. Presses Turks," *The New York Times*, October 8, 2014, available at http://www.nytimes.com/2014/10/09/world/middleeast/isis-syria-turkey-border-us.html?module=Search&mabReward=relbias%3Ar%2C%7B%222%22%3A%22RI%3A16%22%7D&_r=0. On "Levant," see Edward Said, *Orientalism* (New York: Pantheon, 1978), 3, 58, 354.

17,951,639 from the CIA *World Factbook*.[2] IS is responsible for more than a small portion of that toll.[3]

The situation has the United States and its allies flummoxed. Turkey is a NATO country; the U.S. can't simply abandon it. Though the alliance (NATO) was not solely an American concept – it was a Benelux, French, and UK initiative as well – the U.S. was nonetheless the group's prime mover after the Second World War. Still, the Obama Administration has been unwilling to commit to the town's defense. John Kerry, the American Secretary of State, has been running interference for the administration all week. Regarding the situation on the Turkish border, Kerry claimed, "it's important to step back and understand the strategic objective." America's foreign minister didn't articulate precisely what that was. Filling in the gaps, however, and acknowledging that a Pentagon press secretary claimed that it's "clear" there were "towns and cities" IS would "take," one imagines Kerry to be referring to Obama's September 10 statement declaring his intention to "degrade and ultimately destroy" IS.[4] Of course, the notion of ceding ground only to take it later is puzzling; why go backward only to go forward at a later point? Why relinquish territory one ultimately intends to win? It isn't unheard of military strategy, however. It was, e.g., the basic Soviet approach during the Second World War.[5]

Human rights violations follow Islamic State everywhere it goes. The group's victories are often followed by executions and brutal corporal punishment. *The Washington Post*, e.g., has noted the live tweeting of punitive amputations in Maskanah, north of Aleppo. Swords, not surgical instruments, were the implements of choice.[6] We know – at least video evidence indicates – that Alan Henning, a British national bringing aid to refugees, was executed sometime towards

---

2   Central Intelligence Agency, "Syria," *The World Factbook* (2014), available at https://www.cia.gov/library/publications/the-world-factbook/geos/sy.html.

3   The Guardian, "Iraqi Civilian Death Toll Passes in Wake of ISIS Offensive" July 18, 2014, available at http://www.theguardian.com/world/2014/jul/18/iraqi-civilian-death-toll-5500-2014-isis.

4   Again, Landler and Schmitt, "As Islamic State Nears"; The White House, "Statement by the President on ISIL," September 10, 2014, available at http://www.whitehouse.gov/the-press-office/2014/09/10/statement-president-isil-1.

5   See David M. Glantz, *Soviet Military Deception in the Second World War* (London: Routledge, 1989).

6   Liz Sly and Ahmed Ramadan, "Syrian Extremists Amputated a Man's Hand and Live-Tweeted It," *The Washington Post*, February 28, 2014, available at http://www.washingtonpost.com/blogs/worldviews/wp/2014/02/28/syrian-extremists-amputated-a-mans-hand-and-live-tweeted-it/.

the end of the September (September 20 is the date published in *The New York Times*). James Foley, an American journalist, was executed a month before. It's brutal stuff with which IS is involved – more brutal than most of us can imagine.[7]

That these are human rights violations should not be put into doubt. The Universal Declaration of Human Rights (1948) – the primary international rights document – claims the right to life. That's above and beyond the right to "liberty and security of person."[8] The Universal Declaration *also* claims the right to avoid torture and "cruel, inhuman or degrading treatment or punishment" – a point undergirded by yet further rights treaties such as the Convention against Torture and Other Cruel, Inhuman or Degrading Treatment or Punishment (1984) and the International Covenant on Civil and Political Rights (1966) (the latter referencing torture in its seventh article).[9] Now, there has long been a debate as to whether or not the U.S. has violated – and continues to violate – such standards in the "War on Terror." Guantanamo Bay and the Abu Ghraib saga may be the prime examples. There, the U.S. overstepped boundaries for the humanitarian treatment of prisoners as laid-out in the Geneva Conventions (1949) – a treaty to which the U.S. is party.[10] Still, that the U.S. or any other major power may have violated human rights doesn't mean such standards can't be turned back on IS. The "War on Terror" may have two faces: those prosecuting the war, and the terrorists and/or fundamentalists themselves. "Moral panic," it's been claimed – the

---

7   Rukmini Callimachi and Kimiko de Freytas-Tamura, "ISIS Releases Video of Execution of British Aid Worker," *The New York Times*, October 3, 2014, available at http://www.nytimes.com/2014/10/04/world/middleeast/islamic-state-releases-video-of-execution-of-alan-henning-british-aid-worker.html; BBC, "Profile: James Foley: US Journalist Beheaded by Islamic State," August 20, 2014, available at http://www.bbc.com/news/world-28865508.

8   United Nations, "The Universal Declaration of Human Rights" (1948, article 3 [hereafter UDHR]), available at http://www.un.org/en/universal-declaration-human-rights/index.html.

9   Ibid., article 6. See also United Nations, "Convention against Torture and Other Cruel, Inhuman or Degrading Treatment or Punishment" (1984 [hereafter CAT]), available at http://www.ohchr.org/EN/ProfessionalInterest/Pages/CAT.aspx; United Nations, "International Covenant on Civil and Political Rights" (1966 [hereafter ICCPR]), available at http://www.ohchr.org/en/professionalinterest/pages/ccpr.aspx.

10 See Fiona de Londras, *Detention in the "War on Terror": Can Human Rights Fight Back?* (Cambridge: Cambridge University Press, 2011); Richard Ashby Wilson, ed. *Human Rights in the "War on Terror"* (Cambridge: Cambridge University Press, 2005): Philippe Sands, *Torture Team: Rumsfeld's Memo and the Betrayal of American Values* (New York: Palgrave Macmillan, 2009).

loss of ethical compass – may be everywhere. Confusion may reign in a world characterized by intense conflict and levels of violence the likes of which many of us have rarely seen.[11]

Nonetheless, the decision to bomb IS *does* raise fundamental points. The first of those points concerns double standards indeed. The 1993 Bangkok Declaration of the Regional Meeting for Asia of the World Conference on Human Rights, e.g., warns of applying rights standards when one violates rights oneself. There is a "universality, objectivity, and non-selectivity [to] human rights," claims the document, via which no country is welcome to violate rights at any time.[12] Now, the Bangkok Declaration has little legal standing. Though they were debated, not all of its ideas were adopted into the UN regime.[13] Still, the text *does* raise questions as to whether rights violators can also be rights enforcers. E.g., the U.S. remains a death penalty state. The death penalty is *not* fully circumscribed by international law; the Civil and Political Rights Covenant asserts that capital punishment may be deployed for the "most serious crimes" in "*accordance* with the law" (i.e., the death penalty *is* allowed under specially-defined circumstances).[14] Still,

---

11 Gershon Shafir and Cynthia E. Schairer, "The War on Terror and Moral Panic," in *Lessons and Legacies of the War on Terror*, ed. Gershon Shafir, Everard Meade and William Aceves (London: Routledge, 2013), 9–46.

12 United Nations, "Report of the Regional Meeting for Asia of the World Conference on Human Rights" (1993), available at http://daccess-dds-ny.un.org/doc/UNDOC/GEN/G93/125/95/PDF/G9312595.pdf?OpenElement.

13 The Bangkok Declaration was the result of a regional preparatory meeting for the 1993 World Conference on Human Rights – famous for its debates concerning double standards and cultural relativism. The primary result of the conference was the Vienna Declaration and Programme of Action (1993). Now, there's a distinction between statements of principle, like the Bangkok Declaration, Vienna Declaration or in fact the UDHR, and more concrete law embodied in conventions like the ICCPR or CAT. One is theory and the other can be adjudicated upon. Still, as many point out, it's difficult to get to law without theory and, in the case of human rights, documents organized around principle are often used to represent the essentials of the idea. This makes it tough to delineate between concepts with legal effect and those of a more "philosophical" nature. See Michael Freeman, *Human Rights. An Interdisciplinary Approach* (Cambridge: Polity, 2002); David Weissbrodt and Connie de la Vega, *International Human Rights Law: An Introduction* (Philadelphia: University of Pennsylvania Press, 2007); United Nations, "Vienna Declaration and Programme of Action" (1993), available at http://www.ohchr.org/en/professionalinterest/pages/vienna.aspx; Susan Marks, "Nightmare and Noble Dream: The 1993 World Conference on Human Rights," *The Cambridge Law Journal* 53, no. 1 (1994): 54–62.

14 ICCPR, article 6.

documents such as the Second Optional Protocol to the International Covenant on Civil and Political Rights Aiming at the Abolition of the Death Penalty (1989) and the Civil and Political Covenant itself make it clear that it's the preferred position of the UN to move that way (towards abolition [the Civil and Political Covenant refers to countries which have "not abolished the death penalty"; a disdainful tone towards those who have it]).[15] That's but to say that one can ask whether the U.S. has the authority to move on others in the name of human rights when the country may be involved in, if not *direct* rights violations, then at least modicums of behavior skirting on the edge of rights standards themselves.[16]

Of course, it's *also* always a question as to on what terms humanitarian intervention, or military interventions in which human rights are used as a justification, take place. At what point do we combine rights with force, and what do we imagine the grounds of such actions to be? International studies scholar Chih-Hann Chang, for example, has claimed the 1990s as the "golden age" of humanitarian intervention. Entry into conflicts in Somalia, Bosnia and Kosovo are the leading examples. There, force was used to extend the life of rights – that though such actions involved suspending certain rights themselves (the right to life, e.g. [force always involves a threat in that area]).[17] Still, the practice has hardly stopped. UN Security Council Resolutions 1973 (2011 [pertaining to Libya]) and 2178 (2014 [pertaining to Syria]) both reference human rights.[18] World

---

15 See ibid.; United Nations, "Second Optional Protocol to the International Covenant on Civil and Political Rights, Aiming at the Abolition of the Death Penalty" (1989), available at http://www.ohchr.org/EN/ProfessionalInterest/Pages/2ndOPCCPR.aspx.

16 Obviously, this is complex. If one eliminated every state violating some variety of rights from ever engaging in intervention, the number of states that could intervene in deleterious situations would be small and involve few powers with the *capability* to intervene. That doesn't exempt us from asking into the distinctions between acceptable and unacceptable intervention, however. See Giorgio Agamben, *State of Exception*, trans. Kevin Attell Chicago: University of Chicago Press, 2005); Bas de Gaay Fortman, *Political Economy of Human Rights: Rights, Realities and Realization* (London: Routledge, 2011); Elizabeth Wicks, *The Right to Life and Conflicting Interests* (Oxford: Oxford University Press, 2010).

17 Chih-Hann Chang, *Ethical Foreign Policy? US Humanitarian Interventions* (Farnham: Ashgate, 2011). See also Dana H. Allin, *NATO's Balkan Interventions* (London: Routledge, 2002).

18 United Nations Security Council, "Resolution 2178 (2014)," available at http://www.un.org/en/ga/search/view_doc.asp?symbol=S/RES/2178%20(2014); United Nations Security Council, "Resolution 1973 (2011)," available at http://www.un.org/en/ga/search/view_doc.asp?symbol=S/RES/1973(2011).

leaders from David Cameron to François Hollande to Angela Merkel over and above Barak Obama have indicated human rights as the grounds for intervening against Islamic State.[19] IS rights violations feature frequently in the news, reinforcing ideas that they might be the grounds for military intercession.[20] We appear on the cusp of another bombing campaign in human rights' name – that though the "universality, objectivity [and] non-selectivity" of human rights will likely come under duress in the process.[21]

Finally, though, it may be necessary to look at issues of self-determination. That's as self-determination may – *may* – contribute to conflict. Now, it's true: some have claimed anti-colonialism and anti-imperialism as concepts *not, prima facie*, involved with human rights. Anti-colonialism and anti-imperialism may concern national and cultural independences as much as anything else.[22] It's also unclear to what degree IS is involved with anti-colonialism and anti-imperialism as such.[23] Still, both the Civil and Political Covenant and the International

---

19 See Sebastian Payne, "The Likely Partners of Obama's 'Broad Coalition' to Destroy Islamic State," *The Washington Post*, September 11, 2014, available at https://www.washingtonpost.com/news/post-politics/wp/2014/09/11/the-likely-partners-of-obamas-broad-coalition-to-destroy-the-islamic-state/.

20 E.g., Nick Cumming-Bruce, "U.N. Investigators Cite Atrocities in Syria," *The New York Times*, September 16, 2014, available at http://www.nytimes.com/2014/09/17/world/middleeast/un-investigators-cite-atrocities-in-syria.html; Terrence McCoy, "ISIS, Beheadings and the Success of Horrifying Violence," *The Washington Post*, June 13, 2014, available at https://www.washingtonpost.com/news/morning-mix/wp/2014/06/13/isis-beheadings-and-the-success-of-horrifying-violence/.

21 Largely, this is a matter of *jus cogens*: peremptory international law. The idea with *jus cogens* is that there are global situations dire enough to warrant the intervention of global powers even if that means a temporary suspension of supposedly universal rights (e.g., the right to life). That doesn't make *jus cogens* easy to enact, however, nor exempt us from explaining ourselves when we do. See Robert Kolb, *Peremptory International Law – Jus Cogens: An Inventory* (Oxford: Hart, 2015); Elizabeth Wicks, *The Right to Life and Conflicting Interests* (Oxford: Oxford University Press, 2010).

22 See Samuel Moyn, *The Last Utopia: Human Rights in History* (Cambridge, MA: Harvard Belknap, 2010).

23 The goal of IS, it's been written, is to hasten "End Times" – a showdown in which IS' particular variety of Wahhabi Islam gains confrontation with its enemies and establishes an "ostensible [Islamic] super state." There's undoubtedly a theological element to that. Concretely, however, it means that IS "does not recognize modern regional boundaries" in the Middle East, in turn meaning a rejection of the entire history Western interference in the region: from the Sykes-Picot Agreement and the great power mandate system after World War I to modes of cultural interference to the most recent

Covenant on Economic, Social and Cultural Rights assert that "all peoples have the right to self-determination."[24] Cultural groups, not excluding those defined by religion, have the right to shape the contours of their social and political lives. It is true – "peoples" is a tricky issue. Some see "peoples" as representing "imagined communities" as much as anything else.[25] Still, minority representation is an issue in any community. How does one deal with groups endowing themselves with senses of self and seeking representation in worlds in which if they do not, they at least *can* feel outnumbered? How does one negotiate worldviews in conflict – conflicts potentially connected to histories of socio-cultural power relations in which it's not guaranteed that the playing field has been anywhere near level? Is it not incumbent on us to look under radical expression for radicalism's cause, and do we not want to take said causes into account as we make our approach to international affairs? Such issues may be especially acute with IS – situations where a group's ideals fall so far outside global norms that it's unclear how to incorporate them, or if they should be incorporated at all.[26]

These are complex issues. In a globalized world, it's difficult to address concrete political situations without defined standards. Human rights are intended to be such a standard. Rights *should* be norms with high if not universal degrees

---

rash of wars in Iraq and, clearly, Russian and American attempts to influence the fate of Syria. This brings geo-political goals to IS activities over and above simply wild-eyed violence. See Yonah Alexander and Dean Alexander, *The Islamic State: Combating the Caliphate without Borders* (Lanham: Lexington, 2015), 35–6. See also Benjamin Hall, *Inside ISIS: The Brutal Rise of a Terrorist Army* (New York: Center Street, 2015).

24 ICCPR, article 1; United Nations, "International Covenant on Economic, Social and Cultural Rights" (1966, article 1), available at http://www.ohchr.org/EN/ProfessionalInterest/Pages/CESCR.aspx.

25 The idea here is roughly that social groups aren't natural. "Peoples" and "identities" have to be discursively and ideologically constructed – they're not at all organic or "given" quantities on the international plane. See Benedict Anderson, *Imagined Communities: Reflections on the Origins and Spread of Nationalism* (London: Verso, 1983).

26 Clearly, the notion of "incorporating" IS ideals sounds ludicrous – that as they're so strongly opposed to human rights. Still, peacemaking *is* an ambition of the United Nations and the insistence of the International Covenants on self-determinatory rights may make it imperative to hear, if not comprehend, what identities staking political claims have to say. See United Nations, "Charter of the United Nations" (1945), available at http://www.un.org/en/sections/un-charter/chapter-i/index.html; Ana Filipa Vrdoljak, "Self-Determination and Cultural Rights," in *Cultural Human Rights*, ed. Francesco Francioni and Martin Scheinen (Leiden: Martinus Nijhoff, 2011), 41–78. See also Emmanuelle Tourme Jouannet, *What is a Fair International Society?: International Law Between Development and Recognition* (Portland: Hart, 2014).

of consensus. All members of the United Nations – one hundred ninety-three of them – pledge themselves to rights principles. As former UN Secretary-General Kofi Annan has maintained, rights should "cross any border, climb any wall, defy any force."[27] There should be no way around the basic freedoms and privileges with which we're all supposed to be endowed.[28]

That doesn't exempt us from the need for clarity, however. I.e., it may be incumbent on us to articulate precisely where we stand. To the extent that we have them, e.g., it may be necessary to address the use of double standards not just *when*, but *if*, they exist. What happens when rights *don't* cross every "border" scale every "wall" and defy every "force"? What happens when rights, or their practice, *aren't* as present as we'd like – that not only in relation to those involved in obvious violations (say, IS) but in political geographies supposedly maintaining rights as part of their essential *raison d'être* (e.g., modern Western states)? Do we simply call rights off? Do we throw rights out? Or do we allow an imperfect relationship with them in which we sometimes "step outside" of rights such that they might be sustained further into the future?

Such questions repeat themselves in an amplified manner when discussing the use of force.[29] Clearly, there can be grounds for rights' "derogation." We have to reserve the right to intervene in humanitarian crises (genocide or torture, e.g.) lest we seek to relinquish emergency defenses of dignity at all. A world with no possibility for intervention sounds frightening. Still, the *terms* on which intervention takes place *have to* be discussed. It can't be taken for granted that everyone understands what "rights intervention" means and, given that defending *anything* down the barrel of a gun is no easy task, the nature of such acts shouldn't be treated as either comprehensible or easily agreeable to all. Perhaps

---

27 Kofi Annan, "Message by the United Nations Secretary-General," in *Reflections on the Universal Declaration of Human Rights: A Fiftieth Anniversary Anthology*, ed. Barend van der Heijden and Bahia Tahzib-Lie (The Hague: Martinus Nijhoff, 1998), 18.

28 Of course, this applies equally to groups like IS. Their rights violations clearly need to be brought to account. That's while it must be acknowledged that it's markedly more difficult to make demands of non-state actors in relation to human rights than of state actors. See Andrew Clapham, ed., *Human Rights and Non-State Actors* (Northampton: Edward Elgar, 2013).

29 See David Chandler, *From Kosovo To Kabul: Human Rights and International Intervention* (London: Pluto, 2002).

especially when it comes to human rights, we have to be darn careful about what we ask people to do under threat of force.[30]

Again, though, self-determination may be decisive. That's as if not self-determination, at least *recognition*, may – *may* – hold the key to conflict. IS may be many things: extremist group, terrorist outfit, theologically-grounded organization and anti-Western in orientation.[31] The group may scare the pants off us in its appearance as the paragon of violent militarism. Still, it *is* noteworthy that IS is looking to establish an "Islamic state."[32] A political claim accompanies whatever theological issues with which the group sees itself as involved. Therein, it seems necessary to ensure that actions like bombing IS not only "degrade and destroy," but address *why* we "degrade" and "destroy" on the occasions that we do. There's no doubt that "degradation" and "destruction" can be just. I have no interest in amputations and torture, to say nothing of the creation of radically conservato-theological states. Still, it *is* the degradation and destruction of human beings we're talking about. Those are human beings that, like them though we may not, the members of IS (and anyone else coalition bombs hit) in fact are.

---

30 As Michael Walzer notes, this question also attaches itself to issues of "just war": that one might enter conflict justly, yet also that one should able to articulate what that just cause is. See Walzer, *Just and Unjust Wars: A Moral Argument with Historical Illustrations* (New York: Basic Books, 1977).

31 In addition to Alexander and Alexander, *The Islamic State*, see Michael Weiss and Hassan Hassan, *ISIS: Inside the Army of Terror* (New York: Regan Arts, 2015).

32 See especially Alexander and Alexander, *The Islamic State*.

Brussels

Looking for Peace: A Different Approach to Terrorism and Human Rights (March 22, 2016)

Abstract: *Events in Brussels force us to confront the tragedy of terrorism's violence – something both emotionally disheartening and challenging basic rights such as the right to security and sovereignty over one's life. Brussels also challenges us to think about peace, however – a sometimes-forgotten dimension of human rights that may induce us to negotiate with those with whom we usually might not.*

It's happened again – again. Unfortunately, I'd argue, it's something that's happened more often than we think. I refer here not only to recent events such as 9/11, the 2005 public transport bombings in London or the 2004 bombings in Madrid of a similar ilk. I refer to Black September storming the Olympic Village at the 1972 Munich Summer Games and murdering eleven athletes in the process. I refer to the 1976 hijacking of an Air France jet filled with Israeli citizens that ended in their dramatic rescue at Uganda's Entebbe Airport – the first time for that many Westerners that small central African state may have come onto the mental map. I refer to the bombing of Pan Am flight 103 in 1988 in which

"Flag of Belgium." © Miro Novak / *Fotolia.com 96916359*

responsibility was claimed by many, but the tenor of the act and its connection to the provocative Muammar Gaddafi tattooed it with his particular brand of anti-Westernism and anti-imperialistic thought.[1] Now, it *is* difficult to say the

---

1   See Rodney Wallis, *Lockerbie: The Story and the Lessons* (Westport: Praeger 2001). On the larger history of modern terrorism, see Jussi M. Hanhimäki and Bernhard Blumenau, eds., *An International History of Terrorism: Western and Non-Western Experiences* (London: Routledge, 2013); Walter Laqueur, *A History of Terrorism* (New Brunswick: Transaction, 2001). Regarding Gaddafi, the point is not so much that he had a particular variety of anti-imperialism on a theoretical basis. He managed to make a particularly vocal noise on the subject for some years, however, especially in relation to anti-Americanism. See Immanuel Ness and Zak Cope, eds., *The Palgrave Encyclopedia of Imperialism and Anti-Imperialism, vol. 1* (New York: Palgrave Macmillan, 2016), 260.

degree to which Islamic State's (née ISIS') brand of terrorism concerns "anti-imperialism" as such. For some, the group represents but a cultish ideology – "twisted" concepts in which only an archaic Salafism will do and a mockery is made of one of the world's great religions.[2] Still, it's hard to not notice that a portion of the group's rise concerns opposition to the presence of Western troops in the Middle East (IS' al-Qaeda origins) and that their interest in the realization of an immediate caliphate appeals to self-determinatory goals. That's with all acknowledgment of IS' otherwise brutal erosion of what are supposed to be fundamental human rights.[3]

Reflecting on these tragic events – the deep tragedy of Brussels – two dimensions stick out. The first is the crushing – absolutely crushing – sense that there may be nowhere in the world where anyone is anymore unqualifiedly safe. The range of attacks is stacking up now: *Charlie Hebdo* in January 2015, the Bataclan and Stade de France in November 2015, the attempted murder of Lars Vilks in Copenhagen in February of that year (Vilks escaped; a filmmaker and security guard did not) and now the dozens killed at Brussel's Airport and a subway stop in the city top the list of attacks from *Europe* – but one continent – more or less

---

2   As Robin Wright has noted, the IS phenomenon illustrates how the 1916 Sykes-Picot Agreement, carving up large portions of the Middle East among victorious World War I powers, still haunts the modern world. While it's not the only factor contributing to the rise of extremism, the exigencies of state-building coming out from under heavy structures of Western imperialism and colonialism – structures which lasted until after the Second World War – have been so complex that they offer not a small vein in the genealogies of al-Qaeda and IS. See Wright, "How the Curse of Sykes-Picot Still Haunts the Middle East," *The New Yorker*, April 30, 2016, available at http://www.newyorker.com/news/news-desk/how-the-curse-of-sykes-picot-still-haunts-the-middle-east. See also Yonah Alexander and Dean Alexander, *The Islamic State: Combating the Caliphate without Borders* (Lanham: Lexington, 2015).

3   The UN has detailed a massive range of crimes committed by IS simply from its time in Iraq, never mind the group's expansion into Syria. This includes brutality visited on civilian populations and an extensive rape epidemic – to say nothing of utter non-recognition of anything resembling civil rights. See United Nations High Commissioner for Human Rights, "Report on the Protection of Civilians in the Armed Conflict in Iraq: 11 December 2014–30 April 2015" (2015), available at http://www.ohchr.org/Documents/Countries/IQ/UNAMI_OHCHR_4th_POCReport-11Dec2014-30April2015.pdf. Regarding self-determination rights, see Hurst Hannum, *Autonomy, Sovereignty, and Self-Determination: The Accommodation of Conflicting Rights* (Philadelphia: University of Pennsylvania Press, 1990).

within the space of the last year.[4] Now, there's no doubt: Western societies often enjoy heightened senses of security due to what one might see as unfair hoardings of global wealth as well as positions behind an umbrella of what one might consider a disproportionate amount of the world's military might.[5] Still, it feels like we're today confronted with the question of which European capital one might be able to visit in safety and *where* on the continent one might be able to visit without background senses of nervousness or feelings that one has to look over one's shoulder and wonder what might be coming next. On March 18, the Belgian police arrested Salah Abdeslam, the sole survivor of the November action in Paris – an act that, given the tenor of the times, was perhaps bound to garner response. Four days later, in the city in which Abdeslam was arrested (Brussels), bombs began to go off. The fact that response couldn't be stopped is a phenomenon that might give one a serious amount of pause.[6]

Indeed, it might *also* be the case that, whether we like it or not, Brussels reveals, or at least helps to underline, that the so-called "clash of civilizations" is dismayingly real. Advanced as a thesis in the mid-1990s after the fall of the Berlin Wall, political scientist Samuel Huntington argued that culture, as opposed to political ideology or economic concept (issues linked over the roughly five decades of the Cold War) would be the "fundamental source of conflict" and the primary call to arms for all.[7] I.e., rather than the more usual "-isms" – capitalism, communism, socialism, liberal democracy and the like – conflict would happen under the hue of identity; it would involve religion, worldview and senses of the self. What the Germans call *Weltanschauung* would determine not only senses

---

4   Indeed, as *Foreign Policy* notes, the number of *global* terrorist events over the past year or so are almost too numerous to count. Attacks by Boko Haram in Nigeria and Cameroon, IS in Yemen, al-Shabaab in Kenya and suicide bombings in Turkey, however, to say nothing of the November 29–30, 2015 San Bernardino shootings in the U.S., add to the sense of increasingly few global locales as safe. See Megan Alpert, "It's Not Just Paris: From Nigeria to Egypt, 10 of 2015's Worst Terrorist Attacks," *Foreign Policy*, November 16, 2015, available at http://foreignpolicy.com/2015/11/16/its-not-just-paris-from-nigeria-to-egypt-ten-of-2015s-worst-terror-attacks/.

5   E.g., Jeremy Black, *Great Powers and the Quest for Hegemony: The World Order since 1500* (London: Routledge, 2007).

6   For a timeline of events, see The New York Times, "What Happened at Each Location in the Brussels Attacks," March 22, 2016, available at http://www.nytimes.com/interactive/2016/03/22/world/europe/brussels-attacks-graphic.html.

7   Samuel P. Huntington, "The Clash of Civilizations?" *Foreign Affairs* 72, no. 3 (1993): 22. See also Huntington, *The Clash of Civilizations and the Remaking of the World Order* (New York: Free Press, 1996).

of political right, but even *if* "political right" might be considered among the primary global questions at all.[8]

Now, such things may have been a "gimme" come the Eastern Bloc's collapse. The fall of communism left but one ideological option – the supposed "capitalism with a human face" represented so strongly by figures like Clinton and Blair – and as Huntington's great foil in post-Cold War international analysis, Francis Fukuyama, *also* noted, the exigencies of historical change might mean that it was too much to expect *all* global societies to toe a single ideological line. The "wagon train" of international society, Fukuyama maintained, was increasingly headed to a single place: liberal ideals. However, due to the power of individual perspective and the inherent unpredictability of historical processes, there would be "stragglers," and a few socio-cultural wagons might be headed to a completely entirely *different* place.[9] Still, the virulentness of politics' "indigenization" (Huntington term), was hard to predict. Not only did ethnic nationalisms erupt violently from the former Yugoslavia to South Ossetia, Chechnya and Georgia, but "unmodern men in a modern world" became awoken by combinations of cultural globalization and regime-building efforts in locales from Afghanistan to Iraq.[10] In such contexts, it wouldn't just be the worldviews of others ("others") that might be treated as such ("worldviews"). The *West's* supposedly universalist ideologies might gain interrogation on those terms as well.[11]

It's hard to know what to say this. Clearly, West/non-West cultural dichotomies paint a false global picture. It's hard to draw borderlines around one global region and say that one set of concepts exists "here" and not "there." Ideas have complex

---

8   The point here concerns the possibility of fully distinct approaches to politics; that what might be standard points of departure for many parts of global society (particular senses of justice or rights, e.g.) might be seen neither in the same way nor as the point of departure for politics at all. This opens the way to political conflict based on culture. See Huntington, "The West Unique, Not Universal," *Foreign Affairs* 75, no. 6 (1996): 28–46; Frederico Lenzerini, *The Culturalization of Human Rights Law* (Oxford: Oxford University Press, 2014).

9   See Francis Fukuyama, *The End of History and the Last Man* (New York: Penguin, 1992), 338. On the Huntington-Fukuyama relationship, see Richard K. Betts, "Conflict or Cooperation?: Three Visions Revisited," *Foreign Affairs* 86, no. 6 (2010): 186–94. See also See Flavio Romano, *Clinton and Blaire: The Political Economy of the Third Way* (London: Routledge, 2006).

10 See Michael Mazarr, *Unmodern Men in the Modern World: Radical Islam, Terrorism, and the War on Modernity* (Cambridge: Cambridge University Press, 2007).

11 See Makau Mutua, *Human Rights: A Political and Cultural Critique* (Philadelphia: University of Pennsylvania Press, 2002).

ways of wending their ways through vast terrains of cultural space.[12] Still, the "New World Order" of the early 1990s fell apart quickly, and the rise of especially religion as a basis for resistance caught many by surprise.[13] Now, battle cries of "tradition" and "belief" *can* be feigns – they can cover over what may be devious goals, such as holding out easily-consumable elixirs of anger intended to appeal to alienated youth; that when the goal is nothing more than bald grabs for power.[14] Still, there *are* questions as to whether we attempt to detect *why* such appeals might work, and we may need to ask *how* we react when at least *some* point to global trends (say, secularization or "Westernization") and say "those aren't mine." Do we *presume* to know which claims about other's identities are "true" and which ones are "not?" Do we barrel ahead in our indictments, assured we know people's "real" senses of self and that, regardless of how one claims to perceive the world, they need to be tuned into ideas we simply "know" are right? Or do we take a more modest stance in which we say that violence isn't something we want, but that goes for ourselves as much as anyone else? Obviously, such issues gain a heightened level of importance when connected to questions of the use of force – which, in the context of events like Brussels, they're more than likely to be.[15]

I'm again a touch unsure of what to say to this. Generally, difference need be respected. Twenty-first century conditions and the realities of globalization mean, or at least *may* mean, that we have to deal with each other whether we like it or not. The "challenge" of multicultural societies – including global multiculturalism – may be unavoidable.[16] That may be the nature of the "time-space compression" that's

---

12 E.g., David Slater, "Post-Colonial Questions for Global Times," *Review of International Political Economy* 5, no. 4 (1998): 647–78.

13 For a recounting of all of this, see G. John Ikenberry, *Liberal Leviathan: The Origins, Crisis, and Transformation of the American World Order* (Princeton: Princeton University Press, 2011). Of course, religion already had a presence in world affairs via the Iranian Revolution (1979) and the Afghan War in the 1980s. Still, it's the breadth of the appeal to culturo-religious issues that seems to be new. See Jonathan Fox, *Religion, Civilization, and Civil War: 1945 Through the New Millennium* (Lanham: Lexington, 2004).

14 E.g., Stephen Filder, "How Alienated Youth Fall Prey to the Militant Allure of Islamic State," *The Wall Street Journal*, December 5, 2015, available at http://www.wsj.com/articles/how-alienated-youth-fall-prey-to-the-militant-allure-of-islamic-state-1449205294.

15 See, e.g., Henning Trüper, Dipesh Chakrabarty, Sanjay Subrahmanyam, eds., *Historical Teleologies in the Modern World* (London: Bloomsbury, 2015).

16 Jan-Erik Lane, *Globalization and Politics: Promises and Dangers* (Farnham: Ashgate, 2006), 93.

brought global society closer together.[17] That's while one doesn't want to see differ-ence used as an excuse for brutality, or claims to alienation become the grounds for hurting one's fellow women and men. Political realism has to be measured against political idealism, and we have to recognize where history has brought us whether we're fully enamored by the locations in which we find ourselves or not.[18]

In any case, the *larger* issue with which Brussels may confront us is the prob-lem of human rights. I.e., Brussels *may* reveal the contemporary stage as "civili-zationally" conflicted. It may underline us as engaged in sets of culturally-driven battles which have crept increasingly close to the center of the global stage since the Cold War's end. Brussels may *also* ask, however, us to look at the framework through which we *address* such issues; the concepts that many of us hold as our "highest moral precepts and political ideals."[19] Brussels may ask us to look at the *ideas* through which we claim we *seek* to organize politics and the standards to which many of us, anyway, would like to imagine that we hold *ourselves*.

I'd pose the problem as follows. Firstly, as the Universal Declaration of Human Rights (1948) puts it – the Universal Declaration being primary international rights document – everyone has the right to "life." Everyone has the right to live in "liberty and security of person."[20] Everyone should live in "freedom from fear," as the American President Franklin Roosevelt put it in what some mark as an early iteration of the idea (the 1941 State of the Union Address, or the so-called "Four Freedoms" speech). Now, in Roosevelt's version, "freedom from fear" concerned disarmament. It concerned hindering unnecessary "aggression" and stopping the progress of war – comprehensible concerns given the state of global affairs in 1941.[21] The *point* of hindering aggression, however – of hold-ing conflict at bay – was to help the individual conduct his or her business. It concerned inculcations of normality and *not* living on a knife's edge regarding

---

17 See David Harvey, *The Condition of Postmodernity: An Enquiry into the Origins of Cultural Change* (Oxford: Basil Blackwell, 1989).

18 It's a touch old – a point made in the early '90s. The historian Eric Hobsbawm, however, referred to ours as the "Age of Extremes." I'd tend to agree. See Hobsbawm, *The Age of Extremes: A History of the World, 1914–1991* (New York: Vintage, 1994).

19 Samuel Moyn, *The Last Utopia: Human Right in History* (Cambridge, MA: Harvard Belknap, 2010), 1.

20 United Nations, "The Universal Declaration of Human Rights" (1948, article 3 [here-after UDHR]), available at http://www.un.org/en/universal-declaration-human-rights/index.html. See also Rowan Cruft, S. Matthew Liao and Massimo Renzo, eds., *Philo-sophical Foundations of Human Rights* (Oxford: Oxford University, 2015).

21 See Franklin Delano Roosevelt, "Message to Congress 1941" (State of the Union Address), available at http://www.fdrlibrary.marist.edu/pdfs/ffreadingcopy.pdf.

the basic elements of one's life. At stake was degrees of sovereignty; one's ability to control one's existence and being. The philosopher Isaiah Berlin once posed this as a matter of not being hindered by "other men."[22] "Other men," of course, might mean the state. It also, however, might mean *any* group attempting to prevent one from doing as one might like. That includes going to the airport, or getting on a subway train when one wants.[23]

Now, there are qualifications to be made here. What does one do when one feels one's *own* rights have been violated? How does one deal with situations in which one senses that not only the *extreme* ends of one's beliefs are opposed, but that the right to have *any* of the beliefs one does might *also* be at risk (e.g., that the West might be at war with "Islam")? What does one do about not only immediate messes made by, say, Western intervention into non-Western lands, but the potentially *endemic* nature of such interventions and the lack of clarity as to when such interventions might end? What means are available to those who wish to bring *permanent* ends to long-term histories of marginalization and who are dog-tired of asking for recognition? Is there *no* justification for taking the fight so hard to one's enemies – including actions one might condemn as extreme?[24]

From time to time, the global community invokes the concept of *jus cogens*: "peremptory" forms of international law. Coalitions of states have historically maintained the ability to identify circumstances in which they might "derogate" or "degrade" what are generally thought of as fundamental rights – that in order to uphold the rights of others or preserve rights for generations to come (one might deny some the right life in order to stop a genocide or an unjust war, e.g.).[25] In such contexts, one *could* argue that if either political or cultural marginalization were extreme enough – if they were *really* endemic in nature – provisions should

---

22 Isaiah Berlin, "Two Concepts of Liberty," in *Liberty: Incorporating Four Essays on Liberty*, ed. Henry Hardy (Oxford: Oxford University Press, 2002), 179.

23 See Jordan J. Paust, "Human Rights, Terrorism, and Efforts to Combat Terrorism," in *Human Rights and Conflict: Exploring the Links between Rights, Law, and Peacebuilding*, ed. Julie Mertus and Jeffrey Helsing (Washington, D.C.: United States Institute of Peace, 2006), 239–66.

24 Historians Jeffrey Wasserstrom, Greg Grandin, Lynn Hunt and Marylin Young note that human rights in fact has a long history in revolution and insurrection – that as rights are at least partly based on the idea of overturning unjust systems. See Wasserstrom, Grandin, Hunt and Young, eds., *Human Rights and Revolutions* (Lanham: Rowman and Littlefield, 2007). See also Werner Maihofer and Gerhard Sprenger, eds., *Revolution and Human Rights* (Stuttgart: Franz Steiner 1990).

25 See Robert Kolb, *Peremptory International Law – Jus Cogens: An Inventory* (Oxford: Hart, 2015).

be made for insurrection as a means to combat marginalization. I.e., it might be recognized that one *might* take up arms to fight non-recognition as a structurally ingrained phenomenon. Indeed, given the presence of such phenomena in the foundation of modern, liberal democracies as well as post-colonial independences – there might be something to this.[26] Still, we're on a slippery slope. Regardless of questions as to whether the *kinds* of violence employed by groups like IS constitute acceptable reactions to injustice, it's unclear what the *guidelines* for such peremptory rights might be; when and how *specifically* would such rights apply, and in what *form* might one recognize "cultural insurrection" – again, even *if* one recognizes histories of marginalization, which one should? Again, we *might* recognize "cultural-insurrectory" rights; lording over anyone in any sense is hardly within human rights' purview. Still, insofar as *I* can see, there's also no basis for *terror* in international law; I can't find where one gains the right to threaten innocents or, as one might feel is being done to one's own people, undermine the tranquility of societies as a whole. "Peremptory" law *can't* be about making people feel *less* secure than they do today.[27]

Again, all well and good. Rights demand justice, and in any conflict, just behavior has to be asked of both sides.[28] Still, there's another ethic that comes under the heading of international rights. There's another issue that Brussels asks us to look at – another dimension of our "highest moral precepts and political ideals" that events like those in Belgium force us to discuss. That's peace. That's concord. It's the charge us to avoid violence *at all*. It's the request that we might consider how to *deescalate* strife and, really, what the best way is to handle our response when the bombs go off.

Now, we again have to be clear that human rights involve a "right to." Rights involve over the ability to control one's life and the ability to conduct one's

---

26 I simply point to the fact that it is noticeable that certain levels of violent insurrection have been historically accepted in the name of cultural liberation. I.e., if colonial independences are considered to have cultural components, and we keep in mind that those were hardly fully achieved on peaceful bases. That's of course to say nothing about violence as part of events like the American and French Revolutions, or the revolutions of 1848. See again Wasserstrom, Grandin, Hunt and Young, *Human Rights and Revolutions*. See also Martin Thomas, *Fight or Flight: Britain, France, and Their Roads from Empire* (Oxford: Oxford University Press, 2014). See also See also Alastair Crooke, *Resistance: The Essence of the Islamist Revolution* (New York: Pluto Press, 2009).

27 See, e.g., Benjamin J. Goold, and Liora Lazarus, eds., *Security and Human Rights* (Oxford: Hart, 2007).

28 See Francesco Francioni, ed., *Access to Justice as a Human Right* (Oxford: Oxford University Press, 2007).

business as one wants. "Mental integrity" and "security of person," two scholars have noted, are the baseline of any concept of freedoms and privileges.[29] The ability to live as one would like is a reasonable expectation of what one might "receive" through the frameworks of international justice.[30]

Still, rights involve *responsibilities*. Rights ask us to consider the societies we'd like to *create* – the futures we seek to *build*. Rights ask us to speak to the tenor of the milieus in which we desire to lead our lives and what we're willing to *give*. The Universal Declaration is clear. "Peace in the world" should stand alongside "freedom and justice" as international society's guiding light.[31] "Friendly relations" between peoples is the gold standard humanity should *always* seek; liberty and equality lose their luster when achieved down the barrel of a gun. How do we create worlds where we *needn't* fight insurrection because people will be *less* likely to take up arms – that because they *don't* suffer senses of marginalization and they're *not* dog-tired from asking to be heard? How do we ensure that individuals and groups feel included because they've at least been *asked* about global norms – that they gain senses that we've at least *tried* to listen because we haven't contributed to marginalization *ourselves*? Political philosopher John Rawls once maintained that any rights society has to accept a "diversity of opposing and irreconcilable religious, philosophical and moral" views.[32] We *can* say "no." Not everything is ok. Still, we need to ask ourselves how we get to worlds where we're *less* likely to "degrade" rights because we've done what we can to avoid the conditions in which the rights' deconstruction *begins*. How do we hear – listen – such that it's *harder* to say that particular groups haven't been allowed to speak? How do we nod to the fact that others are *present* – that whether we agree with a group's or individual's theology, philosophy, worldview or not?

To me, all this says two things. Firstly, as cease fires are negotiated in places like Syria and Iraq, IS and its allies *must* be brought to the table. Clearly: one doesn't want to overdo negotiating with dictators and murderers; no one needs a reproduction of Munich in 1938 (acquiescing to a terrorist's demands because

---

29 Alex Conte and Richard Burchill, *Defining Civil and Political Rights: The Jurisprudence of the United Nations Human Rights Committee*, 2nd ed. (Farnham: Ashgate, 2009), 3.

30 See Jürgen Habermas, "Private and Public Autonomy, Human Rights and Popular Sovereignty" in *The Politics of Human Rights*, ed. Obrad Savić (London: Verso, 1999), 50–66.

31 UDHR, preamble.

32 John Rawls, *Political Liberalism* (New York: Columbia University Press, 1993), 3–4.

one sought to pursue peace at any price).[33] Still, the U.S. and its allies – most certainly Russia too – have some strange bedfellows, and there are few clean hands in situations involving massive factionalism and humanitarian nightmares on scales many of us can barely contemplate. There may be value in forcing IS to say something out loud about it goals – that in recognized forums as opposed to shady online proclamations or covertly-circulated videotapes. Perhaps our "Others" perceive "civilizational conflict" too, wherein it might be interesting to hear if *they* have suggestions about global coexistence; if they *are* just out for destruction, or if, despite all the madness, they perceive themselves as maintaining rights-based visions *themselves*. Asking doesn't guarantee results. Those who want war can pursue it, and peace can be employed as a ruse. Still, it might be worth evaluating if there's *any* way to proceed without drone strikes, carrier groups or the ground forces that, though in small numbers, are already present in Syria and the borderlands of Iraq. In divided worlds like ours, such approaches might set new precedents in terms of promoting negotiation as opposed to armed posturing as a response to tension and strife.[34]

Of course, *that* can only be done if we reflect on the meaning of such actions. I.e., peace can only be pursued if we understand that peacemaking isn't just oriented towards those with whom we agree, but that the rubber hits the road when we're involved with those whom we imagine we *don't*. Peace involves spanning *broad* divides of difference and confronting what can seem like *oceans of* incomprehension on quite some number of sides. Now, I have no interest in assenting to cross-border, seventh century caliphates. In my view, the primary issue regarding fundamentalism may be less fundamentalism *itself* (the concept) than the practices issuing from it. Among those, gender oppression may be the worst.[35] Still, I *am* interested to *avoid* continuous Syrias, Libyas and Iraqs. I'd

---

33 Munich was the 1938 peace conference intended to placate Hitler by giving him the portions of Czechoslovakia he demanded in exchange for promises of no further aggression; promises he eventually broke. See David Faber, *Munich, 1938: Appeasement and World War II* (New York: Simon and Schuster, 2008).

34 See Chester A. Crocker, Fen Olser Hampson and Pamela Hall, *Dogs of War: Conflict Management in Divided World* (Washington, DC: United States Institute of Peace, 2006); Oliver P. Richmond, *Peace in International Relations* (London: Routledge, 2008). See also Barbara Starr and Jeremy Diamond, "Syria: Obama Authorizes Boots on the Ground to Fight ISIS," *CNN*, October 30, 2015, available at http://www.cnn.com/2015/10/30/politics/syria-troops-special-operations-forces/.

35 See Courtney Howland, ed., *Religious Fundamentalists and the Human Rights of Women* (New York: Palgrave, 1999).

like a world *without* further Brussels, Parises, Londons, Madrids or New Yorks. I'd enjoy the seemingly constant cycles of war to *stop*, and for the world to be free of violence not just for some days, but as the default position for global society at-large. To the extent that others might feel the same way, negotiation with our enemies *has to* begin. Negotiation with our malevolent "Other" must somehow commence. That's as, in the words of the Universal Declaration, the "highest aspirations" of a "common people" *must* trump all. Anything we can do to end humanity's "barbarous acts" has to be considered a gift, and whatever one can do to halt "outrage[s]" against the "conscience" of "[human]kind" should be thought of as a boon.[36] That's in the name of creating atmospheres in which *all* can thrive, and in which we've given *everyone* means to express themselves that don't include putting innocents to death. Such innocents exist in many places. They clearly exist in locales like Raqqa and Aleppo. No fewer, however, exist in cities like Brussels, or any other site of recent terrorist attacks.

---

36 UDHR, preamble, article 1.

Human Rights and American Politics
The Surprising Case of Bernie Sanders
(March 24, 2016)

Abstract: *The democratic socialist Bernie Sanders has been one of the surprises of the American electoral season. Not the least of the surprises Sanders has brought is relatively frequent allusion to human rights principles – unusual in otherwise generally-exceptionalist America.*

Arizona, Utah, and Idaho held presidential primaries and caucuses a couple of days ago – March 22, to be exact – and Bernie Sanders, the sometime-dubbed "insurgent" candidate on the Democratic side, won a couple of them: Utah and Idaho.[1] It was a typical Sanders day. He gained clear support. In what's become increasing political parlance, Sanders "drubbed" Clinton in the states he won – Utah and Idaho; rural states that are generally conservative and in which Democrats tend to be a special kind breed (Obama lost both states handily in 2008 and 2012, e.g.).[2] Clinton won the big prize, though – Arizona (eighty-five delegates [Idaho and Utah have twenty-seven and thirty-seven each]) – and continued a march forward in which, though it's clear there's a taste for something further to the left, especially the young, centrist positions remain the default on the American political spectrum. Clinton, short of an unforeseen catastrophe (something concerning those pesky emails, for example, or perhaps a left over from the 1990s Bill and Hillary closet), will win.

"Flag of the United States." © Miro Novak / Fotolia.com 131291020

Still, Sanders' relative popularity – he *will* gain a significant number of delegates – *has* been hard to predict. I know Sanders in a way; that from his years as mayor of Burlington, Vermont, where he was one of the country's few genuinely left-wing politicians with any modicum of real-time success. I went to high

---

1   On the vocabulary of "insurgent" candidacy, see Jason Horowitz, "Democrats Turn to Hillary after Flirting with Bernie Sanders," *The New York Times*, March 1, 2016, available at http://www.nytimes.com/2016/03/02/us/politics/hillary-clinton-bernie-sanders.html.

2   See The New York Times, "Election Results 2008," available at http://elections.nytimes.com/2008/results/president/map.html; The New York Times, "Election Results 2012," available at http://elections.nytimes.com/2012/results/president.

school in neighboring New Hampshire and, for those of us styling ourselves on what we thought was the *true* political left – something beyond the sometimes-vague progressivisms of the Democratic Party – Sanders was a hero.[3] The Vermont senator supported Jesse Jackson in 1988 – unusual for a white, non-urban politician – he thundered on issues of income inequality, he prodded on issues of social justice, he often pointed to the problematic state of the environment and frequently raised questions of disarmament and world peace (decidedly unusual in that late-Cold War world). Sanders also used the word "socialist" – something which at the time that was a virtual no-go in American life. As young activists, we loved it.[4] When he made it to Congress as an independent in 1990, we loved it even more. Few politicians played outside the two-party system and, again, even fewer dared label themselves with a word common on the European tableau (again, "socialist") yet, outside of highly specific pockets of American culture, was extremely rare to hear. It expanded the political imagination in ways that seemed daring and brave.

Now, Sanders, positions aren't *100%* uncomplicated. He is in fact not *fully* liberal on *every* issue. He *is* as far to the left as it gets on the American spectrum regarding Wall Street reform, financial speculation, affirmative action, disarmament and military cutbacks as well as gender-related issues such as a women's right to choose and equal pay for equal work – to say nothing of his long-term commitment to LGBT rights.[5] It turns out, however, that Sanders is a bit of a moderate on guns.

3　Clearly, the Democrats have been traditional supporters of civil rights and more extensive entitlement programs than their Republican counterparts. Fundamental transformations in the economic system have largely *not* been part of Democratic agendas, however, and, as has shone through in this election cycle, moderate Democratic policies, such as the 1994 Crime Bill, have played into the hands of law and order conservatism with sometimes highly problematic consequences. I simply point to the fact that as one of the country's two major parties, it isn't always easy for Democratic politicians to work outside the broad mainstream of the country's politics. See Thomas Frank, *Listen, Liberal: Or Whatever Happened to the Party of the People?* (New York: Henry Holt, 2016).

4　See Russel Banks, "Bernie Sanders, The Socialist Mayor," *The Atlantic*, October 5, 2015, available at http://www.theatlantic.com/politics/archive/2015/10/bernie-sanders-mayor/407413/.

5　Government research website InsideGov, e.g., ranks Sanders by far the most liberal of the major party candidates – though overall, he falls a hair behind Green Party candidate Jill Stein. See InsideGov, "Ranking Every Candidate from Least to Most Conservative," available at http://presidential-candidates.insidegov.com/stories/4079/ranking-2016-presidential-candidate-least-most-conservative#2-bernie-sanders.

Now, personally, I can't get beyond the idea that, given his determinedly leftward-lean on near everything else, Sanders would *actually* like to see a more European approach to personal firearms (namely, that they're near-impossible to get). Still, Sanders has needed to win election in a rural state (again, Vermont), and he appears to have given a bit on a specific issue in order to stay close to his voters and get his other proposals in. Sanders is no Second Amendment nut. He wants the broad range of loopholes surrounding the purchase of firearms immediately shut (the sale of firearms online and at gun shows, for example).[6] His "D-" rating from the NRA is nonetheless a touch worse (or better, from the NRA's perspective) than Hillary Clinton's "F," and is a grade indicative of a level of pragmatism in a man about whom it's often easy to assume that it's only principle that drives how he thinks.[7]

Sanders is also a surprisingly adept campaigner. His is a curious blend. On one hand, Sanders stays ferociously on message, taking advantage of a weakness his opponent (Clinton) sometimes has (consistency). That nonetheless appears to be both a planned staying on message and not. Sanders appears fully aware of where his strengths lay – the authenticity of his liberal commitments (he's been an activist since the '60s) and his willingness to say things that others often won't. However, Sanders simply rests in those strengths, iterating again and again what he sees as his basic points (heightened civil rights and economic justice, largely).[8] It's a move that creates intense problems for candidates about whom it's difficult to tell if their campaigns just campaigns, or if they *do* concern sets of ideas intended to lead to something larger than themselves.[9]

Indeed, one might also mention that Sanders connects with a wider array of voters than one might assume. Again, his popularity with the young is well-known;

---

6   See Jessica Taylor, "Bernie Sanders Walks a Fine Line on Gun Control," *NPR*, June 24, 2015, available at http://www.npr.org/sections/itsallpolitics/2015/06/24/417180805/bernie-sanders-walks-a-fine-line-on-gun-control.

7   Ellen Brait, "Candidates NRA Ratings: A Telling Reflection of Reactions to San Bernardino Shootings," *The Guardian*, December 3, 2015, available at http://www.theguardian.com/us-news/2015/dec/03/san-bernardino-shooting-presidential-candidates-responses-nra-ratings.

8   Tamara Keith, "The Political Moment Finally Caught Up to Bernie Sanders' Message," *NPR*, May 15, 2016, available at http://www.npr.org/2016/05/05/476927333/bernie-sanders-has-a-message-for-the-political-moment.

9   E.g., Callum Borchers, "Hillary Clinton Acknowledges Voter Concern that She's 'In it for Herself,'" *The Washington Post*, February 21, 2016, available at https://www.washingtonpost.com/news/post-politics/wp/2016/02/21/hillary-clinton-acknowledges-voter-concern-that-shes-in-it-for-herself/.

Sanders typically gains more than two-thirds of Democratic primary voters among the under-thirty crowd.[10] He also gains majority support from those posing themselves as "highly liberal" or going to the maximum edge of what most Americans consider the political left.[11] That's while gaining *some* of the same supporters as the quasi-populist Donald Trump – "anti-establishment" voters attracted to candidates who "tell it like it is."[12] Interestingly, though, while much has been made of Sanders' inability to make inroads among minorities, he's in fact picked up more than marginal support in certain of those areas as well. In the March 15 Ohio primary, e.g., Sanders garnered about of 30% of the African-American vote. Clinton, playing something of the role in relation to Barak Obama that Sanders plays in relation to her concerning Black voters – the clear underdog – received less than 15% in Ohio in 2008.[13] Partly, the discrepancy involves Sanders' strong – some would say impeccable – civil rights credentials. Strangely enough, those are credentials certain Clinton allies, including Civil Rights hero John Lewis, attempted to discredit.[14] It was a bizarre move as Clinton's own civil rights record is nothing to sneeze at itself.[15]

---

10 See Aaron Blake, "Bernie Sanders: The 74-Year-Old's Dominance among Young Voters in One Chart," *The Independent*, March 18, 2016, available at http://www.independent. co.uk/news/world/americas/us-elections/bernie-sanders-democratic-party-us-election-2016-dominance-among-young-voters-chart-a6938911.html.

11 It was at a time when the Democratic primary was more than a two-person race. However, CNN entrance polls in Iowa indicated that Sanders won 58% those who considered themselves "very liberal" as opposed to Clinton's 39% (Martin O'Malley, who was still in the race at the time, garnered 1%). Clinton, scored 58% of those considering themselves "moderate," whereas Sanders scored only 35%. See CNN, "Iowa Entrance Polls," February 1, 2016, available at http://edition.cnn.com/election/primaries/polls/ia/Dem.

12 Tamara Keith, "5 Ways Bernie Sanders and Donald Trump Supporters Are More Alike Than You'd Think," *NPR*, February 8, 2016, available at http://www.npr. org/2016/02/08/465974199/what-do-sanders-and-trump-have-in-common-more-than-you-think.

13 See USA Today, "5 Keys to the Democratic Primaries in Ohio and Texas," March 3, 2008, available at http://usatoday30.usatoday.com/news/politics/election2008/2008-03-04-exit-poll-graphic_n.htm.

14 See Tom LoBianco and Elizabeth Landers, "John Lewis: 'I Never Saw' Sanders at Civil Rights Events," *CNN*, February 11, 2016, available at http://edition.cnn. com/2016/02/11/politics/john-lewis-bernie-sanders-civil-rights/.

15 See Charles P. Pierce, "Why Hillary Clinton's Stint as a Civil-Rights Secret Agent Matters Today," *Esquire*, December 28, 2015, available at http://www.esquire.com/news-politics/politics/news/a40772/hillary-clinton-undercover-civil-rights/.

In any case, beyond the idealism and surprising effectivity – beyond the emergence of a candidacy at which many guffawed when it began – two points stick out to me regarding Sanders' run; two elements shine through that *I* see, anyway, as making his popularity unusual. The first *in fact* concerns socialism, or what appears to be a relative *lack* of fanfare concerning Sanders' identification with the term. Now, it's not that Americans *haven't* met socialism before. Beyond the concept's long influence in academic circles and its use in movements such as the New Left in the '60s and '70s, the country had socialist mayors *before* Sanders; Milwaukee's had two or three of them, in fact (Emil Seidel, Daniel Webster Hoan and Frank Zeidler). Indeed, it's also the case that socialist heroes like Daniel De Leon and Eugene Debs ran multiple times for the Presidency – the latter twice polling between 3 and 6% (1912 and 1920).[16] Now, one should take care: Sanders advocates positions that in places like Europe and Canada are relatively uncontroversial: universal health care, tuition-free college, meaningful welfare benefits, extensive public services, daycare for all and the inculcation of cradle-to-grave social security. Though perhaps not in the *American* mainstream, it's not like such concepts are in no one's mainstream at all.[17] However, it's *also* not the case that no one has advocated such ideas over the course of *American* life. The Socialist Party of America once boasted around 100,000 members and the mutual aid branch of Communist Party USA once had upwards of 200,000 active in its ranks – parties that most *certainly* supported expansion of the welfare state. The role of socialism in unions up to the start of the twentieth century and the importance of fringe yet influential groups such the Industrial Workers of the World (the "Wobblies") in the 1910s and '20s was also significant – movements bringing the banner of inclusion to a great many working men and women who otherwise felt deep disenfranchisement.[18] Indeed, there were also what one might identify as "socialistic" concepts in the ideologies of groups from Students for a Democratic Society to the Black Panthers as well as dimensions of Martin Luther King's 1968 "Poor People's Campaign" – all of which advocated for more grassroots distributions of the national wealth. In fact, whether

---

16 Mary Beth Norton, et al., *A People and a Nation: A History of the United States,* 9th ed. (Boston: Wadsworth, 2007), A16–A21.

17 See Mel Cousins, *European Welfare States: Comparative Perspectives* (London: Sage, 2005).

18 On a small literary note, the kind of atmosphere to which the Wobblies appealed is portrayed in John Steinbeck's 1936 *In Dubious Battle* – a novel set amidst a fruit worker's strike in California in the 1930s. See Steinbeck, *In Dubious Battle* (New York: Penguin, 1978).

it's Franklin Roosevelt's or Lyndon Johnson's minimal – I say *minimal* – inculcations of the welfare state (programs like Social Security, Medicaid and Medicare) or initiatives on state levels such as the provision of broad-based health care in Massachusetts (under Mitt Romney; a Republican!), *some* level of collectivistic, "share-the-wealth" thinking has *long* been present in American life.[19] I'd be shy to say precisely what "socialism" is. Still, unfettered capitalism and notions of everything-addressed-individualistically-all-the-time haven't gone *completely* without critique over the American past.[20] There's been interest social inclusion coupled with *some* form equalitarian economics in *some* sense of the word.[21]

That being said, however, there clearly *is* a history of having to be careful – quite careful – about using the "S" word in American social space. Though not totally *absent* from U.S. history (and no, I'm not saying that Mitt Romney is a socialist), socialists *have* experienced more than a small amount of stigmatization through the larger arc of American life. The 1919–1920 Palmer Raids may have set the tone – that as they brought the U.S. its first "Red Scare" in the context of the Department of Justice's attempt to rid the country of the "collectivists" and "anarchists" supposedly threatening the ideological foundations of the American state. McCarthyism and the House Committee on Un-American Activities in the 1940s and '50s furthered "anti-Red" ideals as the Cold War set in and the Soviets became America's largest threat; the post-World War II expansion of Soviet influence was a boon for those who sought to whip up anti-socialist and anti-communist fervor at home. The 1960s and '70s saw accusations of movements like those against the Vietnam War and nuclear arms as loaded with "commies" and "pinkos" wherein, combined with Reagan-esque designations of the Soviets and their satellites as an "evil empire" – never mind the fact that no socialist party ever polled anything *beyond* the 3–6% twice garnered by Debs – it becomes not *un*fair to say that the larger part of American politics *has* had its doubts about anything from socialist-communist-collectivist ideological spectrum.[22]

19　See John Nichols, *The "S" Word: A Short History of an American Tradition...Socialism* (London: Verso, 2011).

20　See Douglas Charles Rossinow, *Visions of Progress: The Left-liberal Tradition in America* (Philadelphia: University of Pennsylvania Press, 2008).

21　For more on definitions of socialism, see Peter Lamb, *Historical Dictionary of Socialism*, 3rd ed. (Lanham: Rowman & Littlefield, 2016).

22　See Larry Ceplair, *Anti-Communism in Twentieth Century America: A Critical History* (Westport: Praeger, 2011); Carl Freedman, *Nixon's America: A Study in Cultural Power* (Hants: Zero, 2012). Indeed, figures like King were also circumspect about invoking any kind "socialistic" vocabulary in public space as it was always controversial that

I over-generalize. Considering my own memories of the late '80s and early '90s, however – I was sixteen when the Berlin Wall came down in 1989 – it seems that when the Cold War ended, most Americans were happy to say "goodbye to all that."[23] Though its flame had always been just a flicker at home, history had finally proved socialism *qua* concept wrong, and by hook or by crook, the whole idea could be thrown out. Those on the supposed "right" side of history could finally utter "good riddance."

I'm not exactly sure what's changed. Again, Sanders supporters are young – "millennials," as such – and it may be that within the bounds of *that* age group, many feel they *can* say "goodbye to all that." I.e., many in their twenties and thirties appear to feel uncompelled to join in the anti-socialist paranoia of their parents' and grandparents' generations; notions of "Reds" hiding under anyone's bed seem noticeably non-*de rigueur*. As one commentator has offered, that might be because "socialism" now means Occupy or the "Battle of Seattle" (1999). Socialism may have come to mean the movements emerging from the 2008 financial crash or deriving from 1990s responses to globalization.[24] "Socialism's" meaning may have morphed from one of the world's many Marxism's into a kind of postmodern hodgepodge of interests in economic justice and varied achievements of social progress (the simultaneously vague-yet-precise "we are the 99%!").[25] Indeed, understandings of American *history* may have changed. The drive for recognition by minority groups, immigrant communities and the working class may be so mainstream by now that it's hard to flat-out indict the calls for social justice with which such groups have so often been involved. That includes petitions for things like welfare and basic social services – again, causes that socialism historically embraced.[26] In any case, the tenor if not around "socialism," then at least "social democracy" or "democratic socialism" (Sanders' preferred terms), appears decidedly

---

some figures important for Civil Rights – Bayard Rustin and Paul Robeson, for example – were explicitly involved with socialist parties and groups. See Paul Le Blanc, ed., *Black Liberation and the American Dream: The Struggle for Racial and Economic Justice* (Amherst: Prometheus, 2003); Michael Eric Dyson, *I May Not Get There with You: The True Martin Luther King, Jr.* (New York: Free Press, 2000), 230.

23 Eric Hobsbawm, "Goodbye to All That," in *After the Fall: The Failure of Communism and the Future of Socialism*, ed. R. Blackburn (London: Verso, 1991), 115–25.

24 See Martin Bak Jørgensen and Óscar García Agustín, eds., *The Politics of Dissent* (Frankfurt am Main: Peter Lang, 2015).

25 Nick Gillespie, "The Secret Language of Millennials," *Time*, July 11, 2014, available at http://time.com/2974185/millennials-poll-politics/.

26 See John David Skrentny, *The Minority Rights Revolution* (Cambridge, MA: Harvard University Press, 2002).

different. On November 18, Sanders held a speech Georgetown University to describe his version of the idea. Largely, he harkened to Rooseveltian New Dealism,
Johnson-esque "Great Society" concepts, bits of left unionism and paeans to civil
rights with some good-old-time-religion Debs fervor thrown in. Relative to the
reaction Sanders might have received a decade or two ago (to say nothing of three,
four or five), the media, public and other candidates hardly made a peep. It was as
though nothing much had happened at all.[27]

Now, that's all interesting: the idea that socialism isn't *totally* unknown in
American life, though it's a good while since the term featured so centrally in
national debate (to say nothing of in a *positive* sense). The *second* point I find
provocative regarding Sanders' campaign, however, is its relationship to *human
rights*. I.e., I'm provoked by the relationship of Sanders' candidacy with the global
community's most basic humanitarian ideals – our "highest morals precepts and
political ideals," as it's been put; the concepts which should define *all* political systems and which, theoretically, no government should forget.[28] Now, this is tricky.
Especially as the latter days of the campaign have featured a number of large
industrial states, Sanders' message has sometimes veered towards economic pro-
tectionism, leading to tones sometimes sounding pseudo-nationalistic as much
as universalist-egalitarian (the usual terrain of human rights [the notion has
roughly been the protection of American workers]).[29] Clinton has also made *her*
overtures to international privileges as the *likely* winner of the Democratic primary kicked off her campaign in New York's Roosevelt Island "Four Freedoms"
Park – a kick-off in which she referenced FDR's 1941 speech in which he argued
that all deserve "freedom of speech," "freedom of worship," "freedom from want"
and "freedom from fear;" vocabularies reproduced near-exactly in central documents of international rights.[30] Clinton also sometimes phrases women's issues as

27 See again Tupy, "Bernie is Not a Socialist."
28 Samuel Moyn, *The Last Utopia: Human Rights in History* (Cambridge, MA: Harvard
    Belknap, 2010), 1.
29 See Steven Pearlstein, "What Bernie Sanders Would Do to America," *The Wash-
    ington Post*, March 18, 2016, available at https://www.washingtonpost.com/news/
    wonk/wp/2016/03/14/can-bernie-sanders-turn-the-united-states-into-denmark-an-
    investigation/.
30 See Jeffrey A. Engel, "The Four Freedoms: FDR's Legacy of Liberty for the United
    States and the World," in *The Four Freedoms: Franklin D. Roosevelt and the Evolution
    of an American Idea*, ed. Jeffrey Engel (Oxford: Oxford University Press, 2015), 8.
    See also Franklin Delano Roosevelt, "Message to Congress 1941," available at http://
    www.fdrlibrary.marist.edu/pdfs/ffreadingcopy.pdf; United Nations, "The Universal

human rights issues specifically, which they clearly are.[31] Still, Sanders has made certain statements that are startlingly clear. On March 7, e.g., Sanders participated in a Fox News town hall – none-too-friendly territory for left-wingers, as viewers of American television will know. Towards the start of the event, Sanders was asked by host Brett Baier, who did quite well with the interview, in fact, to describe his (Sanders') approach to single-payer, universal health care. Now, Sanders, the Socialist-*cum*-Independent-*cum*-Democrat, invoked a line of argumentation that he often uses: that there's single-payer health care in similarly industrialized states, the cost of drugs for older and disadvantaged citizens is high, and that a public system might be more efficient to run than the maze of private health care networks defining the American approach. It was practicalities and comparative points, mostly. Sanders was about to go on. Baier, however, interrupted him. He asked Sanders from where he thought such broad-scale rights came (that one might be guaranteed health care, ensured social services or be universally offered access to welfare). From where do people deserve such broad levels of social and political consideration – that they might be *guaranteed* something, as opposed to having to "work" for it? Sanders' answer was as clear: "from being a human being." From one's humanity alone. From the fact that one belongs to the human species. With a single phrase, Sanders summed up the entire meaning of international human rights.[32]

Now, the surprise comes at a number of levels. Firstly, the U.S. has had a complex relation with international rights ideals. In many ways, the country was decisive for human rights' basic formulation. Conceptually, the U.S., along with France, might be the historical birthplace of institutionalized rights. That's via Enlightenment-era democratic-revolutionary vocabularies of rights as "inalienable" and something one has by birth – that all deserve "life, liberty, and the

---

Declaration of Human Rights" (1948, preamble [hereafter UDHR]), available at http://www.un.org/en/universal-declaration-human-rights/index.html.

31 Amy Chozick, "Hillary Clinton's Beijing Speech on Women Resonates 20 Years Later," *The New York Times*, September 5, 2015, available at https://www.nytimes.com/politics/first-draft/2015/09/05/20-years-later-hillary-clintons-beijing-speech-on-women-resonates/. See also Julie Peters and Andrea Wolper, eds., *Women's Rights, Human Rights: International Feminist Perspectives* (London: Routledge, 1995).

32 Rights historian Micheline Ishay, e.g., has written that the essence of human rights is that one simply has them via belonging to the "human race." Humanity alone determines (or should) one's access to fundamental rights. See Ishay, *The History of Human Rights: From Ancient Times to the Globalization Era* (Berkeley: University of California Press, 2004), 3.

pursuit of happiness," as the Declaration of Independence (1776) phrases it; that "all men are created equal," or should at least strive to treat each other as such.[33] They were stirring words at the time, and though there's a ways to go to realize them, such ideas set deep precedents for the notion of ingrained liberties and privileges. That was again by insisting on the theoretical inherentness of justice, and the inseparability of rights from the person.[34]

Still, human rights involve more modern milieus. Specifically, human rights involve twentieth-century international law – something for which the U.S. was *also* important. I.e., much of what we *today* think of as human rights (an internationalist ethics and global set of legal standards) comes from the UN in the late 1940s – the UN being an organization behind which and the U.S. was a driving force.[35] Now, there were parts of the American government that fought the UN's focus on rights. There were forces that wanted the UN to focus on national sovereignty, international security and the balance of power.[36] Still, be it a matter of the vision of the Roosevelts, the State Department trying to garner the support of American civil society groups for the UN project at-large (groups like the NAACP or League of Women Voters), or any number of well-placed idealists within American officialdom who sought the broadest possible realization of internationalist frameworks, the United States ultimately *did* push for the human rights cause.[37] American political capital deployed in defense of "full-bodied" inter- and transnational liberties was important – that as it was increasingly clear come the '40s that the U.S. was now the most powerful country in the world.[38]

That being said, however, the picture hasn't always been so simple. U.S. attitudes towards human rights have hardly always been a resounding "yes!" No doubt, the country played a fundamental role in bringing rights ideas to the international community, and the world will always owe Rooseveltian humanitarianism a significant debt. However, the U.S. has also had high levels of tension with precisely the same ideals. That involves rights *violations*, yes – interventions

---

33 National Archives, "Declaration of Independence" (1776), available at https://www.archives.gov/founding-docs/declaration-transcript.

34 See Lynn Hunt, *Inventing Human Rights: A History* (New York: W.W. Norton, 2007); Jonathan Israel, *Democratic Enlightenment: Philosophy, Revolution, and Human Rights 1750–1790* (Oxford: Oxford University Press, 2011).

35 See Roger Normand and Sarah Zaidi, *Human Rights at the UN: The Political History of Universal Justice* (Bloomington: Indiana University Press, 2008).

36 Ibid.

37 Ibid., 112–4.

38 The vocabulary of "full-bodied" is borrowed from Moyn, *The Last Utopia*, 28.

from Nicaragua to Vietnam in support of some curious dictatorships, as well as the propping up of dubious regimes from Chile to Zaire.[39] It's also a matter, however, of the fact that the U.S. has tended to support particular *kind* of rights – what are usually referred to as "civil and political rights," or free speech, freedom of religion, the legal recognition of the individual and senses of the right to privacy and the protection of the individual against the state. Now, that's not wrong. The ability to be recognized by courts, keep the government out of parts of one's life and say what one thinks are liberties desired by most, if not all. Many want personal autonomy and the right to think for themselves.[40] *Economic and social* rights, however, are *also* part of rights' picture. I.e., as human rights phrase it, one is supposed to have "a standard of living adequate for the health and well-being of [oneself] and [one's] family." One should have "food, clothing, housing and medical care." One should have access to education, including higher education when possible, as well as the possibility of leisure and the knowledge one will have work if one wishes.[41] Human rights aren't anti-free market. The right to own property "alone" *is* enshrined in international law.[42] Still, *always* leaving society's welfare to what economic philosopher Adam Smith termed the "invisible hand" is *not* within the boundaries of what rights are supposed to achieve.[43] Referencing socialism again, it's in part *because* such ideas (socio-economic guarantees) were advanced by socialist states that they garnered resistance from the U.S. The U.S. is one of the few countries *not* to ratify the International Covenant on Economic, Social and Cultural Rights (1966), the primary international covenant concerning socio-economic justice – a reality connected to the fact that it unfortunately seems that there remain certain fronts on which the U.S. can't let the Cold War go.[44]

Now, *that* point then jives with the idea that, despite particular invocations of rights ideals – more or less supporting political rights and, yes, promoting

---

39 See Richard A. Melanson, *American Foreign Policy since the Vietnam War: The Search for Consensus from Nixon to George W. Bush*, 4th ed. (London: Routledge, 2015).

40 UDHR, article 25.

41 Ibid., articles 23, 26.

42 Ibid., article 17.

43 See Adam Smith, *The Wealth of Nations* (New York: Bantam, 2003), 292.

44 See Normand and Zaidi, *Human Rights at the UN*, 139–242; Johannes Morsink, *The Universal Declaration of Human Rights: Drafting, Origins & Intent* (Philadelphia: University of Pennsylvania Press, 1999), 157. See also Rhoda E. Howard-Hassmann and Claude E. Welch, Jr., eds., *Economic Rights in Canada and the United States* (Philadelphia: University of Pennsylvania Press, 2006).

the initial foray into international rights concepts at-large – Americans and American politics can be quite guarded about their willingness to appeal outside their own borders for *any* manner of political concept, human rights or not. I.e., Americans are *ideologically* protectionist in addition to whatever other protectionisms with which the country might be involved. This manifests itself in a number of ways. One is an unwillingness to join the ICC (the International Criminal Court in The Hague) – the international body concerned with war crimes, crimes against humanity and issues of genocide. The objection technically concerns American soldiers and the American military potentially becoming subject to unfair litigation – that given America's extensive involvement in world affairs. That's though many argue that more than a small part of the issue *really* concerns national sovereignty and a desire to not have to respond to anyone else's political whim.[45] Another example of American "rights isolation" *is* that willingness to ratify one variety of rights (civil and political) but not another (those concerned with socio-economic issues). One hundred and sixty-four states are party to the Economic and Social Covenant; not the U.S., though, and the Obama Administration continues to stay away.[46] There's also an unwillingness to participate in *regional* rights agreements such as the American Convention on Human Rights (1969; a document sponsored by the Organization of American States, in which the U.S. plays a major role).[47] I gloss. However, Sanders and Clinton ran smack into such issues in the Democratic primary's first debate. Speaking in Las Vegas – perhaps the maximal symbol of the Wild West free-marketism against which Sanders often rails – he (Sanders) was asked about his advocacy of expanded social security, tuition free universities and the break-up of financial institutions whose size makes them too big to fail. He was asked about his economic proclivities and his advocacy of a relatively socialized American life. Where did he get such a model, he was asked, and why did he

---

45 See Sarah B. Sewall and Carl Kaysen, *The United States and the International Criminal Court: National Security and International Law* (Lanham: Roman & Littlefield, 2000).

46 See Philip Alston, "U.S. Ratification of the Covenant on Economic, Social and Cultural Rights: The Need for an Entirely New Strategy," *The American Journal of International Law* 84, no. 2 (1990): 365–93: Kevin Robillard, "10 Treaties the U.S. Hasn't Ratified," *Politico*, July 24, 2012, available at http://www.politico.com/gallery/2012/07/10-treaties-the-u-s-hasnt-ratified/000303-003927.html.

47 The American Convention on Human Rights is the primary rights document of the Organization of American States. See Organization of American States, "American Convention on Human Rights" (1969), available at http://www.oas.org/dil/treaties_B-32_American_Convention_on_Human_Rights.pdf.

think it right? What was the rationale behind such ideas and could he explain the ins and outs of his thought? "I think we should look to countries like Denmark, like Sweden and Norway, and learn from what they have accomplished for their working people," Sanders maintained. The U.S. should emulate nations where social services *are* addressed as matters of universal privilege, banking *is* far more regulated and, paid for by tax, tuition-free higher education *is* made available to all. We should concern ourselves not only with national standards but *international* standards as well.[48] Then something funny happened. Clinton, whether she meant to or not, reacted with what might be thought of as a proto-typical American statement. "I love Denmark," she maintained. Clinton didn't want to take a *negative* tone towards European democracies; close allies well-regarded on scales of international justice. "But we are not Denmark;" "…we are the United States."[49] I.e., while Clinton *herself* may have had an interest in varieties of universal rights ideals – and evidence indicates that she does – *qua* candidate, she was careful to suggest that America might resolve its problems its *own* way; that the U.S. was under no obligation to respond to laws whose origins lay outside its borders. America could *choose* to participate. However, the United States could also *except* itself from such standards; what other states did was a matter of their own affairs. This opened questions as to at what point one *is* bound to larger norms, or if international ideals may *always* be trumped by the particularities of national life.

Now, we have to be clear. If one is discussing civil and political rights, though the country has problems in terms of structural discrimination, incarceration rates, distributions of social power and the influence of money on politics, there's rough consensus that the *architecture*, if not always the execution, of the American system aligns with the standards of basic rights. Attempts to measure democratic practice generally rank the United States high. The Economist Intelligence Unit, e.g., ranks the U.S. as the world's twentieth most democratic state. That involves freedom of information, political plurality as well as the ability of citizens to influence the workings of government. Those are clear elements of

---

48   CNN, "CNN Democratic Debate – Full Transcript," October 13, 2015, available at http://cnnpressroom.blogs.cnn.com/2015/10/13/cnn-democratic-debate-full-transcript/. For more on the "Nordic Model," see Niels Finn Christensen, et al., ed., *The Nordic Model of Welfare: A Historical Reappraisal* (Copenhagen: Museum Tusculanum Press, 2005); Jon Magnussen, Karsten Vrangbæk and Richard B. Saltman, eds., *Nordic Health Care Systems: Recent Reforms and Current Policy Changes* (Maidenhead: Open University Press, 2009).

49   CNN, "CNN Democratic Debate."

human rights – wherein, despite specific problems, many of the civil and political dimensions of the American system work.[50]

Still, what to do in instances where the U.S. is *not* in accordance with or *doesn't* commit itself to what are *supposed* to be universal standards? What happens when the U.S. *can't* be affected by condemnations of Guantanamo Bay or Abu Ghraib, or the United States *doesn't* guarantee citizens health care, minimal living standards, essential social services or other dimensions of what are supposed to be privileges that all should maintain? What happens when, if so much is left to individual initiative, the individual doesn't make it through? What happens when social services are inadequate, or military interventions *don't* accord with humanitarian practice? Should the U.S. get a free pass based on ideas that one *only* has to accept "the nation" as determining the outlines of justice? Do we *really* participate in erosions of ideas that there are values to which *everyone* should respond, and that those might be more than matters of lip service, or a wink and a knowing nudge? Do we *always* claim that "this is us, we do things this way and whatever you might want from us based on extra-national ideals amounts to your tough luck"? Or do we acknowledge that higher standards *exist*, and that *all* have particular rights regardless of what one or the other state at one or the other time may or may not deem just?

It seems – seems – that Sanders thinks the latter. Sanders *appears*, anyway, concerned with addressing universal, or extra-national, ethics and thinking beyond practices of simply assenting to what one or the other state "usually" says is right. He seems interested in *some* address to universal morality, and not beliefs in "particular" paths laying out "specific" legal visions based on the uniqueness of this or that "people." It appears that Sanders is willing to consider what *all* developed states should do, and propose baselines outside of which no country should ever tread. Again, many issues mark the Sanders campaign: income inequality, campaign finance reform, health care, tuition-free college, gender discrimination, the fate of the poor and runaway Wall Street speculation. One *can* argue, as the U.S. in a certain way traditionally does, that intellectual self-development – the "full realization" of the self and the mind's intellectual freedom – are rights' *ultimate* point. One can argue that a life *only* marked by economic sustenance or access to doctors isn't a full life at all.[51] Still, Sanders sees them as linked. In

50 The Economist Intelligence Unit, "Democracy Index 2015: Democracy in the Age of Anxiety" (2015), available at http://www.yabiladi.com/img/content/EIU-Democracy-Index-2015.pdf.

51 See, e.g., Ari Kohen, *In Defense of Human Rights: A Non-Religious Grounding in a Pluralistic World* (London: Routledge, 2007).

his view, the central question is achieving "one person, one vote." The central question is how to level the playing field so that *all* have substantive social statures and equal voice. Such ideas mean commitments to civil rights, yes: breaking down walls of discrimination and acknowledging all as actors with free speech and meaningful thought. It *also*, however, means that no one should exist without a living wage. It means that when one can't work, legally-bound guarantors should secure the individual a dignified existence and help them find a job. It means that access to doctors shouldn't be viewed as a privilege – it's something that everyone should have as a matter of course. It suggests that if one *doesn't* have "freedom from want," one will be hard-pressed to find the *time* to think – that "full bellies" are important for democracy too.[52] Such commitments mean considering the *raison d'être* of states and asking what happens if we view citizens not through national lenses first, but through *human* lenses instead. It means asking if the goal is to sustain national ideals, or if there might be a more basic set of human objectives to reach. It means saying that there might be particularities to what nations want, but that there are certain baselines they should never move beyond. Outside of activists and NGOs, such universalist vocabularies are rare to hear in American life. Save unusual candidates like the handful of socialists who have tried to enter the presidential ring, or third party candidates like those of the Green Party (or even smaller organizations, like the Working Families Party), it's rare to hear a full human rights based platform on the American tableau.[53] Sanders has done something provocative in bringing such a fleshed-out set of human rights ideals to the center of U.S. political debate.

I'll thus end with this. I wouldn't for a moment argue that states aren't sovereign. Part of rights *is* allowing social polities to establish their own ways of life. "All peoples have the right of self-determination…[and may] determine their political status and freely pursue their economic, social and cultural development," both the Civil and Political Rights Covenant and the Economic and Social Covenant maintain.[54] Indeed, the U.S. is hardly the only country to invoke

---

52 See Rhoda Howard, "The Full Belly Thesis: Should Economic Rights Take Priority over Civil and Political Rights?: Evidence from Sub-Saharan Africa," *Human Rights Quarterly* 5, no. 4 (1983): 467–90.

53 See Green Party of the United States, "Platform 2014," available at https://d3n8a8 pro7vhmx.cloudfront.net/gpus/pages/121/attachments/original/1436484918/2014_Platform.pdf?1436484918.

54 United Nations, "International Covenant on Civil and Political Rights" (1966, article 1), available at http://www.ohchr.org/en/professionalinterest/pages/ccpr.aspx; United Nations, "International Covenant on Economic, Social and Cultural Rights"

nationalistically-oriented concepts. Today, significant crises surrounding migration in Europe have led to intense claims of sovereignty and arguments that states have the ability to simply assert their boundaries and say "that's it." There are heavy invocations of national particularity and varieties of assertions that that particularity should be politics' the ultimate grounds. Indeed, in the developing world in the twentieth century, revolution after revolution took place in the name of "the nation" and in relation to claims that peoples are "sovereign" (one can't just pooh-pooh the idea of nations' rights to decide).[55] Still, most analysts agree that universal rights *are* predicated on the idea that the fundaments of one's privileges are first and foremost a function of the fact *that* one exists as opposed to *where*. Universal rights are based on ideas of inherent value, and concepts that there are privileges particular social customs, parliamentary decrees or national judicial systems can't, or at least *shouldn't*, just strip away.[56] At issue are ideas that there's an "us" that extends *beyond* one's country, and that all communities deserve tending to on at least *somewhat* equal bases. That's not to say that appeals to such standards are easy to effect. It *is* to say, though, that one can't appeal to standards that either aren't recognized or simply don't exist.[57]

To that extent, I find it interesting to note that Sanders has called for a "political revolution." Offhand, I'd say that's a revolution he'll be hard-pressed to get.

(1966, article 1), available at http://www.ohchr.org/EN/ProfessionalInterest/Pages/CESCR.aspx.

55 Ironically, Denmark – just as an example (and as one which Sanders oft-points to as to what the U.S. *might* be like) – is one of the European states to ask for the largest range of exemptions from EU (read "larger international") obligations. That's in the form of exemptions to migration standards, as well as recent acts like the resurrection of border controls. See Lee Miles and Anders Wivels, *Denmark and the European Union* (London: Routledge, 2013); Noha Shawki and Michaelene Cox, eds., *Negotiating Sovereignty and Human Rights: Actors and Issues in Contemporary Human Rights Politics* (Farnham: Ashgate, 2009); Nuno Ferreira and Dora Kostakopoulou, eds., *The Human Face of the European Union: Are EU Law and Policy Humane Enough?* (Cambridge: Cambridge University Press, 2016); Peter Calvert and Susan Calvert. *Politics and Society in the Developing World* (London: Routledge, 2014).

56 See Morsink, *Inherent Human Rights: Philosophical Roots of the Universal Declaration* (Philadelphia: University of Pennsylvania Press, 2009), 21.

57 This is a general point about human rights: their ability to shape the international environment even though they can be hard to realize and applied unevenly. Imagine a world *without* human rights standards to which to appeal. See David Kinley, Wojciech Sadurski and Kevin Walton, eds., *Human Rights: Old Problems, New Possibilities* (Cheltenham: Edward Elgar, 2013).

Virtually the entire right of the American political establishment wonders at undoing American exceptionalism, and his opponent on the Democratic side, though more sympathetic to a globalist ethics, also plays more to "take-the-American-system-as-it-is" mindsets. Indeed, beyond Sanders, the Greens and the range of small, alternative parties, there remains little overture in the U.S. to senses that there are *any* rights that might trump those of the nation-state. Still, I wonder: perhaps the Sanders movement might be the start of something new. Perhaps the Sanders movement represents something that may become more mainstream as a younger generation moves increasingly to center stage. Again, Sanders hammers all comers among the young; eighteen to thirty-five-year-olds are an explicitly liberal group. Sanders' supporters have also been engaged, providing his rallies with huge turnouts; they've been vocal, both online and in the street, and a particular activism has been opened with his entry onto the primary stage. There are no guarantees. People often become more conservative as they get older. Still, it *is* intriguing to think about an American milieu in which rights positions – *human* rights positions – might become the norm; that all, or at least *most*, mainstream candidates in American politics would address rights through those of the *human* community first as opposed to the particularities of the national state. Indeed, *were* such trends to become fully realized, it might return the U.S. to a time when it exhibited clearer leadership on the front of universal justice, and the country became exceptional because of its *promotion* of international rights standards as opposed to its skepticism towards them. Unfortunately, we're probably some years away from such a moment. That's while extraordinary things are happening this election cycle – the Sanders phenomenon not least among them.

In the Footsteps of Potsdam
The Cecilienhof and the Glienicke Bridge
(March 30, 2016)

Abstract: *The historical scenery of the German city of Potsdam is evocative – especially of Cold War strife and intrigue. Potsdam is also, however, evocative of the contributions that Cold War ideologies made to human rights.*

I visited Potsdam over the weekend – an intensely, intensely interesting place. There are two periods, it seems, that dominate the city: the eighteenth-century rule of Frederick the Great, the most important of the Prussian kings, and the post-World War II/ Cold War era in which Potsdam was more than once the center of geopolitical vortices. Frederick, perhaps the standard bearer for enlightened despotism (progressive rule from above), brought the royal residences to town – the most well-known being the Versailles-like Sanssouci Palace – and over the course of his father's reign and his own, Prussia was coaxed from the ranks of yet another central European princely state to the status of a great power on par with any of Europe's more established behemoths (Great Britain, Russia and France most noticeably). The emergence of the "iron kingdom," as one historian has put it, nonetheless wasn't the end of Potsdam's anchoring of the European past.[1] In the wake of the cataclysm sometimes taken to have *finally* brought Prussian militarism to an end (World War II),

"Cecilienhof Palace in Germany." © *igorp1976 / Fotolia.com. "View to Glienicke Bridge, Potsdam, Germany."* © *CeHa / Fotolia.com 103034959; 98820053*

the powers that conquered Germany – Britain, the Soviet Union and the United

---

This essay is dedicated to Annette Georgi for all the wonderful conversations about German history and life under the Cold War.

1   See Christopher Clark, *The Rise and Downfall of Prussia: 1600–1947* (Cambridge, MA: Harvard Belknap, 2009).

States – met in the Berlin suburb (Potsdam) to iron out control over Europe and figure out how post-War Germany in specific should be run. With the division of Europe, and sitting smack in the middle of the Soviet occupation zone, Potsdam came to feature one of the few border crossings between East and West Berlin in the form of the Glienicke Bridge. Some serious exchange of spy material happened over that otherwise unremarkable green-iron expanse. The most famous was the 1962 exchange of Soviet spy Rudolf Abel for Gary Powers – Abel being a long-time Soviet operative in the United States and Powers the pilot of an American spy plane shot down in Soviet air space in 1960. The next most famous was the *Refusenik* activist Natan Sharansky for Czech spymaster Karl Koecher in 1986. That exchange more or less coincided with the beginning of a shift in Soviet policy in which Jews were allowed to emigrate from the Soviet Union to settle in Israel – a small step, one might argue, in the liberalization if not end of the Soviet state.[2]

It *is* the Cold War history that gets you the most. You can feel it; you can breathe it. You almost feel as though you can reach out and touch it. It's a history directly rooting the contemporary world and the circumstances we find ourselves in today. While there are good questions to ask regarding what European history would have looked like without the rise of Prussia, we're *still* trying to figure out the meanings of politics since the end of the Cold War. Indeed, Germany was *itself* a microcosm of mid-twentieth century *raisons d'état* in terms of investments in either liberal democracy or socialistic-communism. It's also the case that many of the central figures from Cold War Potsdam simply *feel* closer. In terms of the Potsdam Conference (the unofficial name for the "Three Powers Conference of Berlin" [July–August 1945]), there's no doubt that Stalin, Truman and Churchill (later Attlee) came from a different time and place. None were born in the twentieth century and, for a good part of their lives, it was the *1914–8* war that came to mind when one said "the War" as opposed to the Second World War, like today. In fact, as opposed to, say, the peacemakers of the First World War, the peacemakers of the Second somehow *looked* like us. Their suits looked like ours – well, Truman's, Churchill's, and Attlee's, anyway (Stalin preferred his generalissimo's uniform) – and they went to, from and around the city in transport that looked not a great deal unlike how we'd show up at a conference ourselves: in automobiles, passenger trains and airplanes with a modern feel. Indeed, it was also partly at Potsdam that the world entered the nuclear age – during the proceedings, Truman announced to Stalin the U.S.' possession

2   Christopher Hilton, *The Wall: A People's Story* (Gloucestershire: The History Press, 2001), 297.

of a "new weapon" the country intended to use against Japan – that though espi-
onage on the Manhattan project made the existence of the A-Bomb a possibility
of which Stalin was already aware.[3] If you're over forty – part of Generation "X"
or the "Baby Boom" years – you'll remember parts of the Cold War. Not least of
those memories might be of the nuclear build-up that, as one historian put it, can
make one feel fortunate to have come out of the period alive.[4]

Now, as one follows Truman's, Stalin's, Churchill's and later, again, Attlee's
footsteps around the Tudor-inspired Cecilienhof Palace (where the Potsdam
Conference took place), or one contemplates the stare-downs and prisoner exchanges that occurred over locales like the Glienicke Bridge, it is in fact Stalin's
and the Soviets' presence that one feels the most. Truman cut a familiar figure.
He wore folksy hats – American semi-Stetson, semi-Fedoras – and his body
moved in that open, shoulders-squared-to-you-way with a ready smile that it
sometimes seems only Americans can pull off. Churchill and Attlee, though different between themselves (one was the Conservative Party leader and one the
leader of the left-leaning Labour), were of a different ilk. Both were British-bred,
exuding something of an Old-World charm; Churchill in particular projected a
kind of Victorian sense of right (indeed, Churchill's first year in politics was the
last year of Victoria's reign).[5] Still, they were *democratic* politicians who had to
respond to the will of their people. Indeed, Attlee's succession of Churchill at the
Potsdam Conference was a product of the fact that, in the first post-War election,
Churchill's Conservatives lost to Attlee's Labour. Stalin was simply a different
kind of cat. Wearing a pared-down version of the dictator's uniform ("high command casual," one might call it [the Soviets eschewed much ornamentation in
those early years]), the leader of the USSR very much projected the sense that his
politics emerged from a different kind of charge. The elections Stalin responded
to were largely shams – it was always a "my God, the party leadership got 99%
stamp of approval!" kind of thing – and, among the Allies, *winning* the war had
also cost the Soviets by far the highest price. Upwards of twenty million Soviet
citizens and soldiers paid for their country's victory with their lives (roughly half
the total for the war at-large).[6] Indeed, the *point* of the politics from which the

3   See Michael Neiberg, *Potsdam: The End of World War II and the Remaking of Europe*
    (New York: Basic, 2015), 243.
4   See John Lewis Gaddis, *The Cold War: A New History* (New York: Penguin, 2005), x.
5   See Norman Rose, *Churchill: The Unruly Giant* (New York: Free Press, 1994).
6   See Priscilla Mary Roberts, *World War II: The Essential Reference Guide* (Santa-Barbara:
    ABC-Clio, 2012), 30. It should also be noted that at the start of the Soviet project, there
    was some commitment to expanded democracy, at least compared to what it had been

Soviet Union emerged – revolutionary Leninism – was also different. That was not so much accepting things as they were, but rather making the world anew.[7] All this lent a particular intensity to the air as Stalin and his seconds entered the Cecilienhof's negotiating spaces or stared at the capitalist "Other" over borderlines like the Glienicke Bridge. Compared to Truman, Churchill, and Attlee, "Uncle Joe" and his cohorts simply offered a different kind of feel: harder – more ruthless, somehow. It was tied to a different kind political faith.[8]

Of course, one *also* feels the Soviets' presence in part because their world no longer exists. I.e., historical proximity brings intimacy; it brings an electricity to our relations with the past. It also, however, underlines what's no longer there. Guided by Moscow, Eastern Bloc states sought to solidify an alternative way of life – one where, at least theoretically, solidarity was valued over individualism and "bourgeois" ideals were left to the past. Structures of oppression should be broken, and a greater egalitarianism would rule the day. This was not a project, however, that would ultimately win. For one, the West wouldn't *let* it win. Though always somehow holding the upper hand in Cold War *Realpolitik* – the West was simply wealthier (socialism and communism largely took hold in poorer parts of the world) – there was almost always *some* mode of pressure, be it economic or military, maintained on the USSR and its allies. Now, Western military and economic strategizing in relation to the Soviets may not have been the ultimate factor "breaking" the Communist Bloc. Historians point to a range of factors, from flat economies to cultural stagnation and the uninspired dreariness of the communist social world.[9] Western *Realpolitik* didn't help, however, as it most certainly pushed down on a system that was rust-laden at best and corrupt at

---

under Czarist Russia, via emphasizing workers' councils ("Soviets"). As almost all historians are clear on, however, this was pushed to the side in the name of consolidating Bolshevik power and, by the time Stalin consolidated control, any kind of ground-up democratic practice existed in name only. See Samuel Farber, *Before Stalinism: The Rise and Fall of Soviet Democracy* (London: Verso, 1990).

7   "The revolution," Lenin claimed, "does not need historians." The point was the creation of new societies and, in fact, clear modes of breaking from the past. In Robert K. Massie, *The Romanovs: The Final Chapter* (New York: Random House, 1996), 257.

8   See Robert Service, *Stalin: A Biography* (London: Pan, 2010).

9   See Dick Combs, *Inside the Soviet Alternate Universe: The Cold War's End and the Soviet Union's Fall Reappraised* (University Park: Pennsylvania State University Press, 2008); Robert Strayer, *Why Did the Soviet Union Collapse?: Understanding Historical Change* (London: Routledge), 114.

worst.[10] As one political theorist has put it, *qua* concept or idea, socialism and communism may not have provided "gravely defective form[s] of recognition."[11] The *goal* of Soviet the system *was* greater inclusion and heightened social recognition. Still, in what's often referred to as socialism's "real, existing" form, "defective recognition" may have been what one got. A "worker's paradise" the Eastern Bloc exclusively was not.[12]

Now, that being said, surveying the red-veloured negotiating room at the Cecilienhof or the spaces of stare-downs and barbed-wire at places like Glienicke – a few concepts come to mind. A few ideas theoretical and conceptual present themselves as one encounters history's locales and tries to listen to the echoes of the past. The first is that, despite their abundance of problems, there may be a strange *hole*, or *vacuum*, left by the disappearance of the Soviet Union and its satellite states. There may be something *lost* with the collapse of a Europe that, east of the longer stretch of the Elbe, *was* constituted exclusively of socialist states. Again, Soviet communism was again an oft-troubling enterprise. Though again claiming to derive from popular sovereignty and what were supposedly more thoughtful forms of expression than were had in the West – "sugary sentimentalism" and "castrated eroticism," Soviet Bloc authorities claimed, were the intellectual offerings of the capitalist world – the response of communist nations may have been even *worse*.[13] Over the roughly seventy years of its existence, thousands if not millions were jailed or exiled for thinking the wrong way. It took little time after the start of the Russian Revolution in 1917, e.g., and then again with the establishment of Eastern European communist regimes in the late-1940s, for orthodoxy to be reinforced by surveillance and secret police (it's noticeable that the Soviet Cheka, the country's first covert police force, was formed near-immediately after the start of

---

10 See Michael Voslensky, *Nomenklatura: The Soviet Ruling Class* (New York: Doubleday, 1984).

11 Francis Fukuyama, *The End of History and the Last Man* (New York: Penguin, 1992), xix.

12 This isn't to downplay socialism's successes. It should be noted that more than half of the world's population lived under the banner of socialism come the mid-twentieth century – and that wasn't always a matter of coercion over choice. Still, the larger evaluation of most historians is that the system ended up nowhere near achieving the goals it intended to reach. See Robert Service, *Comrades!: A History of World Communism* (Harvard: Harvard University Press, 2007).

13 Alan M. Ball, *Imagining America: Influence and Images in Twentieth Century Russia* (Lanham: Rowman & Littlefield, 2003), 182.

the revolution, in December 1917).[14] Oral histories provide thousands of tales of people feeling the need to look over their shoulder when discussing even mildly controversial topics in public space. Indeed, cases like the East German Stasi provide dramatic lessons as, when their offices were stormed at the regime's end, more than one hundred and seventy-eight – *one hundred and seventy-eight!* – kilometers of surveillance files on the country's own citizens were found – enough to line-up between the city of Hamburg and the Baltic Sea port of Rostock (hardly just next door).[15] Of course, that just compounds what we already know. When figures like Czechoslovakia's Alexander Dubček attempted to institute "socialism with a human face" in 1968 (socialist economics with a more liberal politics on top), the powers that be crushed the move with troop battalions and tanks. Supporting dissent movements was not high on the agenda of the Soviet high command.[16] The Hungarian Revolution was similarly broken in 1956 as dissidents who had damaged the "cause of defending the power of the working class," as it was phrased in *apparatchik*-speak, were hauled off to jail and incarcerated *en masse*.[17] Of course, the East Germans constructed a wall to keep people *in* – a wall featuring landmines and tripwires on the *East* German side as opposed to the other way around (some one hundred thirty-nine people are imagined to have been killed at the border between East and West Berlin).[18] No doubt: America and the West committed *their* crimes too. From bombing Vietnamese, Cambodian and Laotian villages to rubble to racial segregation in the American South to the police in countries like West Germany killing students like Benno Ohnesorg when they demonstrated against the West's support for corrupt rulers like Iran's Shah, "free democratic" and capitalist culture brought *its* share of "blood, torture [violence and] death"[19] Liberal-capitalist societies were hardly the bastions of saints. That doesn't exempt

14 Christopher Andrew, *KGB: The Inside Story of Its Foreign Operations from Lenin to Gorbachev* (New York: HarperCollins, 1997).

15 Barbara Miller, *The Stasi Files Unveiled: Guilt and Compliance in a Unified Germany* (New Brunswick: Transaction, 2004), 5: Peter Malloy, *The Lost World of Communism: An Oral History of Daily Life Behind the Iron Curtain* (London: BBC Books, 2009).

16 See Günter Bischof, Stefan Karner and Peter Ruggenthaler, eds., *The Prague Spring and the Warsaw Pact Invasion of Czechoslovakia in 1968* (Lanham: Lexington, 2010).

17 In Basil Dmytryshyn, *USSR: A Concise History*, 4th ed. (New York: Charles Scribner and Sons, 1984), 592. See also Victor Sebestyen, *Twelve Days: The Story of the 1956 Hungarian Revolution* (New York: Pantheon, 2006).

18 See Fredrick Taylor *The Berlin Wall: 13 August 1961–9 November 1989* (London: Bloomsbury, 2006).

19 Fredric Jameson, *Postmodernism, or the Cultural Logic of Late Capitalism* (Durham, NC: Duke University Press, 1991), 5. See also Peter L. Hahn and Mary Anne Heiss, eds.,

communism from *its* crimes, however. Be it internment and labor camps such as Perm-35, where Sharansky was held, the wire-tapping and surveillance by organizations like not only the Stasi or KGB but lesser-known services like the Polish SB, Romanian Securitate or Czech StB or the massive levels of control over the press and public information, socialist systems involved violations – serious ones – of basic civil rights. They overstepped even mildly-conceived notions of individual liberty and private space. That's while espousing liberatory impulses and ideas that, eventually, socialist solidarity would save the world from crimes whose nature was even *worse* – the inequalities of the global marketplace, or the fact that capitalism meant that some lived quite well while others could hardly get by.[20]

Still, were the questions of socialism not questions we should *ask*? I.e., while we can understand the idea that the "liberation" of those who labor and the "freeing the poor" might be flimsy excuses for demolishing free speech or undoing civil liberties, was it not *also* important to look at the history of privilege not only in modernity, but over the larger trajectory of human time, and interrogate if free markets and capitalist consumerism really *were* history's "end?"[21] *Especially* given issues like segregation, poverty and the behavior of capitalist powers in places like Vietnam, was it so *deadly* clear that, in the battle of modern ideas, one side was "right" and the other simply "wrong?" I again won't grieve the disappearance of the Soviet system. It wasn't *all* prison camps and the crushing of Prague Springs. The guarantee of people's right to work and cradle to grave care by the state were real.[22] Living standards in some places – East Germany especially – weren't relatively good, and there was ideological thaw under figures like Khrushchev and Gorbachev.[23] Still, from Honecker to Ceaușescu to even Gorbachev in his crackdown on Lithuania in the course of the Soviet Union's death-throes, the strong-arming

Empire and Revolution: The United States and the Third World since 1945 (Columbus: The Ohio State University Press, 2001).

20 See Natan Sharansky, *Fear No Evil*, trans. Stefani Hoffman (New York: Public Affairs, 1988); See, e.g., Stéphane Courtois, et al., *The Black Book of Communism: Crimes, Terror, Repression*, trans. Jonathan Murphy and Mark Kramer (Cambridge, MA: Harvard University Press, 1999); George G. Brenkert, *Marx's Ethics of Freedom* (London: Routledge, 1983).

21 This was Fukuyama's thesis: that the end of the Cold War represented an end to a particular battle in the history of ideas, and that liberalism – capitalism too, by association – had "won." Moreover, that was in accordance with a particular individualism ingrained in human nature. See Fukuyama, *The End*.

22 See, e.g., J.L. Porket, *Work, Employment and Unemployment in the Soviet Union* (New York: Palgrave Macmillan, 1989).

23 See Malloy, *The Lost World of Communism*.

never quite stopped. There was often a sense that the system was *against* its people as much as for them. As one historian of the USSR has put it, the lines of such tendencies may be long. Figures like Lenin may have turned liberation into a goal to be pursued at any cost wherein, as communism proceeded, a certain momentum may have developed around oppressive practices through which they became employed as a matter of course.[24] For many, this made the end of the Cold War a reason to celebrate. One could finally say "goodbye to all that."[25]

Again, though: *was* capitalism *really* better? Did, or *does*, commercial production for profit – and the deeply conformist pop cultures often accompanying it – really represent the best we can do? *Are* we in just societies when *anyone* starves or goes homeless while others have so much? For all the decrying of "determinist" views of history in which liberal philosophers sometimes engage, the existence of an alternative system – one which sometimes *did* support the little man and in some ways *did* shared the wealth – meant that one had to consider one's opinions and at least engage in *conversation* regarding political choice. One had to interrogate what progress *meant*, and it wasn't *necessarily* obvious that one's beliefs would be the same as all's. At least the *boundaries* for political debate were less pre-prescribed. *That* might be the void left by the Soviet system and the disappearance of the Eastern Bloc: that one had to *argue* for concepts of liberation and understand that there were serious alternatives regarding socio-political ends. It was the *possibility* of something else – the idea that alternatives were at least being *tried*. It was the notion that particular modes of idealism weren't to be dismissed directly out of hand.[26]

---

24 Richard Pipes, *The Russian Revolution* (New York: Vintage, 1990), xxii.

25 Eric Hobsbawm, "Goodbye to All That," in *After the Fall: The Failure of Communism and the Future of Socialism*, ed. R. Blackburn (London: Verso, 1991), 115–25. It should be noted that there was a tinge of irony attached to Hobsbawm's notion of "goodbye to all that." I.e., he also held the opinion that something was lost in the process – a particular level of idealism and critique of the inequities of capitalist life. Still, Hobsbawm acknowledged a historical moment in which a highly complex project was able to fade into the past.

26 Russell Jacoby also raises this point in *The End of Utopia: Politics and Culture in the Age of Apathy*: that the contemporary world has lost the utopian ideal, and not for the better. We now feel higher justice is little worth fighting for because what we have is somehow "right." This damages activist causes and the project of humanitarianism – a point bearing relations to that raised by Hobsbawm in "Goodbye to All That." See Jacoby *The End of Utopia: Politics and Culture in the Age of Apathy* (New York: Basic Books, 1999), 1–28.

Clearly, these are important issues. Again: have we found ourselves beyond the age of political choice? In the absence of socialism, *is* it possible to think beyond the parameters of received ideals (the rectitude of liberal-capitalism, e.g.)? *Have* we reached the pinnacle of freedom with the fall of the Soviet world even in view of its police apparatuses and atmospheres of dreariness – that though acknowledging that the Soviet system made *some* attempts at social justice? It's hard to say. Communist parties were roundly defeated when systems opened and elections were held in '90 and '91. Given a choice, many sought to throw out several decades of communist past. That's though some *do* point out that a particular socio-critical *élan may* have slipped away with "real, existing socialism's" end. In any case, *another* issue Potsdam brings to the fore, or at least occurred to *me* as I explored the city's sites, is that of *human rights*. I.e., confronting Potsdam's historical scenes, I began to wonder how we can concretely think about the systems that faced each other over the Cold War period in relation to the concepts we *today* imagine to be our "highest moral precepts and political ideals."[27] How can we think about the Cold War years and "Western" and "Eastern" political philosophies in relation to the conceptual regime which may have displaced *both* approaches as our ultimate point of political appeal? How do we read elements of Cold War life in relation to the standards we *now* use to judge the past? That's with some years of distance – it now nearing thirty years since the first cracks were put in the Berlin Wall.

Now, there's again the significant – massive, really – levels of human rights *violations* perpetrated by both sides. Again, there are particular ins and outs regarding the multiple regimes that Soviet history maintains. Not everything was Stalin-like brutality or rule with an iron fist. Socialist culture made real contributions to global society – significant modernization projects in the developing world are attributable to Soviet support, e.g. – and people had their everyday lives. Indeed, if you could cut through the orthodoxy, parts of communist education systems were actually quite good, and some would argue that conditions for women were better in the East than in the West. A certain idealism was encouraged and solidarity was promoted as a cultural goal.[28]

27　Samuel Moyn, *The Last Utopia: Human Rights in History* (Cambridge, MA: Harvard Belknap, 2010), 1.

28　See Mervyn Matthews, *Education in the Soviet Union: Policies and Institutions Since Stalin* (London: Routledge, 1982). See also Gleb Tsipursky, *Socialist Fun: Youth, Consumption, and State-Sponsored Popular Culture in the Soviet Union, 1945–1970* (Pittsburgh: University of Pittsburgh Press, 2016); Jeremy Friedman, *Shadow Cold War: The Sino-Soviet Competition for the Third World* (Chapel Hill: Duke University Press, 2015);

Again, though, the total number civil rights violations accompanying various Soviet and Eastern European regimes *is* impressive. At their height, Soviet gulags held between two and three *million* people – large numbers of whom were identified as "enemies of the state" or in need of ideological "reeducation."[29] Political disappearances – situations where, on the grounds of political conviction or activism, individuals were simply arrested and no one was informed of their fate, numbered in quantities difficult to count. One scholar of the period has noted that "counter-revolutionary activities" was a ubiquitously powerful legal phrase via which, once gone, it wasn't expected the accused would ever come back.[30] Again, voting – "voting" – was a dubious affair in the Eastern Bloc. Until the late '80s, if there was more than one party on the ballot ("party" – they were always subsumed under the main communist bloc), its representatives were chosen by socialist authorities, and one's choice was usually voting either "for" or "against."[31] That's again above and beyond the nervous nature of living in societies where one couldn't be sure of who was listening and what it was ok to say or not. Yet again, visiting various Stasi museums in Germany – one of the countries most forthcoming about the extent of communist oppression – one is confronted with the flabbergastingly large number of ways in which the government watched its citizens. At its height, the Stasi employed some 174,000 informants. That's in a country with roughly 16 million people. The numbers in relation to the KGB have been posited as one out of every eighteen Soviet adults.[32] That's extensive – invasive – surveillance indeed.

Donna Harsch, "Communism and Women" in *The Oxford Handbook of the History of Communism*, ed. S.A. Smith (Oxford: Oxford University Press, 2014), 488–503.

29 Mark Mazower, "Violence and the State in the Twentieth Century," *The American Historical Review* 107, no. 4 (2002): 1169.

30 Nanci Adler, "In Search of Identity: The Collapse of the Soviet Union and the Recreation of Russia," in *The Politics of Memory: Transitional Justice in Democratizing Societies*, ed. Alexandra Barahona De Brito, Carmen González-Enríquez, Paloma Aguilar (Oxford: Oxford University Press, 2001), 275.

31 Systems weren't identical. To take the East German example, however, one "chose" whether or not one would vote privately in a voting booth (it was frowned upon if you did) and one either voted for an entire list of candidates, or crossed the list out (in which case, it was unclear precisely *who* one had voted for). See Das Bundesarchiv, "Wahlen in der DDR," available at https://www.bundesarchiv.de/oeffentlichkeitsarbeit/bilder_dokumente/03298/index-14.html.de.

32 Miller, *The Stasi Files*, 4. It's worth noting that a similar amount of informers in the contemporary U.S. would mean about 3.5 million people informing for the FBI.

Again, though, the West watched its citizens – just ask Martin Luther King or Malcolm X – and serious Cold War atrocities were *absolutely* committed in democracy's name. From El Salvador and Nicaragua to Korea and Vietnam, dictatorial governments were supported by the U.S. and its allies, and problematic – extremely problematic – military interventions were made in the name of holding the fall of the communist "dominoes" back. One historian has argued that dating to the overthrow of the Hawaiian monarchy in 1893, the United States has more or less retained a foreign policy based on regime change, and organizing its allies around such projects during the Cold War was a primary foreign policy goal. From Patrice Lumumba to Iran's Mosaddegh, there seems to be something to this point. Simply put, in the mid-twentieth century, "Soviet aggression" became a ubiquitous term used to cover-up some ghastly stuff.[33] Be it the House Committee on Un-American Activities, the McCarthy hearings or sponsoring the murder of developing world leaders who took Western-critical positions – never mind the behavior of Western European governments towards what they saw as "radical" groups – the liberal ("liberal") West had own behaviors to answer for. Cold War intrigue left few looking particularly good.[34]

Still, there's funny way in which the Cold War may have also given human rights a major *assist*. There's a way in which the Cold War may have *contributed to* human rights' cause, or at least the concept's spread *qua* idea. It's a controversial point. However, previous to the 1970s, human rights ideas *qua* concept played a bit *less* of a role in international affairs than one might think. Largely, Soviet and Western powers promoted their *own* ideologies as the concepts representing history's "end," or which would "save the world." It was frequently but *implicit* that it was larger "rights" with which the Cold War's various "-isms" were concerned (socialism, communism, capitalism, liberal democracy and the like). Put more plainly, it might be typical for *us* to talk about "human rights" as the goal of political life. *We* might evaluate ideologies in terms of how they accord with higher, theoretically "non-political" ideals – privileges that all people should maintain. For ideologues in both systems, however, the point was often those systems in and of *themselves*; one achieved rights *through* one or the other ideology as opposed to appealing to rights ideas *as such*. This often left human rights in something of a

---

33 Stephen Kinzer, *Overthrow: America's Century of Regime Change from Hawaii to Iraq* (New York: Holt, 2006), 1. See also Ludo de Witte, *The Assassination of Lumumba*, trans. Ann Wright and Reneé Fenby (London: Verso, 2002).

34 See Odd Arne Westad, *The Global Cold War: Third World Interventions and the Making of Our Times* (Cambridge: Cambridge University Press, 2005). See also Peter Stearns, *Human Rights in World History* (London: Routledge, 2012), 124–60.

"paralysis."[35] It meant that standards *not* framed first and foremost through "capitalism," "liberalism," "socialism," or "communism" were often nudged aside.[36]

Now, the idea of a Cold War human rights "deep freeze," as it's been put – the notion of an ideological downplaying of rights in favor of other vocabularies – *is* intriguing. It again reveals human rights as an idea a bit more in the historical background than we might think. Still, in the context of peacemaking in the '70s – moments where the Soviets, the Americans and their allies momentarily backed off each other – as well as, ironically, in the context of one side accusing the other of various *crimes*, the *opposite* also became true: *qua* concept, "human rights" sometimes became an increasing point of *appeal*. 1970s and '80s American administrations, e.g., used "human rights" to put pressure on Soviet states regarding issues of democracy and free speech. Rights were used to explain the 1980 Moscow Olympic boycott under Jimmy Carter, they were an important bargaining chip in relation to the 1975 Helsinki Accords, and Ronald Reagan used the vocabulary to indict the Soviet Union as an "evil empire." Indeed, rights were used to explain *why* it was important to defend capitalism and liberal democracy in various parts of the world – perhaps especially Central America, where, across the '70s and '80s, the U.S. became increasingly active.[37] Of course, the USSR shot back that it had its *own* variety of rights (socio-economic principles), and that the West had no patent on concepts of liberty. *Socialism* was defending human privileges with *its* Cold War interventions, from backing leftists in Eritrea to the support of the Nicaraguan Sandinistas in their fight to rid societies of corrupt privilege. Indeed, Soviet Premier Leonid Brezhnev even released a *book* with human rights in the title as part of this debate.[38] At the end of the day, such back and forth, though tortured, may have *helped* the promotion of larger rights ideals. As "human rights" became increasingly understood to at least from time to

---

35 Micheline R. Ishay, *The History of Human Rights: From Ancient Times to the Globalization Era* (Berkeley: University of California Press, 2004), 228.

36 Moyn's *The Last Utopia* is very much organized around this idea. I refer readers to that work for further explanation. See also Jan Eckel and Samuel Moyn, eds., *The Breakthrough: Human Rights in the 1970s* (Philadelphia: University of Pennsylvania Press, 2014).

37 See William M. LeoGrande, *Our Own Backyard: The United States in Central America, 1977–1992* (Durham, NC: University of North Carolina Press, 1992). See also Jerome J. Shestack, "Human Rights, the National Interest, and U.S. Foreign Policy," *The Annals of the American Academy of Political and Social Science* 506 (1989): 17–29.

38 Leonid Brezhnev, *Socialism, Democracy and Human Rights* (Oxford: Pergamon, 1980).

time hold a level of *rhetorical* usefulness, the concept regained some of the power that the Cold War had drained away.[39]

Indeed, *that* point becomes heightened when one realizes that as fraught with self-contradictions and violations of basic justice as both the Soviet and Western systems were, *behind* the ideas facing off against one another at locales like the Cecilienhof or swapping prisoners across the Glienicke Bridge were, in certain ways, those providing human rights' conceptual *grounds*. I.e., liberal and socialist ideals *both* exist within rights ideals and form important ground floors for rights thought as we think of it today. Now, historical reality can again not be ignored. Regarding Soviet society, "all the instruments" of later oppression *may* have been laid out in the Russian Revolution's formative years.[40] Bolshevik concepts of "revolutionary vanguards" and demands to create a "new man" – one not tainted by "bourgeois" pasts – may have lent themselves to the emergence of police states and non-democratic control. They may have led to ranges of situations in which one wasn't sure *what* kind of legal or philosophical world one had ended up in (again, *police states* in freedom's name?). Yet again, however, communism wasn't *just* the KGB. "Real, existing socialism" wasn't *only* hauling off dissidents in the middle of the night or encouraging dubious modes of ideological control. Socialist and communist governments brought large numbers of social advancements and privileges to broad ranges of groups – from women to national minorities to members of the working class itself. A little historical imagination can be useful. The sense of transformation felt as women gained legal equality with men – a major result of the Russian Revolution – must have been astounding. It helped break what were centuries of stifling patriarchy.[41] It must have also been deeply inspiring to no longer hear defenses of social of rank – to hear Europe's aristocratic worlds challenged by concepts of brotherhood and the idea that no one deserved to live in poorer conditions than anyone else. It must have been further dramatic to have education become *much* more widely available, and the doors thrown open to massively greater participation in civil service and government bureaucracy. It must have been astounding to have the state declare that it would assure food on your table and a chicken in your pot – that if one starved, it was only because everyone else did as well. Whatever their absolutisms, all Soviet and Eastern Bloc leaders had to provide at least *paeans* to such ideals. They had to

---

39 See also Daniel Thomas, *The Helsinki Effect: International Norms, Human Rights, and the Demise of Communism* (Princeton: Princeton University Press, 2000).

40 Pipes, *The Russian Revolution*, 790.

41 See Rochelle Goldberg Ruthchild, *Equality and Revolution: Women's Rights in the Russian Empire 1905–1917* (Pittsburgh: University of Pittsburgh Press, 2010).

speak to the possibility of social equality and material betterment. That was as, in terms of its intellectual history, such concepts were the heart of socialist life. No resource should be left to an elite, and the means of life should be guaranteed for all.[42]

That idea – *some* modicum of socio-economic fairness – provides one current in human rights thought: the idea that, over and above rights to free thought and speech, if not precisely full economic *equality*, societies should at least guarantee basic standards of *living* for all. I.e., socialism departs from the idea that political equality demands *social* equality, and *social* equality – real equality between a plurality's multiple groups – involves at least a *modicum* of the equal distribution of wealth (i.e., economic and social equality go hand-in-hand). Now, there are degrees of this. Purer socialists – "committed" Marxists, if one will – don't want inequality *at all*. The moment at which *anyone* profits off the labor of another or holds a different social status is the moment at which oppression sets in (indeed, for stricter Marxists, racial and gender oppression were really matters of economic exploitation; women and ethnic minorities would be truly freed when they became *economically* emancipated).[43] Of course, one *can* loosen the strings on such ideas. One *can* suggest, without regard to the specific levels of wealth one may or may not have, that all should at least be guaranteed the means to *exist*. One must pay at least *minimal* heed to the material person and guarantee the right to *minimally* satisfactory material lives. *That*, as opposed to fully-blown odes to economic equality, is what's enumerated in human rights: that "everyone has the right to a standard of living adequate for the health and well-being of himself and of his family," as the Universal Declaration of Human Rights (1948) puts it, or that "food, clothing, housing and medical care and necessary social services" are privileges *all* should enjoy, as are education and the right to work.[44] One needs to make sure that the larger collective provides for those in need, and that individuals don't fall through the cracks. Such ideas, however, are related to the wider history of socialist thought. They derive from notions of looking closely at the individual as a creature with material foundations and the

---

42 See, e.g., Rodney G. Peffer, *Marxism, Morality, and Social Justice* (Princeton: Princeton University Press, 1990).

43 See Geoff Boucher, *Understanding Marxism* (London: Routledge, 2012).

44 United Nations, "The Universal Declaration of Human Rights" (1948, article 25 [hereafter UDHR]), available at http://www.un.org/en/universal-declaration-human-rights/index.html; United Nations, "International Covenant on Economic, Social and Cultural Rights" (1966), available at http://www.ohchr.org/EN/ProfessionalInterest/Pages/CESCR.aspx.

principle, as Marx put it, that people should give "from each according to their ability [and] to each according to their needs."[45] They have to do with recognizing that free speech without bread is a difficult project. No – in the context of the UN, communist states weren't the only countries to push for socio-economic rights. Some liberal powers supported them too. There's nonetheless a reason why Eastern Bloc countries pushed so heavily for such rights and, even in the West, that socialist parties were often their most vocal sites of support. Such issues were a matter of socialism's *raison d'être*.[46] Simply put, significant parts of documents such as the Universal Declaration, if not the very *existence* of documents like the International Covenant on Economic, Social and Cultural Rights (1966), owe more than a small debt to socialism and socialist states' insistence on *some* level of economic fairness. They emerged in no small part because of socialism's claims to, if not of socio-economic equality, then at least an acceptable material existence for all.[47]

Of course, the *other* side of human rights *are* the so-called "liberal rights": rights such as freedom of speech, freedom of religion and freedom of conscience. The other side of human rights is the right to participate in government and be recognized equally in court. Rights' "other side" involves *habeas corpus* and the guarantee that, if one commits a crime, one's day in court will come. "Civil and political rights," they're called, and as one scholar has characterized it, at issue is "voice": freedom of thought and the idea that, absent the ability to say one's piece, personhood is degraded, or loses its worth.[48] Again, socialists made the argument that there was little reason to discuss free speech unless one had access to bread. One can't eat speech, they maintained.[49] It has *also* been noted, however, that one can't petition for bread without *voice* – that guaranteeing the right to

---

45 Karl Marx, *Critique of the Gotha Program* (Rockville: Wildside, 2008), 27.

46 The goal of socialism, Leonid Brezhnev once wrote, was to secure "in reality the rights of the working man whatever his nationality" and to assure the "right to work, education, social security, free medical aid, rest and leisure and the like" – things either "secondary" or "unacceptable" in the West. See Brezhnev, *Socialism, Democracy and Human Rights*, 82.

47 See Roger Normand and Sarah Zaidi, *Human Rights at the UN* (Bloomington: Indiana University Press, 2008). See also Johannes Morsink, *The Universal Declaration of Human Rights: Origins, Drafting & Intent* (Philadelphia: University of Pennsylvania Press, 1999): Ishay, *The History*, 117–72.

48 Joseph Slaughter, "A Question of Narration: The Voice in International Human Rights Law," *Human Rights Quarterly* 19, no. 2 (1997): 406–30.

49 Bob Canon, "Marx, Modernity and Human Rights," in *Constructing Marxist Ethics: Critique, Normativity, Praxis*, ed. Michael J. Thompson (Leiden: Brill, 2015), 179–80;

articulate oneself ensures one's ability to speak up for one's needs. Out of its long-held tradition of political liberty, the West pushed hard for *those* rights – ideals *also* constituting significant parts of documents like the Universal Declaration, and forming the grounds of treaties like the International Covenant on Civil and Political Rights (1966). That push was based on the idea that it was really *there* that the heart of human rights lay.[50]

I'm not sure where I fall in such debates. Clearly, life is devalued without free thought and expression. *Esprit*, as the French call it – the active, reflective self – is central to who we are. Echoing some of philosophy's most famous words, it may be that I "am" because I "think." Forget the mind and we may be discussing a human life worth little.[51] Take away intellectual freedom and we may have a dry existence.

Still, humanity's physical nature can't just be ignored. There's no "mind" to consider *absent* the body.[52] One need keep the mind *alive* to have *any* kind of speech. Indeed, more than just "bare life," as it's been called, one might consider if the person should perhaps be endowed with enough material resources such that the quality of one's life won't involve noticeably *fewer* opportunities to reflect and formulate one's thoughts than anyone else.[53] My stomach may not deserve to rumble particularly more than the mayor's or my banker's. That is, however, rights; they ask for *both* – attention to the "spiritual" *and* "material" self. Though there may be certain things that we've lost – a certain critical edge to reflection in our neo-liberal worlds – such things may be the *boon* of our post-Cold War years. It may be a gift that we can discuss the multiple sides of rights without "-isms" and "-ologies" looming so heavily in the background. Though we should not forget the *scope* of our political possibilities, there is virtue to the idea that

---

Peter Lamb, *Historical Dictionary of Socialism* (Lanham: Rowman & Littlefield, 2016), 209–12.

50 See again Normand and Zaidi, *Human Rights*.

51 See, e.g., Amélia Oksenberg Rorty, "Descartes and Spinoza on Epistemological Egalitarianism," *History of Philosophy Quarterly* 13, no. 1 (1996): 35–53. The reference is to Descartes' famous "I think, therefore I am."

52 One can't lead a life based solely on concepts in "the brain," Marx maintained – again underlining the connection of such points to the history of socialism. See Karl Marx and Friedrich Engels, *The German Ideology: Part One, with Selections from Parts Two and Three and Supplementary Texts*, ed. C.J. Arthur (New York: International, 1993), 8.

53 See Giorgio Agamben, *Homo Sacer: Sovereign Power and Bare Life*, trans. Daniel Heller-Roazen (Stanford: Stanford University Press, 1998).

we might worry about *humanity's* victory as opposed to the victory of one or the other ideological "camp."[54]

Still, as important as such issues are – as important as contemplating the nature of rights or the winding paths of Cold War history might be – the *final* point that Potsdam may drive home is the evocative nature of the historical scene. I.e., above questions of communist or capitalist rights and wrongs or the intellectual legacies of ideas maintaining high levels of contemporary significance (again, human rights), one of the *basic* powers in considering Potsdam's personalities and locales may be encountering the force of the historical imagination. Perhaps the most intense dimension of touring the city's sites is understanding the significance of *lieux de mémoire*, French historian Pierre Nora once called them: "sites of memory" and locales of reflections.[55] It's discovering places where we *can* think about the past, and where problems of ideology, global conflict and the genealogies of our *own* times are placed so saliently in front of us.

In many ways, Potsdam moves slowly; the city maintains a staid veneer. When one arrives, the town appears as wanting to demonstrate little about itself. The markers the municipality uses to indicate its historical sites are modest, and one can but vaguely hear greater Berlin in the background. Indeed, insofar as its historical sites *are* concerned, it *is* Sanssouci that sticks out the most. The Cold War locations are visually less lavish, lacking the eighteenth century's Rococo touch. Now, thinking about Nora, his discussion of *lieux de mémoire* in fact came in relation to *France* – locales evoking a *nation's* memory and providing connections between the present and *national* times gone by. At issue were locales like Versailles, the Louvre, the Pantheon, the Eiffel Tower, the Bibliothéque Nationale and their meaning for the *French* people. It was the constitution of a *nation-state's* identity and the sinews of that identity's emergence over time. Still, Nora wasn't *unaware* of the *world* importance of such sites. Nora maintained a sense of the meaning of such places to both European history and world civilization at-large. Indeed, as Nora notes, the "national" and "international" are hard to tear apart. Places like the like the great buildings of Paris become interesting *nationally* in part because they represent ideals and experiences to which a *larger* community relates; sites elucidating something for us *all* and appealing to sets of imaginations

---

54 It's now become common to refer to the "indivisibility" of human rights: that one right can't be detached from another, or at least that the different varieties of rights are related to one another. See Daniel Whelan, *Indivisible Human Rights: A History* (Philadelphia: University of Pennsylvania Press, 2011).

55 See Pierre Nora, ed., *Rethinking France: Les Lieux de Mémoire (Volume 1: The State)*, trans. Mary Trouille (Chicago: University of Chicago Press 2001).

which extend beyond a specific nation's borders and walls.[56] Simply put, that's what we have with Potsdam. We have a *lieux de mémoire* in precisely that sense. Much is evoked – international interventions and Cold War crimes; *Realpolitical* conflict, the history of political principle and the contexts in which such principles evolved. We have a sense of something German – a Central European state at the heart of global storms – yet something emblematic for a larger community; something central for understanding *world*-historical states and the pathways many took through them. The city offers rare moments – stark yet quiet confrontations with massive scales of conflict as well as contemplations of intrigues both local and global. We see long lines in the history of political thought – lines simultaneously challenging and feeding into concepts that maintain significance, perhaps *ultimate* significance, today. We need to listen carefully to such sites. We need to walk on the pathways and in the footsteps of such locales, allowing their presence to speak. We need to stand in the places where history was made and hear the voices of the past. Ultimately, that's in the name of more fully-rounded understandings of what is and has been at stake in terms of the torsion of ideas and the conflicts to which torsion can lead. It's to learn what's at risk when ideologies face off against one another, convinced of their rectitude though they may have been. It's also, however, to reflect specifically on concepts such as *human rights* – the ways of an *idea's* origins and the challenges *it* poses. That's such that we might take the ideological tools available to us and use them in ways that hopefully won't involve prisoner exchanges or the need to divide up continents in terms of whose ideas may exist where and what we're willing to do to keep the other's out. Simply put, in our day and age, the Cecilienhof and Glienicke Bridge have a great deal to teach.

---

56 Ibid., viii.

Iron Bridges
Crackdowns, Crackdowns
(April 2, 2016)

Abstract: *We know that Recep Tayyip Erdoğan's Turkey is challenging international rights standards, especially in relation to democracy and freedom of the press. With recent crackdowns such as that again the newspaper* Zaman, *however, Erdoğan is in fact attacking the heart of human rights: free expression and the spaces that facilitate the operation of the free-thinking individual.*

Turkey, as many know, is supposed to be the bridge between East and West. In many ways, it is. The vast majority of the country (Anatolia) lies on the Asian continent, where the capital Ankara lays, and the country maintains a long border

"Flag of Turkey." © Miro Novak / Fotolia.com 132441773

with the state at the center of so much of contemporary international affairs (Syria) in addition its borders with other Middle- and Near Eastern states with high levels of centrality to today's global goings-on (Iran and Iraq most specifically). Turkey also maintains membership in organizations with decided levels of meaning to Mid- and Near-East politics such as the Organisation of Islamic Cooperation and maintains borders with Armenia and Georgia, important states in the Eurasian region in which Russia has historical interests.[1] That's while a chunk of the country's geography lies in *Europe* (Istanbul is split between the two continents), and the Ottoman Empire as it existed into the nineteenth century included not only the European part of Istanbul but other European capitals as well (e.g., Sofia and Belgrade). I've always been impressed by that: the idea of an actual bridge spanning the physical and cultural boundaries of East and West; a kind of continuum running from the Occident to the Orient and back. It bespeaks a level of cosmopolitanism that few of us can easily claim to have.[2]

---

1   Organisation of Islamic Cooperation, "Member States" (2016), available at http://www.oic-oci.org/oicv2/states/?lan=en#.

2   See, e.g., Vojtech Mastny and R. Craig Nation, eds., *Turkey between East and West: New Challenges for a Rising Regional Power* (Boulder: Westview, 1996).

Indeed, the cultural dimensions of this *are* interesting. As many will also know, modern Turkey was carved out of the defunct Ottoman Empire – the regional power throughout North Africa and the Mid-East from the sixteenth through the nineteenth centuries – and, emerging as the country's leading figure in the wake of the First World War (the Ottomans, German allies, were soundly defeated), Atatürk, the founder of modern Turkey, sought to break the nation away from the traditions marking the roughly five-hundred-years of the Ottoman sultanate. That included issues like expanding the country's industrial base. It also, however, included the disbandment of courtly privileges, a massive overhaul of the nation's education system, the abolition of Islamic courts, the transformation of the alphabet from Perso-Arabic to Latinate, throwing out of the Ottoman fez, paring down on religious dress and, perhaps most importantly, establishing a modern democratic system that in 1934 also brought women into the fold – a concept that would have inconceivable but a few short decades before.[3] The official stance – defining for post-1923 Turkey ('23 being the year the Republic of Turkey was declared [October 29]) – is that the country is a secular state: secularism being a concept important enough for the military to be granted a special charge to oversee. In fact, the army *has* intervened in national politics in secularism's more than once – the 1980 coup and the 1997 "military memorandum" being perhaps the most famous examples.[4] Now, religion isn't *necessarily* new to major party politics in Turkey – its over-emphasis was the supposed the grounds for the 1997 ouster of Prime Minister Necmettin Erbakan, whose government that was brought down by that year's "memorandum" (a kind of coup with the coup). Still, secular commitments and basic interests in civil society have been profoundly challenged with the rise of Recep Tayyip Erdoğan, an advocate of a noticeably more religious and culturo-conservative state. Since rising to the prime ministership in 2003 and then the presidency in 2014, Erdoğan's been busy. He's stacked the courts with religiously sympathetic judges – judges who have thrown out demands that couples have legally-binding civil marriages before religious ceremonies can be performed (a move some have suggested might reinvigorate practices such as polygamy and child marriage) – he's finagled the replacement of a number of secular public schools with *imam–hatips* (schools involving religious training), he's reintroduced long-dropped restrictions on the sale of alcohol in

---

3   See Jacob M. Landau, ed., *Atatürk and the Modernization of Turkey* (Boulder: Westview, 1984).

4   See, e.g., Sam Kaplan, "Din-u Devlet All Over Again?: The Politics of Military Secularism and Religious Militarism in Turkey Following the 1980 Coup," *International Journal of Middle East Studies* 34, no. 1 (2002): 113–27.

terms of when and where it might be sold (something that had long been thought of as of no particular importance in the supposedly secular Republic) and his judges have handed down prison sentences to critics of the regime like the pianist Fazil Say and the writer Sevan Nişanyan (Say's sentence was suspended; Nişanyan's was not).[5] Of course, one hardly need mention the 2013 crackdowns on protestors in Istanbul's Gezi Park in which eight people were killed, thousands were tear gassed and hundreds were water cannoned as they petitioned for basic rights to free speech and government transparency.[6] It's a recognized trend in Turkey by now: vaguely religious, authoritarian rule eroding what's supposed to be a liberal state. Many wonder if, in the midst of all this, Turks supporting more cosmopolitan points of view can anymore find a place in national political life.[7]

Erdoğan's done it again. It's old news by now. However, on March 4, the Turkish government took control of the country's largest newspaper, *Zaman* ("Time") for picking up on issues that while hardly new, have the potential to eat into the President's power base. Corruption scandals have been rife in Turkey, especially since 2013, when dozens of officials in the Justice and Development Party (AKP [*Adalet ve Kalkınma Partisi*]) were discovered to have been involved in everything from bribery and fraud to money laundering to even, it seems, the smuggling of gold.[8] *Zaman*, initially supportive of the AKP, felt the need, like any decent paper, to do its due diligence. That meant keeping abreast of scandal, reporting on it and offering commentary on what it discovered as it went along. Erdoğan, who's hassled newspapers before, saw this as too much. Utilizing a running feud with former ally Fethullah Gülen – an influential ex-imam in self-imposed exile in Pennsylvania in the United States – the Turkish President

---

5   Guillaume Perrier, "Fazil Say, jugé pour blasphème et pour l'exemple," *Le Monde*, October 17, 2012, available at http://www.lemonde.fr/culture/article/2012/10/17/fazil-say-juge-pour-blaspheme-et-pour-l-exemple_1776748_3246.html#CUiuQLvI7BTgXJQL.99. See also Constanze Letsch, "Turkish Parent Complain of Push Towards Religious Schools," *The Guardian*, February 12, 2015, available at http://www.theguardian.com/world/2015/feb/12/turkish-parents-steered-religious-schools-secular-imam-hatip. See also M. Hakan Yavuz, *Secularism and Muslim Democracy in Turkey* (Cambridge: Cambridge University Press, 2009).

6   Efe Gürcan and Efe Peker, *Challenging Neoliberalism at Turkey's Gezi Park: From Private Discontent to Collective Class Action* (New York: Macmillan, 2015).

7   See Abdullah Bozkurt, *Turkey Interrupted: Derailing Democracy* (Izmir: Blue Dome Press, 2013).

8   See Berivan Orucoglu, "Why Turkey's Mother of All Corruption Scandals Refuses to Go Away," *Foreign Affairs*, January 6, 2015, available at http://foreignpolicy.com/2015/01/06/why-turkeys-mother-of-all-corruption-scandals-refuses-to-go-away/.

accused the paper of contributing to a supposedly Gülen-led effort to run what Erdoğan calls a "parallel state" (a state within a state, somehow). Now, there *are* questions as to what *Gülen* is up to. Some have suggested that his *Hizmet* ("Service") movement is something of a New Age cult, injecting its own brand of religiosity into Turkish life (*Hizmet* has grown rapidly, and its workings sometimes appear secretive).[9] Beyond the fact that it's a large-scale, widely-read daily, however, it's unclear *what Zaman's* crimes were, and it's also the case that, regardless of the particular allegiances the paper may or may not have, attacking *any* legitimate newspaper's offices and disbanding its editorial board represents a less-than-subtle move against freedom of speech and liberty of the press. Video of the crackdown is dramatic. Recalling scenes that have become common on Turkish streets, demonstrators protested by bringing signs, chanting slogans and invoking the usual rights-based *esprit*. It wasn't unlike civil rights demonstrations one can see many places in the world on any given day. The police ran right through them, though, using water cannons and rubber bullets. They crowbarred their way into the newspaper's building and forced their way into its offices. The move left an impressive trail of hurt people and destroyed property in its wake.[10]

The whole scenario troubles me on two levels – potentially three. The potential "third" level simply concerns the emergence of an increasingly authoritarian state. Clearly, few democracies *don't* have their troubles, and Turkey remains nominally that: a democracy. In the U.S. in the '50s and '60s, e.g., Civil Rights demonstrators met the power of the police more than once, tasting everything from water cannons to dogs as they petitioned for social inclusion and democratic rights.[11] In the '60s and '70s, anti-war demonstrators had more than one run-in with everyone from National Guardsmen to local police as they protested for troops to get out of Vietnam and the country tone down its engagement in Cold War *Realpolitik* (few will of course forget the shootings at Kent State in 1970). Events like May '68 in Paris and riots in places like Brixton in the UK

9   BBC News, "Profile: Fethullah Gülen's Hizmet Movement," December 18, 2013, available at http://www.bbc.com/news/world-13503361.

10 See Safak Timur and Tim Arango, "Turkey Seizes Newspaper, Zaman, as Press Crackdown Continues," *The New York Times*, March 4, 2016, http://www.nytimes.com/2016/03/05/world/middleeast/recep-tayyip-erdogan-government-seizes-zaman-newspaper.html.

11 See Horace Huntley and John W. McKerley, eds., *Foot Soldiers for Democracy: The Men, Women, and Children of the Birmingham Civil Rights Movement* (Urbana: University of Illinois Press, 2009); Charles DeBenedetti and Charles Chatfield, *An American Ordeal: The Antiwar Movement of the Vietnam Era* (Syracuse: Syracuse University Press, 1990).

in the '80s involved heavy confrontations between activists and the authorities as students' rights, minority rights, and essential social privileges were taken up as issues throughout Europe and the West.[12] As open societies whose openness in part concerns the negotiation of power (that's partly what democracies do [negotiate power]), it might be inevitable that social processes will sometimes involve at least the *potential* for violence, including from the state.[13] Still, it's the *sustained* nature of what's taking place in Turkey that worries me. Claiming to want to cultivate a "pious generation," Erdoğan's methods seem anything but.[14] The Turkish President seems involved with bold-faced thuggery – an approach in which there's little attempt to even *justify* crackdowns except to say that they concern "subversives" and "terrorists;" old saws for any strongman looking to centralize his or her power.[15]

My *primary* points, however – points "one" and "two" – concern the relation of Erdoğan's actions to the refugee crisis in Europe and Turkey's status in NATO (point one), and then problems of not only democracy, but how religiously-leaning states *can*, anyway, relate to problems of basic human rights (point two). Regarding the first issue, both Europe and the United States have much to answer for. While there's no doubt that the number of migrants attempting to cross European borders poses extensive logistical challenges, Europe's collective response has degenerated to a point where the EU has essentially agreed to *pay* Turkey more than 3 billion Euros to take illegal refugees back – an agreement the two parties recently made. That involves EU states returning refugees to a country (Turkey) whose ability to handle the numbers crossing its *own* borders has exceeded all reasonable limits (Turkey is often refugees' first stop as part of the longer journey to Europe, and the conditions for the more than 2.5 million in Turkish camps are universally considered poor).[16] Yes: mass migration is complex. Good

---

12 E.g., Kristin Ross, *May '68 and its Afterlives* (Chicago: University of Chicago Press, 2008); C. Hamnett, "The Conditions in England's Inner Cities on the Eve of the 1981 Riots," *Area* 15, no. 1 (1983): 7–13.

13 See Susan Bickford, *The Dissonance of Democracy: Listening, Conflict, and Citizenship* (Ithaca, NY: Cornell University Press, 1996).

14 See Simon Tisdall, "Recep Tayyip Erdogan: Turkey's Elected Sultan or an Islamic Democrat?" *The Guardian*, October 24, 2012, available at http://www.theguardian.com/world/2012/oct/24/recep-tayyip-erdogan-turkey.

15 Aydogan Vatandas, *Hungry for Power: Erdogan's Witch Hunt and Abuse of State Power* (New York: Blue Dome Press, 2013).

16 The concrete dimensions of the deal are that the EU will take one refugee declared eligible for asylum in return for each refugee that didn't apply for asylum or had their case rejected. This is massively controversial as grounds for rejecting asylum can be

suggestions about how to handle all the dimensions of Europe's migrant crisis may not be rife.[17] Still, the EU has engaged a money-for-people deal based on pressure from right-wing parties that play to not-always-subtly ethnicized and religicized visions of "the nation" and who aren't much interested in seeing the cultural complexion of the continent change much in the first place.[18]

That's then been tied to agreements to accelerate the consideration of Turkish membership in the EU – a point under negotiation since 2005. I.e., in part *because* there's been criticism from the both the "European purist" right and the humanitarian left (the latter critical of Turkey's record based precisely on issues like the crackdown on *Zaman*; the former skeptical of diluting the ethnic core of Europe's "nations"), negotiations with Turkey about EU membership *had* come close to being put totally on hold. In light of Turkey's encroaching authoritarianism, the country, in the vocabulary of one EU official, had been told to clean up its "act;" it had been asked to reach at least *minimal* levels of civil liberties and free speech before it might be allowed to enter the bloc.[19] However, given that Europe now prefers *not* to handle its own refugee crisis and has decided to make hard distinctions between refugees with "legal" and "illegal" status (can a person be "illegal?"), mum's been the word on issues like *Zaman*, and there's a chance for Turkey to get at least *part* of what it wants regarding forward motion on joining the bloc. That's then been exacerbated by relative silence from the U.S. – that as Turkey forms NATO's frontline with the Middle East. I.e., in view of the conflict with Islamic State and, in certain ways, Syria's Assad regime, Obama Administration criticism of Erdoğan has been relatively mild as there's been a need to keep

---

varied, reasons for *not* applying for asylum can be varied, and it's a situation that seems to characterize some refugees as "legitimate" and others as "not" – that over and above the massive number of refugees, especially from Syria, with which Turkey is trying to deal. See Patrick Kingsley, "EU-Turkey Refugee Deal: Staff Shortages and Rights Concerns Pose Twin Threat," *The Guardian*, April 1, 2016, available at http://www.theguardian.com/world/2016/apr/01/refugee-deal-threatened-by-lack-of-staff-and-concern-at-turkish-human-rights.

17 BBC, "Why Is the EU Struggling with Migrants and Asylum?" March 3, 2016, available at http://www.bbc.com/news/world-europe-24583286.

18 See, e.g., Matteo Garavoglia, "The EU-Turkey Dirty Deal on Migrants: Can Europe Redeem Itself?" *Brookings*, March 14, 1016, available at https://www.brookings.edu/blog/order-from-chaos/2016/03/14/the-eu-turkey-dirty-deal-on-migrants-can-europe-redeem-itself/.

19 Jennifer Ranking, "EU Strikes Deal with Turkey to Send Back Refugees," *The Guardian*, March 18, 2016, available at http://www.theguardian.com/world/2016/mar/18/eu-strikes-deal-with-turkey-to-send-back-refugees-from-greece.

Turkey on side. Following *Zaman*, the American President simply noted that he's "troubled" by the Turkish government's attack on the press and suggested that the country should be "reminded" of its commitments to democracy and people's ability to speak.[20] Given NATO's dedication to promoting "democratic values," that's weak-kneed stuff. That's to say nothing of the idea that the organization is hardly supposed to support dictatorships *within* its ranks.[21]

Now, fair enough – we need to keep eyes out for authoritarianism and moments at which dubious political projects are supported by democratic states. Hypocrisy deserves to be highlighted and international actors held to account. Still, I'd suggest that we need to dig deeper regarding the realities surrounding Turkey's crackdowns against free speech. There are *more* fundamental truths we need to address when liberal inquiry is put under duress and the right to think out loud is curtailed. Turkey – at least the Erdoğan government – is clearly attacking human rights; the country has levied an assault on freedoms we're all supposed to have. Still, that attack isn't only on human rights in a *general* sense. It's on the *heart* of the freedoms and liberties with which we're all supposed to be endowed. Erdoğan has taken a pot shot at the *essence* of our supposedly "highest morals precepts and political ideals."[22] He's dug at the *core* of the concepts involved in the liberties that are supposedly inherent to everyone.

We might think of it this way. Human rights are usually broken into two categories: "civil and political rights" and "economic, social and cultural rights" (very roughly, rights concerning free speech and individual choice and rights concerned with economic resources). Historically, the two haven't been weighted equally as socio-economic rights can be difficult to enforce. I.e., socio-economic rights, as opposed to civil and political rights, involve decisions about the "reallocation" of wealth – something which isn't always easy to effect (it's no small

---

20 See Dexter Filkins, "Erdogan's March to Dictatorship in Turkey," *The New Yorker*, March 31, 2016, available at http://www.newyorker.com/news/news-desk/erdogans-march-to-dictatorship-in-turkey; Nahal Tooshi, "Obama 'Troubled' by Turkish Leader's Crackdowns," *Politico*, April 1, 2016, available at http://www.politico.com/story/2016/04/obama-turkey-press-media-221483.

21 NATO, "What is NATO" (2016), available at http://www.nato.int/nato-welcome/index.html. Of course, NATO isn't "supporting" a dictatorship as such. Turkey is still nominally a democracy and no one is congratulating the country on its authoritarian turn. Still, the alliance is supposed to *protect* democracy – a task that doesn't seem helped when at least one of its governments may not be particularly democratic itself.

22 Samuel Moyn, *The Last Utopia: Human Rights in History* (Cambridge, MA: Harvard Belknap, 2010), 1.

thing to establish standards saying that states *must* spend money in particular ways – that especially if they're poor).[23] Still, the *idea* behind socio-economic rights is that voting, open journalistic practice, free social communication and participation in civic institutions are, if not meaningless, then at least *difficult* to accomplish if one can't eat. The idea is that intellectual life is predicated on the realities of physical existence, wherein one needs to at least minimally meet material needs. Rights experts often talk about an "indivisibility" to all rights. That means participating in government, yes, and the ability to speak one's mind. It also means, however, considering how to get people sufficient economic resources such that they *have* a life about which to express themselves and in relation to which they might exercise free thought at all.[24]

Again, all well and good. Full bellies are needed, and that means pushing for material well-being. Still, rights aren't just about "bare life." Rights concern *more* than just physical existence – a standard, as one philosopher notes, that even the vilest of states have at least *sometimes* managed to guarantee (even concentration camps, it's been noted, from time to time kept people alive).[25] No; rights are intended to involve the "free and full" development of the human "personality." Human rights should address the exercise of "conscience and reason" – the capacities of the intellect and the ability of individuals to engage in the realization of who they are.[26] Rights should concern the fulfillment the self and becoming subject to as few limitations as possible – that in terms of how one might discuss one's ideas and imagine the possibilities of one's being. One sociologist has noted rights as concerning not only personal security and freedom from fear but the creation of social and political systems allowing us to *expand* our senses of self and widen our horizons.[27] Rights concern the possibility of "narrat[ing] one's story," as one scholar has put it: saying something about our senses of how we want

---

23 Kenneth Roth, "Defending Economic, Social and Cultural Rights: Practical Issues Faced by an International Human Rights Organization," *Human Rights Quarterly* 26, no. 1 (2004): 65.

24 See, e.g., United Nations, "Vienna Declaration and Programme of Action" (1993, article 1, section 5), available at http://www.ohchr.org/en/professionalinterest/pages/vienna.aspx; Daniel J. Whelan, *Indivisible Human Rights: A History* (Philadelphia: University of Pennsylvania Press, 2011).

25 See Giorgio Agamben, *Homo Sacer: Sovereign Power and Bare Life*, trans. Daniel Heller-Roazen (Stanford: Stanford University Press, 1998), 61.

26 United Nations, "The Universal Declaration of Human Rights" (1948, articles 29 and 3), available at http://www.un.org/en/universal-declaration-human-rights/index.html.

27 Jürgen Habermas, "Private and Public Autonomy, Human Rights and Popular Sovereignty," in *The Politics of Human Rights*, ed. Obrad Savić (London: Verso, 1999), 61.

the world to be.[28] Of course, narrating one's story without a *medium* through which to narrate it is difficult indeed. That's where a free press comes in.[29]

That makes sense – Erdoğan has trampled over rights that not only many take for granted but we *should* take for granted and, in the process, trampled over the *essence* of rights as well. Erdoğan's gone after rights as about the free, reflective spirit – something which may be the absolute heart of what human rights are about. Still, we may need to look yet *more* closely the nature of Erdoğan's agenda. We may need to narrow down what his policies are oriented *towards*. Again, gestures towards, if not a fully authoritarian then at least *more* authoritarian state, seem clear. Erdoğan has called for "order" in Turkish society and proposed not only "respect" but "discipline" as the basis of national life.[30] It's yet again strongman stuff – declaiming "lacks of [national] direction" and decrying "wanton" idlenesses supposedly leading to "treasonous" intellectualisms like *Zaman's*.[31] Still, it's not just "order" to which Erdoğan appeals – it's not just criticizing the "loose" nature of modern society and its "wanton" ways. Erdoğan has *also* been asking for order in the context of a more *Islamic* state – the more "pious" society he claims he wants to create.

Now, Islam isn't the problem here. I.e., Islam is no more or less authoritarian or "absolutist" than anything else. Many religions have their fundamentalisms, and some strange politics have been made in the name of many gods.[32] Still, when state authority emerges on *any* theological basis, it *can* eat into popular sovereignty – ideas that the *people* are those to whom the state has to respond above and beyond anything else. The "social contract," democratic theorist Jean-Jacques Rousseau once maintained, should determine the contours of political life. The "general will" is that to which should form the basis of states.[33] Indeed, even when there *is* momentum for states to be founded in theology – something that modern history

---

28 Joseph Slaughter, "A Question of Narration: The Voice in International Human Rights Law," *Human Rights Quarterly* 19, no. 2 (1997): 406–30. See also John Steel, *Journalism and Free Speech* (London: Routledge, 2012).

29 See, e.g., Barbie Zelizer and Keren. Tenenboim-Weinblatt, eds., *Journalism and Memory* (New York: Palgrave Macmillan, 2014).

30 See Jenny B. White, "The Turkish Complex," *The American Interest*, February 2, 2015, available at http://www.the-american-interest.com/2015/02/02/the-turkish-complex/.

31 Juan José Linz, *Totalitarian and Authoritarian Regimes* (London: M.E. Sharpe, 2000).

32 See Karen Armstrong, *The Battle for God: A History of Fundamentalism* (New York: Random House, 2000).

33 Jean-Jacques Rousseau, *The Social Contract*, trans. Maurice Cranston (New York: Penguin, 1968).

has seen more than once – it's hard to claim *that* as popular belief unless one allows the people to *speak*. Religion can't be claimed as a state's *true* foundation if the members of the nation can't say what they in fact *believe* (and how do you accept expression as genuine when one isn't guaranteed the ability to speak as one will?). That's the rub with Erdoğan's Turkey: he seems to be shrinking the space to think, or at least *say* in a manner that seems genuinely open. It will become increasingly difficult to tell *what* people want as free expression decreases as part of the political atmosphere under Erdoğan's AKP.

Now, given history's complexity – the multiple paths we take to get where we are – it's difficult to expect all societies to be the same. One *could* argue – and some have – that Turkish democracy and republicanism were artifacts brought "from above": that they were the ideals of educated elites as much as concepts organic ("organic") to the nation as such. Many Turks in the '20s wanted reform; there were popular interests in ending Ottoman rule, and it's not for no reason that Atatürk maintains hero status as the founder of the modern Turkish state.[34] Still, democratic revolutions *can* be top-down affairs, and not all democratic beliefs accord with what *in fact* might be significant parts of popular sentiment.[35] Indeed, defenders of liberalism *themselves* note that we may have to live with multiple relations to rights. There may be "liberal" peoples in which societies underline participatory-democratic liberty – places where, though the security of the society may well be in hand, free expression is highlighted and a premium is placed on liberty of mind. There may also, however, be "decent hierarchical peoples": states not *always* respecting free speech but trying to look after welfare and society's at-large safety.[36] Perhaps Turkey is the latter. Perhaps the Erdoğan government is attempting to ensure social cohesion even though it eats into freer forms of expression and broader concepts of intellectual right. Perhaps Erdoğan's authoritarianism preserves *something* even if some of us might not understand precisely what that is.[37]

---

34 See again Landau, *Atatürk and the Modernization of Turkey.*

35 See, e.g., Ellen Kay Trimberger, *Revolution from Above: Military Bureaucrats and Development in Japan, Turkey, Egypt, and Peru* (New Brunswick: Transaction, 1978): Jacob M. Landau, ed., *Atatürk and the Modernization of Turkey* (Boulder: Westview, 1984).

36 See John Rawls, *The Law of Peoples* (Cambridge, MA: Harvard University Press, 1999).

37 *The New Republic*, e.g., has noted that Turkey is "stuck" with Erdoğan partly because his party's popularity derives in part from its "law and order" platform – a sense of supposed stability in the social body and a pulling back from more Western-style, supposedly "loose" social attitudes. It's a difficult concept for those automatically gravitating towards liberalism. Such concepts are nonetheless based at least in part on the idea that

I'm not unsympathetic to such arguments. One doesn't want to be so heavy-handed with rights that one refuses to accept multiple viewpoints and insists that *all* societies *must* be the same. We shouldn't ignore the fact that rights *themselves* insist on our ability to think along different lines. Again, liberal perspectives involve accepting a "diversity of opposing and irreconcilable political, religious, and moral doctrines."[38] We have to be careful about pointing at a world around us and always insisting "be like us." Still, *some* sense of civil liberties must be present. *Some* concept of free speech and freedom of mind should be on hand. Free expression *is* an artifact of rights ideals, and the international community asks societies to move *towards* the recognition of basic intellectual freedoms as opposed to away from them.[39] Via internationally-sanctioned ideals, freedom of the press and public communications should proceed relatively unhindered. Democracies that function as such shouldn't oft-suspend rights in "emergency's" name. Conspiratorial senses of protecting against "states within states" shouldn't constitute politics' grounds, and states should take care with appealing to what higher powers "reveal" to explain deviations from international norms. If rights *are* to be suspended, there needs to be clear proof put before the international community as to what the problem is, and one need explain to *what* standards one is appealing in terms of the rights one is about to repeal. I'd put it this way: if it's power in relation to Europe or the "West" that Erdoğan seeks, he's played the game well. He's been able to do what he wants with little sanction, and he may have *improved* Turkey's *Realpolitical* position on a global scale. That's above and beyond Erdoğan's ability to control the levers of state. Erdoğan has perhaps been shrewd, elevating the AKP to precisely where he wants it to go.

As such, I'm not against a shrewd political operator. Advocates for fundamental rights need them too. Politics can involve putting a little elbow grease into pursuing the goals one seeks, and even politicians we admire have to cut their deals. Still, Erdoğan's using more than just elbow grease. He's doing more than just "mixing things up," or getting into the "fray." Erdoğan's injunctions against civil liberties are heavy, and his crackdowns against free speech frequent and intense. His erosion of rights is thorough, and his attacks on his enemies swift. To this observer, anyway, Turkey's political atmosphere feels like hard metal: the

---

expressive rights aren't always held forward by all members of society as the primary values to which one must react (e.g., tradition or order might hold equal sway). See Kaya Genç, "Why Turkey Stuck with Erdogan," *The New Republic*, November 2, 2015, available at https://newrepublic.com/article/123322/why-turkey-stuck-erdogan.

38 See Rawls, *Political Liberalism* (New York: Columbia University Press, 1993), 3–4.

39 E.g., Michael Ignatieff, *The Rights Revolution* (Toronto: House of Anansi Press, 2000).

invocation of iron lines of intimidation and fear. The government's actions feel like a steel baton against liberty: a cold spike against freedom from worry about sanction if one says what one thinks or wants. *If* Turkey is the bridge between East and West, it feels at the moment an iron one: a hard crossing defined by the controlling attitudes of a semi-authoritarian regime undergirded by the icy struts of calculated disinterest from Europe and the U.S. – that as the latter focus on their own concerns and respond to political pressures in their own back yards. It makes one think. The lead weight of political pressure becomes heavier when rights' surface is fractured through crackdowns and the billy-clubbing of demonstrators. Authority feels cold when it involves crowbarring open the doors of journalistic offices and attacking demonstrators in the street. As I see it, the question is whether, *qua* global community, that's what we want: do we want the bridge spanning Europe and Asia to be an iron one? Do we want an illiberal regime in the front ranks of our partners and allies? Or do we seek more liberal bridges – more liberties in the nations to which we relate and with which our business is extensive? I'm in favor of the latter. If rights – the essence of rights – holds much good, our response to Erdoğan needs to be noticeably more robust than it's been.

The Arc of a Blue Note

Clark Terry and the Quiet Sound of Human Rights (April 4, 2016)

Abstract: *The loss of jazz trumpeter Clark Terry represents a loss of an unsung human rights hero: a quiet progressivist who brought change simply through the being of his art and belief in the power of education.*

Clearly, the American Civil Rights Movement is one of the defining movements in the larger push for international human rights. In part, that concerns the country's unique relationship with the idea. Other than France, few states more clearly laid out the basic dimensions of rights concepts in their formative years at the end of the eighteenth century with rights being called "unalienable" in the U.S.' Declaration of Independence (1776) wherein, along with French revolutionaries' use of the same vocabulary in the Declaration of the Rights of Man and Citizen (1789), a precedent became set for governments' equal treatment of their citizens. Now, *human* rights, as opposed to "national rights," or rights based in state polities, don't rely on people being "citizens." "Human

"Jazzmusic." © *Jürgen Fälchle / Fotolia.com 62149902*

rights" should be present whether one calls a specific country "home" or not.[1] Still, the parity of peoples before their governments represented a significant step forward for the cause of international justice at-large.

If one dates the American Civil Rights Movement from 1954 to 1964 – *Brown versus Board of Education* to the Selma to Montgomery marches (a typical dating) – one encounters many of the mid-twentieth century's powerful rights figures: Martin Luther King, Malcolm X, Julian Bond, Thurgood Marshall, Jesse Jackson, James Bevel, John Lewis, A. Phillip Randolph, Rosa Parks and Stokely Carmichael, among others. If one *expands* one's sense of Civil Rights to encompass more than just those who advocated peaceful resistance (X was already there; Carmichael would gravitate in that direction) and one takes a chronological view of the Movement in which it involved more than just the events

---

1   See, e.g., Samuel Moyn, *The Last Utopia: Human Rights in History* (Cambridge, MA: Harvard Belknap, 2010), 26.

leading directly to the 1964 Civil Rights Act, accounting for Civil Rights includes everyone from Sojourner Truth to Harriet Tubman to Frederick Douglass to Booker T. Washington to Marcus Garvey to W.E.B DuBois to Bobby Seale, Huey Newton and Angela Davis to Eldridge Cleaver, Kweisi Mfume, Roy Innis, Ben Jealous, Cornell Williams Brooks and many, many more. Civil Rights snakes through the history of the republic; it's a "peoples' history" in which the promise of American democracy has been both expanded and challenged.[2] Still, the Civil Rights Movement was more than just an American phenomenon. Outside the U.S., figures such as DuBois, King and the Black Panthers were household names for activists fighting imperialism and discrimination abroad.[3] Politically conscious African-Americans followed the politics of Kwame Nkrumah and Jomo Kenyatta in their state-building efforts from Ghana to Kenya. Figures like X and DuBois bridged the gap between political and economic rights as they sought not only voice at home but economic freedom elsewhere.[4] Onlookers from Ho Chi Minh to Nelson Mandela and Stephen Biko viewed Civil Rights in the context of their *own* struggles, seeing the Movement as an occasion for solidarity in the fight against marginalization and oppression wherever they were to be found.[5] On both domestic and global scales, Civil Rights engendered aspirations for equality and the humane treatment of peoples in whatever context one might wish to discuss.

The relationship of Civil Rights to the arts has always been complex. Many were clear: "education is indoctrination if you're white," the writer James Baldwin maintained; "subjugation if you're black."[6] Novels like Baldwin's *Go Tell It On the Mountain* (1953), Ralph Ellison's *Invisible Man* (1952), plays like LeRoi Jones' *Dutchman* (1964) and poetry collections like Gwendolyn Brooks' *In the Mecca* (1968) investigated racial tension, offering critical views on what might be the most complex problem in American history (the relations of Black and White).[7] African-American painters have unfortunately been less well-known.

---

2   Howard Zinn, *A People's History of the United States: 1492-Present* (New York: Harper, 2004).

3   See Kevin, Gaines, "The Civil Rights Movement in World Perspective," *OAH Magazine of History* 21 no. 1 (2007): 59.

4   See Daniel S. Lucks, *Selma to Saigon: The Civil Rights Movement and the Vietnam War* (Lexington: University of Kentucky Press, 2014).

5   See again Gaines, "The Civil Rights Movement."

6   In Geoffrey Hughes, *Political Correctness: A History of Semantics and Culture* (Malden: Blackwell, 2010), 73.

7   E.g., Cornell West, *Race Matters* (Boston: Beacon, 1993).

Barkley L. Hendricks, Marie Johnson Calloway, and Barbara Jones-Hogu all made names for themselves; they were shown and garnered acclaim. That was nonetheless often with a lower profile than many of their literary and written word contemporaries. Still, from the Harlem Renaissance on, the African-American arts maintained a distinctly political streak. While never undoing the art as art (no one but no one could deny the beauty of a Langston Hughes or Maya Angelou poem, e.g.), politics often informed the precise form and content of what much produced under the rubric of Black arts movements should be.[8]

To that extent, it's interesting to note that many of the absolute heavyweights in what might not only be the seminal African-American art specifically but the seminal American art *generally* – jazz – sometimes shied away from politics. Figures like Charlie Parker, Dizzy Gillespie, Ella Fitzgerald, Thelonious Monk, Miles Davis and John Coltrane weren't *a*political. Racial advancement was surely a part of their *œuvre*.[9] Still, as cultural critic Gerald Early has put it, not all "saw jazz as a kind of protest music."[10] Status on the jazz scene didn't necessarily translate to taking a political stance. There are multiple reasons for this. One is the relative acceptance of jazz by White society; in the larger mainstream, boundary-pushing was good, but revolution too much. The "literal" overturning of social structure, it's been argued, was not what many listeners sought.[11] Others were so focused on the art that the politics simply fell away. Stanley Crouch has made this point in relation to Charlie Parker – a figure for whom "counter-culture" may have been the watchword as much as "political revolt."[12] Others were simply unsure of *which* way to turn as it was unclear what it meant to be "political" one week and a "musician" the next.[13] Of course, many took stances about which there could be no doubt. Works like Charles Mingus' "Fables of Faubus" from 1959's *Mingus Ah-Um* offered stark responses to issues like Arkansas governor Orval Faubus'

---

8   See Sharon F. Patton, *African-American Art* (Oxford: Oxford University Press, 1998); Michael G. Cooke, *Afro-American Literature in the Twentieth Century: The Achievement of Intimacy* (Yale: Yale University Press, 1986).

9   Ingrid Monson, *Freedom Sounds: Civil Rights Call Out to Jazz and Africa* (Oxford: Oxford University Press, 2007).

10 In Waldo E. Martin, Jr., "Miles Davis and the 1960s Avant-Garde," in *Miles Davis and American Culture*, ed. Gerald Early (St. Louis: Missouri Historical Society Press, 2001), 113.

11 Nicholas Evans, *Writing Jazz: Race, Nationalism, and Modern Culture in the 1920s* (New York: Garland, 2005), 102.

12 See Stanley Crouch, *Kansas City Lightening: The Rise and Times of Charlie Parker* (New York: Harper Collins, 2013).

13 Crouch, *Considering Genius: Writings on Jazz* (New York: Perseus, 2009).

refusal to integrate Little Rock schools – a turning-point in the longer arc of Civil Rights. Masterworks like Duke Ellington's *Black, Brown and Beige* (1943) portrayed the entire history of Afro-America in tonal form, including the strife and conflict that were surely a part of that past. Many embraced the aesthetics of Afrocentrism as figures from Pharaoh Sanders to Sun Ra marked jazz with a style that said "Black is mine" and that the music's home was in Afro-America as much as anywhere else.[14] Still, the larger acceptance of jazz *qua* art as well as a crafts-manship exceeding image and word (jazz didn't always involve the *text* that tends to drive political life) allowed swing, bebop, and free form to move in and out of politics in ways that other arts could not. Crouch has maintained that it's tempt-ing to impose "ethnic politics" on jazz music when they're not always there.[15] It's a challenge that those of us who too often to see the politicization of all aspects of African-American life may have to accept.

Still, the sheer power of the art – jazz's confrontation of listeners with some-thing so totally new – made it difficult for the music, perhaps along with soul, *not* to be the soundtrack for many of the changes afoot. As Early puts it, politics may have been "implicit in the act of a black person making [their] art under the conditions [in which] he or she were making it."[16] Though many insisted that politics *weren't* their *modus operandi* (Davis was particularly known for this), social situatedness and the tenor of the times may have brought reflections on socio-cultural relations whether one looked for them or not. This resonates. I'm twenty years too young to remember Civil Rights' heyday. My sense of the Move-ment comes from controversies around public school bussing in Boston at the end of the '70s, the rise of figures like Jesse Jackson and Al Sharpton in the '80s and the new Black consciousness of figures like Spike Lee as the '80s closed and the '90s began.[17] Still, when the first bars of "Two Bass Hit" from Davis' *Mile-stones* (1958) came on, or the opening bass line from Coltrane's *Love Supreme* (1965) hit the hi-fi, it was hard not to hear the sound. It was hard *not* to hear the

---

14 See Stephen Howe, *Afrocentrism: Mythical Pasts and Imagined Homes* (London: Verso, 1998).

15 Crouch, *Considering Genius*, 4. See also Anke Weber, Wesley Hiers and Anaïd Flesken, *Politicized Ethnicity: A Comparative Perspective* (New York: Palgrave Macmillan, 2016).

16 In Martin, Jr. "Miles Davis and the 1960s Avant-Garde," 133. See also Marc Anthony Neal, *What the Music Said: Black Popular Music and Black Public Culture* (London: Routledge, 1999).

17 See Ollie Johnson and Karin Stanford, eds., *Black Political Organizations in the Post-Civil Rights Era* (New Brunswick: Rutgers University Press, 2000).

call to change. One simply *had* to move forward. That was to the beat of a totally different drummer than anyone had ever heard before.

Behind the towering figures of King and X, Davises Angela and Miles and the monoliths that are Coltrane, Mingus, and Ellington were others. Figures from Daisy Bates to Dorothy Height to Nikki Giovanni to Mary McLeod Bethune to perhaps even Paul Robeson and Bayard Rustin were known. They were giants in their times. *With* time, however, we may have benefited from their legacies as much as *fêted* them; we may have inherited the gains they left us as much as acknowledged them as their authors. Though sitting in the pantheon, they're figures sometimes dancing on the edge, fading from view when we turn from decided moments of memorialization back to the mundane concerns of our daily lives.

It's a bit more than a year ago now. However, having been away from the U.S. and the maw of its cultural goings-on for some time, I was surprised to find out that the jazz trumpeter and flugelhornist Clark Terry had died – Terry being a figure I once had the pleasure to meet (a handshake at a workshop; nothing more). A few years older than Davis and also hailing from St. Louis, Terry taught Miles a bit. Terry might have *been* Miles had he been as committed to being personally obtuse and musically confrontational. He wasn't.[18] Terry was but one of the great stylists; a tunesmith and master of the craft. And, indeed, *what* a craft. Terry played with almost all the greats – from Gillespie, Basie and Ellington to Sonny Rollins, Herbie Hancock, and the Modern Jazz Quartet. He played in front of Presidents, blowing his horn on the White House lawn on more than one occasion. He was a hero in Europe, once garnering the *Ordre des Arts et des Lettres* by the government of France – the most prestigious award that country offers for artistic achievement.[19] Terry was the first black regular in a TV network band, gaining acclaim on the popular *The Tonight Show* and then staying on for ten more years. And he taught. All the time. The Berklee College of Music. The University of New Hampshire. The Manhattan School of Music. The New England Conservatory. Youth orchestras he started himself. Jazz camp after jazz camp; lesson after lesson. Indeed, Terry's influence was so great that in his last years and months, his hospital room was akin to a Grand Central Station of jazz. Everyone from Wynton Marsalis to Quincy Jones stopped in to say "hi." That's while remaining a connoisseur's figure – known, but not a star, recognized,

---

18 Clark Terry, *Clark: The Autobiography of Clark Terry* (Berkeley: University of California Press, 2011).

19 See Felix Contreras, "Clark Terry, Ebullient Jazz Trumpeter, Has Died," *NPR* February 22, 2015, available at http://www.npr.org/blogs/ablogsupreme/2015/02/22/386127400/clark-terry-ebullient-jazz-trumpeter-has-died.

but in a quiet way. Terry's modest personality never allowed for nor demanded anything more.

What Clark Terry did was slowly equalize. Through a dedication to crafts-manship, a passion for teaching and a focus on the music, Terry slowly nudged Black, White, Brown, Latino, Asian, African and European closer together. He assisted racial concord by focusing on the art and letting the politics play them-selves out as they would. The furies of hot solos to resolved themselves in Terry's presence in moments of the kind perhaps only music can provide – as they are, without pressure or asserting that things must to be a particular way. In a life like that, one hears the quiet sound of human rights: the drumbeat of persistence, tolerance and moderation accompanying the drama, brashness and militancy that's often necessary too. It's the arc of a blue note: a note without which perhaps music generally – but most certainly jazz – can ever do.

What to Do with the Kingdom?
Rights and Cultural Life
(April 6, 2016)

Abstract: *What human rights sense do we make of Saudi Arabia? The country obviously challenges a range of international rights standards. It also, however, raises the question of what to do with rights in the face of fundamental cultural difference.*

I caught a provocative documentary the other day – a piece from *Frontline*, the investigative journalism series produced by an affiliate of the American Public Broadcasting Service (WGBH) that's generally known for its thought-provoking, in-depth pieces. *Frontline* has won awards for a number of films: its series on terrorism in the wake of 9/11, its work on Dick Cheney's influence in the Bush, Jr. White House, issues of national importance such as the 1993 siege of the Branch Davidian complex in Waco, Texas and problems of pressing *international* importance such as the use of torture in the so-called "War on Terror."[1] The series' most recent piece, "Saudi Arabia Uncovered," draws material from a group of younger activists who filmed daily life in the Saudi king-

"Location Saudi Arabia. Red Pin on the Map." © Zerophoto / Fotolia.com 90206782

dom. It's hard-hitting stuff. Revealed is something beyond the show cities, the resorts, the high traffic business areas and what for Westerners anyway, are the often-provocative images of members of the royal family in their *bisht* and *keffiyeh*. One sees slums – you'd be surprised how much of the country lives in poverty – one witnesses the actions of the often-heard-of but little-seen religious police, one sees government crackdowns against pro-democracy demonstrations and one witnesses the intensely punitive practices used for violations of "state security" – that to say nothing of punishments meted out on the basis of the country's notoriously strict interpretations of *Shari'a* law. It's not viewing for the faint-hearted. There are

---

1 The "War on Terror" vocabulary has of course been dropped because of its pejorative nature. Obviously, however, it was the major vocabulary characterizing the larger part of ten years (more) of international conflict – and remains so whether we like it or not. See Jay Solomon, "U.S. Drops 'War on Terror' Phrase, Clinton Says," *The Wall Street Journal*, March 31, 2009, available at http://www.wsj.com/articles/SB123845123690371231.

executions in the street – beheadings, sometimes with swords. Headless bodies are occasionally hung in public space, intended to send a message to the populace at-large. Women are harassed in shopping malls for having made-up their faces or going about unaccompanied by men. The lash is used as punishment, and one sees images of the overt segregation of women in governmental space – visual manifestation of gender-based differences in rights and privileges. If one pays attention to international goings on, such things are hardly news. Saudi Arabia gets a fair amount of press for its heavy-handed, religiously-based approach to law.[2] Still, having such issues brought home graphically is another matter. It bears concrete witness to what it seems that more than a few Saudis see as part of everyday life. There's nothing like a good piece of film work to put one in the middle of the scene.

The bugaboo in all this is what Saudi Arabia represents. I.e., the country has a drastically complex history. As many may know, the shape of the contemporary Middle East owes much to British and French displacements of Ottoman power at the end of World War I – an event providing the outlines of modern Iraq, Kuwait, Egypt, Syria, Jordan, Lebanon, Israel and the Palestinian Territories (most are results of the old Mandate System – the post-World War I agreement splitting formerly Ottoman and German holdings between the victorious Allied powers). It was also in negotiation with British interests that many of the states of the Arabian Peninsula came into being as well (Bahrain, Qatar, and the United Arab Emirates [they weren't Mandate states; however, the British were the reigning power]).[3] Saudi Arabia darts in and around this past. Wresting areas like al-Hasa from the Ottomans as early as 1913 (al-Hasa being more or less the eastern province of the contemporary Saudi state), Ibn Saud, Saudi Arabia's father, kept his distance from the 1916–1918 Arab Revolt – the partly British-jiggered rebellion against Ottoman rule intended to create a unified Arab nation.[4] Focusing instead on the consolidation of his *own* rule, Saud gained hegemony over what we today know as the Saudi Kingdom, including Islam's holy cities of Mecca and Medina, by the mid-1920s. Much was done to unify the country – not the least of which included

---

2   E.g., Adam Taylor, "The Facts – and a Few Myths – about Saudi Arabia and Human Rights," *The Washington Post*, February 9, 2015, available at https://www.washingtonpost.com/news/worldviews/wp/2015/02/09/the-facts-and-a-few-myths-about-saudi-arabia-and-human-rights/.

3   See M.E. Yapp, *The Near East since the First World War: A History to 1995* (New York: Pearson Longman, 1996).

4   See James Joseph Schneider, *Guerilla Leader: T.E. Lawrence and the Arab Revolt* (New York: Bantam, 2011).

marrying a daughter from each of the country's important tribes.[5] Still, perhaps the crux of the unification enterprise involved a series of actions that brought politics and religion into the abiding mix for which we largely know Saudi Arabia today. The initial conquest of the Arabian Peninsula came with the help of the Ikhwan – a band of nomadic warriors who adhered to a strict version of Wahhabist Islam. The Ikhwan fought hard for Saud and then, with the consolidation of his rule, sought to push on into what is today Jordan, Iraq and Kuwait – that in the name of spreading a kingdom of the faith. Saud opposed this move as it challenged British sovereignty in the region – a showdown with the world's then-foremost military power being something that Saud sought to avoid. In an act of religious fervor, the Ikhwan revolted. In what some would say was a deeply disloyal move, Saud put down their rebellion, using other troops to suppress, brutally, his band of religious warriors. Still, especially since he had become the caretaker of Islam's most holy sites – the Kaaba and Al-Masjid al-Haram in Mecca – Saud's crushing of the Ikhwan had to be done with the support of the religious authorities in Riyadh; the *Ulema*, or religious council which, in the Saudi case, was the religious family descending from the founder of Wahhabism, Muhammad ibn Abd al-Wahhab.[6] This created a powerful and perhaps historically-determining cultural configuration. Political authority would rest with the king and royal family – the House of Saud, as such. Wahhabi clerics would maintain power over religion and things spiritual. However, as religion and the state were supposed to be two sides of the same coin, the clerics would also have a direct role in government by way of ensuring that royal decisions conformed with their brand of *Sharia* law. It's interesting: one Middle East scholar has noted that an early draft the Saudi Constitution was, in fact, no constitution at all. It was but a written line noting that "all administration is in the hands of his Majesty King ʿAbd al-ʿAzīz ibn Saʿūd. His Majesty is bound by the laws of *Sharia*."[7] In reality, constitutions needn't be mapped out as one needed but pious Muslims to act them out.[8]

---

5   See Madawi al-Rasheed, *A History of Saudi Arabia*, 2nd ed. (Cambridge: Cambridge University Press, 2010), 74–5.

6   See Jon Armajani, *Modern Islamist Movements: History, Religion, and Politics* (Oxford: Blackwell, 2011).

7   Yapp, *The Near East*, 189.

8   It should be noted that a more extensive "Basic Law" has been in place since 1992. See The Kingdom of Saudi Arabia, "Saudi Arabia: The New Constitution," *Arab Law Quarterly* 8, no. 3 (1993): 258–70.

Now, the fundamentalism never disappeared.[9] I note this because, come the post-World War II era, most, though not all, of the last vestiges of colonial rule were wiped from the map. Peoples from Africa to the Middle East to Southeast Asia could at least in principle decide for themselves.[10] For many, this meant modernization and secularization – engagements, serious ones, with economic and social development. In the Middle East, this was often prosecuted under the heading of "Arab Nationalism," the leading example of which was Egypt under Nasser. Arab nationalism had a lot of ins and outs. It was hardly pro-Western. During the Cold War, more than a few Arab states, largely at Nasser's urging, ended up firmly in the Soviet camp. Arab Nationalism also defended Third World interests – newly independent states that were more than occasionally critical of their old colonial masters.[11] Still, by way of its commitment to largely secular states with modern political architectures (overtures to broad-based popular sovereignty and parliamentary systems, to say nothing of the idea of the nation-state itself), Arab nationalism comes into the panoply of forces that, as one voice has expressed it, "shaping and reshaping Arab life" whose "origin and provenance" lay at least *partly* in the West. I.e., concepts like "socialism," "liberalism" and "capitalism" became the watchwords of development, and, adopting the model developed by Europeans in the nineteenth century, the idea was that modern peoples should have "nations" and their bureaucratic accoutrements.[12] Again, this again would be of little consequence except to the extent that it made Saudi anti-modernism and religiosity noticeably stick out. This was even *more* so after the 1938 discovery of oil made the Saudi kingdom a significant player on the international stage (oil brought Saudi Arabia especially close to the United States as the latter needed oil reserves in the Second

---

9 I'm not wild about the word "fundamentalism." On one hand, it projects a particular fervor for an idea, which is fitting: Saudi Arabia isn't trying to be milk toast. It can nonetheless seem dismissive when applied to entire countries or cultures and paper over the causes and nuances behind complicated movements. See Torkel Brekke, *Fundamentalism: Prophecy and Protest in an Age of Globalization* (Cambridge: Cambridge University Press, 2012).

10 John Springhall, *Decolonization since 1945: The Collapse of European Overseas Empires* (New York: Palgrave MacMillan, 2001).

11 See Bassam Tibi, *Arab Nationalism: Between Islam and the Nation-State* (New York: St. Martin's, 1997).

12 See Sadik J. Al-Azm, "Western Historical Thinking from an Arabia Perspective" in *Western Historical Thinking: An Intercultural Debate*, ed. Jörn Rüsen (New York: Berghahn, 2002), 121.

World War and strategic air bases afterwards – the foundation of the famous "oil for security" deal that's been defining for Saudi-American relations).[13]

Now, some Saudi conservatism has been innocuous enough. The country kept television out until the mid-1960s; the first television broadcast being a 1965 reading of the Koran.[14] The Kingdom has also but one movie theater – an IMAX in the city of Al Khobar, on the country's East Coast (that for close to 30 million people). There's the usual ban on alcohol and anything else that might intoxicate – what one can find is generally reserved for tourist areas. All predictable enough, and not necessarily dangerous.[15] Much of that becomes *less* innocuous, however, when one realizes that cinemas *had been* allowed until a conservative religious revolt in the late '70s demanded a tightening of religious laws (the 1979 occupation of the Grand Mosque in Mecca), people are *lashed* for violating laws surrounding alcohol (the drunk tank is one thing; the drunk *lash*, though?) and while TV as such may be of little consequence – does one *really* need reruns of *I Love Lucy* or *Three's Company* to lead a full life? – if the question is free speech and the dissemination of information, we're on decidedly different terrain. Indeed, one is *really* on different terrain when one realizes that men can practice polygamy but women can't, that people can be whipped for the "immorality" of being homosexual, that if one steals, the price might be losing one's hand, and if one is a Saudi citizen, one is disallowed from practicing any religion *but* Islam.[16] Perhaps I'm unsophisticated. However, it seems there's been an attempt – a not unsuccessful one – for Saudi Arabia to posit itself as the exemplar conservative-Islamic state. The country has offered itself up as the embodiment of what it means to insist on a radically distinct cultural point of view. That's meant Saudi Arabia lining itself up against secular-liberal mainstreams in terms of how one might organize social norms and the cultural ideals one might promote.[17]

---

13 Indeed, President Eisenhower for a time tried to advance the cause of Saudi Arabia as an alternative Arab leadership to the Nasserite neo-socialist state. See Salim Yaqub, *Containing Arab Nationalism: The Eisenhower Doctrine and the Middle East* (Chapel Hill: University of North Carolina Press, 2004).

14 See David Commins, *The Wahhabi Mission and Saudi Arabia* (London: I.B. Tauris, 2010), 110.

15 See Simon Ross Valentine, *Force and Fanaticism: Wahhabism in Saudi Arabia and Beyond* (London: Hurst, 2015), 90.

16 Valentine, *Force and Fanaticism*, 217.

17 This is a role also very much played by Iran, though from a Shiite as opposed to Sunni perspective. See Ann Elizabeth Mayer, *Islam and Human Rights: Tradition and Politics*, 5th ed. (Boulder: Westview, 2013).

For me, two issues emerge here – potentially with a third tacked on. The first of those concerns the starkness of some of the realities of Saudi life. Authoritarian regimes exist – at least two of the world's major states, Russia and China, can be characterized as such – and it's no secret that few states that *don't* struggle with issues concerning fundamental rights. The Economist Intelligence Unit, e.g. – a branch of *The Economist* magazine that provides one of the world's leading democracy indices – asserts no less than fifty-one countries as full-on authoritarian. That's a touch more than a quarter of the world's states.[18] Saudi Arabia comes off as one of the worst, ranking 160th out of 167 (the seven countries *under* Saudi Arabia are Turkmenistan, Equatorial Guinea, the Central African Republic, Chad, Syria and North Korea).[19] Saudi Arabia, however, is also not *necessarily* that far off of Turkey or Russia (88th and 102nd, respectively) – both states party to the oft-tooted-as-successful European Convention on Human Rights (1950).[20] Indeed, there are also worries about the fate of democracy in the exemplar "West" (the resurgent right has brought some relatively heavy insistences on law-and-order itself).[21] I just mention that because it's a heck of a job to say precisely who is authoritarian and who is not. Many of us may live in countries that are more authoritarian than we'd like.

Still, part of what the *Frontline* documentary illustrates is that Saudi Arabia's harsh social practices aren't rumor – they aren't the figment of an "Orientalist" imagination and, regardless of the massive building binges present since the '70s which the country's clerics apparently found to *match* their visions of *Sharia* law (they did the same with the basing of American troops on Saudi soil in Iraq Wars I and II), the country *isn't* just a bastion of oil wealth where rights violations extend to, say, insisting that women cover up bit or, "ha-ha, they have some hang-ups with women drivers, and isn't that good as the subject of a joke or two?" Saudi Arabia is a country where people's *heads* can be removed for

---

18 The Economist Intelligence Unit, "Democracy Index 2015: Democracy in the Age of Anxiety," available at http://www.yabiladi.com/img/content/EIU-Democracy-Index-2015.pdf.

19 Ibid.

20 Council of Europe, "Chart of Signatures and Ratifications of Treaty 005: Convention for the Protection of Human Rights and Fundamental Freedoms" (2016), available at http://www.coe.int/en/web/conventions/full-list/-/conventions/treaty/005/signatures?p_auth=PemigZhB. See also John D. Montgomery, "Fifty Years of Human Rights: An Emergent Global Regime," *Policy Sciences* 32, no. 1 (1999): 79–94.

21 These concerns are made clear in the Economist Intelligence Unit's report. See Economist Intelligence Unit, "Democracy Index 2015."

blasphemy. Saudi Arabia is a country where there's an absence of *any* freedom of conscience in ways many of us would expect. People can be *whipped* for consuming items they shouldn't, and women taking minor – *minor* – steps towards personal self-expression can find themselves confronted by religious authorities. That's behavior one might expect from Islamic State or Taliban-run regions. It's *not* something one expects from a major international player with a central position on the global stage.[22] Again, we have the video evidence to prove it: people lying prone on the ground sometimes begging for their lives – the begging ending with the lowering of a curved saber and a body separated from its head. The berating of women in public on their way to a manicure – that because they decided to put on a bit of rouge or make themselves up. Women bullied to get out of cars because they attempted to drive – their actions then reported to their "men" (husbands, fathers, uncles and the like). It makes for jarring scenery; pictures with a high level of visceral intensity indeed.[23]

Still, we *do* have to note that it's in part *because* of the executions, the lashings, the amputations, the denial of women's rights and the organization of society so deeply around religious law that the country has something to stand for. I.e., though the two countries may be mortal enemies (the extreme poles of the infamous Sunni-Shi'a split), perhaps along with Iran, no state has more strongly struck out against Western values and presumptions and, in engaging the social laws that it has, suggested that not *every* culture maintains the same relationship with notions of justice or ideas of social relations and the organization of society's members. No two states may have gone *further* in taking stands for alternative political cultures and cultural politics. Now, there are complexities here. It *has* been argued that fundamentalist regimes, be they Sunni, Shi'a or anything else, don't necessarily reflect popular sentiment. Islamic culture scholar Ann Elizabeth Mayer, for example, has suggested that the attempt of fundamentalist states to deviate from international norms is tied to "governmental policies... designed by ruling elites to reinforce states' prerogatives" and *not* authentic senses of tradition or theologically-evolved arguments about cultural distinction or particularist claims to "justice" and "truth."[24] What many take as a disinterest in

---

22 See Noah Feldman, *The Rise and Fall of the Islamic State* (Princeton: Princeton University Press, 2008).

23 It's also worth noting that the footage provided in the film was acquired at considerable risk. The film notes that some of those involved in collecting the footage now have to live in exile or have been taken into custody. See James Jones (producer), *Saudi Arabia Uncovered* (United States: WGBH, 2016).

24 Mayer, *Islam*, 16.

rights – indeed, Iran executed twice as many people as the Saudis in 2013 – may concern less "indigenous" worldviews or "native" understandings of law than the advancement of *claimed* versions of Islam that are used as political tools to crack down on protests or grant authority to institutions and courts that might prop-up regimes.[25] As Mayer notes, one can read a range of relationships between Islam – even conservative varieties – and fundamental rights. The Iranians, e.g., formulated a not *fully* illiberal constitution *after* the 1979 Revolution – a draft crafted by more popular hands that was ultimately done away with upon reaching the grasp of the religious elite.[26] The Saudi royal family *easily* relates to the West – many both live in and have been educated in *precisely* the cities and institutions that Saudi clerics often decry (that to say nothing of the business contacts).[27] Indeed, the Ikhwan raised such criticisms of Ibn Saud already in the 1920s – notions that the Saudi king had become too "worldly." To the extent that such contradictions persist, one wonders whether the intensity of Saudi Arabia's supposedly "particularist" approach is really about *religion*, or if the primary issue is an elite's relationship with power writ-large. "Cultural distinction" may be a guise – one helping an aristocracy to sustain its own interests.

It's tough to say. Stretching out around such problems, "tradition" might be what one takes it to be. Societies may be "imagined communities," one theorist has offered, wherein the distinction between the saying of truth (discourse) and more "objective" historical realities is difficult to tell.[28] Say enough times "this is Islam," or "this is Christianity" or "this is Judaism" and perhaps it is (who among us would like to claim ultimate truth on theological issues?).[29] Still, movements pushing regimes in conservato-culturalist directions – the 1979 Iranian Revolution or the occupation of the Grand Mosque in Mecca the same year,

---

25 On worldwide execution numbers, see Leila Haddou, "Death Penalty Statistics. 2013 By Country," *The Guardian*, March 27, 2015, available at http://www.theguardian.com/world/datablog/2014/mar/27/death-penalty-statistics-2013-by-country. See also Human Rights Watch, "Saudi Arabia: 100 Executions Since January 1," June 16, 2015, available at https://www.hrw.org/news/2015/06/16/saudi-arabia-100-executions-january-1.

26 See Mayer, *Islam*, 34.

27 See As'ad Abu Kahlil, *The Battle for Saudi Arabia: Royalty, Fundamentalism and Global Power* (New York: Seven Stories Press, 2004).

28 Benedict Anderson, *Imagined Communities: Reflections on the Origins and Spread of Nationalism* (London: Verso, 1983).

29 This is obviously a relatively intense epistemological point. I refer, however, to works Michel Foucault's *The Order of Things*. The point is less "imagine something and that's reality" and more the ability of social knowledge to condition individual senses of truth. See Foucault, *The Order of Things* (New York: Vintage, 1966).

e.g. – emerged from not *un*popular sentiments in which, theologically "correct" or historically "organic" or not, culture and faith appear to have driven protest and played key roles in demands for fundamentally changed regimes.[30] Again, it was after the Grand Mosque revolt that Saudi cinemas became restricted. It was also at that point that millions of dollars were invested in conservative religious schools and radical theologians were increasingly allowed into the country to influence the culture of the Saudi state (indeed, it's there that critics point to as the moment at which Saudi Arabia became the focal point for the radicalism sometimes claimed to have contributed to 9/11).[31] Such moves have not always been the preference of the well-educated, cosmopolitan royal family itself. Some in the royal family have in fact expressed regret for allowing too far of a rightward, religio-culturalist swing.[32] Still, as one could say was the case when it struck allegiances with the Ikhwan and the *Ulema*, religious authorities, if not the society at-large, asked the House of Saud to stand for something – a conservative worldview bound to a highly particular vision of Islam. In general, that's what it's done.[33] The Saudi state has chosen to stake out a specific territory in the patchwork of world cultures – one deeply touched by religion, and embracing less the future than the past.

This throws us into tensions between cultural perspectives and international rights (point two). I.e., in view of such issues, we come to a place where regardless of how many people "organically" maintain a set of beliefs – regardless of how "authentic" particular concepts may or may not be – there's a claim that worldview *exists*, and some are staking claims to perspectives running afoul of what many, anyway, recognize as fundamental international rights. I.e., some *are* claiming specific understandings of the world and the sovereignty to create societies along those lines. Now, there *are* arguments to be made that human rights are a worldview themselves. Rights are generally seen as emerging from the tradition of the Enlightenment West, and rights' dispersion *qua* idea can be seen to follow the expansion of Western culture out to the rest of the globe.[34] That expansion (colonialism is another word for it) has *de facto* often *not* respected the rights of *other* cultures to have *their* worldviews. It has *not* always understood

---

30 Yaroslav Trofimov, *The Siege of Mecca: The 1979 Uprising at Islam's Holiest Shrine* (New York: First Anchor, 2008).

31 See Commins, *The Wahhabi Mission*.

32 Ibid. See also Jihan El-Tahri (director), *House of Saud* (United States: WGBH, 2005).

33 See Hegghammer, *Jihad in Saudi Arabia*, 24.

34 See, e.g., Robert Aldrich and Kirsten McKenzie, eds., *The Routledge History of Western Empires* (London: Routledge, 2014).

that not *all* will conform to supposedly "rational" ideals of what constitutes the "free" or "liberated" individual or specific notions of "progress" for either the nation or the individual as such.[35] That's while, as more than one social scientist has noted, multiple civilizationally-based senses of justice *can* be translated into rights concepts, and representatives of wide ranges of philosophical and religious perspectives pose themselves as concerned with universal justice. One *can* view human rights as an idea with many flowers. It's not just given that one can pin rights down to *one* mode of thought or singular way of defining human good.[36]

That's important. One doesn't want to put rights into an unnecessarily small box. One need allow more than just *European* history to have contributed to ideas of human rights. Still, regardless of how many streams of thought may or may not flow into rights, or how much one might be able to translate traditions of justice from multiple cultures into specific iterations of contemporary ideals of freedoms and privilege, rights *do* maintain baseline content. Not *anything* goes in human rights' name or the name of international justice. According to the global community's primary rights document – the Universal Declaration of Human Rights (1948) – "everyone is entitled to all [basic] rights and freedoms... without distinction of any kind." All should have access to all human privileges, including non-discrimination along the lines of "race, colour, sex, language, religion, political or other opinion, national or social origin, property, birth or other status."[37] Gender discrimination, for example – say, denying women the right to vote or stand for office – is *not* allowed. One can't hound women for going somewhere alone. One can't tell women that men can do one thing – drive, for example – yet tell women themselves that they're not allowed to do the same

---

35 As historian Lynn Hunt suggests, the view behind human rights largely involves the self-contained or delimited individual: a notion of individual personhood largely defined by the individual mind, individual body and presupposition of free will and scientific, as opposed to, say, theological, rationality. History's "end" becomes either freeing or realizing that person. See Hunt, *Inventing Human Rights: A History* (New York: W.W. Norton, 2007).

36 E.g., Abdullahi Ahmed An-Na'im, ed., *Human Rights in Cross-Cultural Perspectives: A Quest for Consensus* (Philadelphia: University of Pennsylvania Press, 1992); Jean H. Quataert, *Advocating Dignity: Human Rights Mobilizations in Global Politics* (Philadelphia: University of Pennsylvania Press, 2009); David Penna and Patricia Campbell, "Human Rights and Culture: Beyond Universality and Relativism," *Third World Quarterly* 19, no. 1 (1998): 7–27.

37 United Nations, "The Universal Declaration of Human Rights" (1948, article 2 [hereafter UDHR]), available at http://www.un.org/en/universal-declaration-human-rights/index.html.

themselves. One can't harass someone in public space because their standards of decorum are supposed to be different than someone else's. The power of work like *Frontline's* is that it shines a light on such discrimination.[38] Yes, issues like genocide might constitute top-tier rights violations. Religious anger about face rouge or improper dress might seem like comparatively small change.[39] Still, no matter how you slice it, human rights provide *no* room for the demotion of *anyone* to second-class status. Such concepts fall outside the bounds of any sense of non-discriminatory liberties at all.[40]

The funny thing is that the death penalty is *not* necessarily proscribed by rights norms. The International Covenant on Civil and Political Rights (1966) – one-third of the International Bill of Human Rights (the Universal Declaration and the International Covenant on Economic, Social and Cultural Rights [1966] are the other two-thirds) – states that the "sentence of death may be imposed… for the most serious crimes in accordance with the law in force at the time of the commission of the crime."[41] The death penalty *can* be used with careful – extremely careful – legal prescription. Indeed, it's a practice of which Saudi Arabia is hardly the only country to avail (fifty or so countries retain the practice – the U.S. included).[42] Still, the Civil and Political Covenant notes that such conditions apply to "countries which have not abolished the death penalty" – a point making it plain the UN isn't particularly happy about states' retention of its use.[43] Moreover, "torture or cruel, inhuman or degrading treatment or punishment"

---

38 It should be noted that, as stated in *Frontline's* documentary, the Saudi state claims it's at least *trying* to eliminate abuses by at least the religious police. There are members of the Saudi government that also regret the level of power given to religious authorities in the wake of the 1979 Grand Mosque occupation. Still, the conservative religious practices mentioned here are more or less allowed to persist, and the moment doesn't quite appear nigh for fundamental change. See Jones, *Saudi Arabia Uncovered*. See also El-Tahri *House of Saud*.

39 In part, this relates to the idea of *jus cogens*, which supposedly address the most non-derogable human rights. Genocide is often discussed in this context, e.g. See Robert Kolb, *Peremptory International Law – Just Cogens: A General Inventory* (Portland: Hart, 2015).

40 See Niamh Reilly, *Women's Human Rights* (Cambridge: Polity, 2009).

41 United Nations, "The International Covenant on Civil and Political Rights" (1966, article 6 [hereafter ICCPR]), available at http://www.ohchr.org/en/professionalinterest/pages/ccpr.aspx.

42 See Roger Hood and Carolyn Hoyle, *The Death Penalty: A Worldwide Perspective* (Oxford: Oxford University Press, 2015).

43 ICCPR, article 6.

is prohibited by human rights, no exceptions allowed.[44] That clearly concerns Western violations like photographing naked, hooded bodies in military prisons in Iraq, or water boarding persons who have been "rendered" to black sites.[45] It also, however, involves lashing people or using amputation as part of justice ("justice"). It involves any pain that might be involved in stoning someone due to infidelity and all causations of suffering because one drank or smoked something one shouldn't. Such levels of religiosity, if indeed that's what such things are about, contravene *any* sense of internationally-recognized ethics. That's regardless of how much one might claim cultural distinction or the particular "angle" of one's worldview.

Indeed, it's also, and perhaps lastly, the case that human rights grant little if not freedom of conscience, freedom of religion and freedom of speech. I.e., the freedom to think as one wants, including about spirituality, is an essential right. Now, state religions exist; Norway and Denmark, for example – hardly bastions of radical conservatism – both maintain state churches. Costa Rica – also a promoter of liberal principles – asserts Roman Catholicism as the "religion of the state."[46] Notions of national self-determination – a concept that *does* fall within human rights' purview – means that peoples, including those who might define themselves religiously, can constitute their political lives and organize their societies as they want. Still, that can't be done *il*liberally. One can't run societies on *exclusionary* bases. There *must* be roles for minority faiths and the ability to arrive at one's *own* theological conclusions. It's chilling when one is given visual access to a society and realizes that were one to profess an alternative faith, one would have no place to run. It feels a bit like George Orwell's *1984* playing out in a church. The priesthood is Big Brother, and the temple is really the state.

Still, the point is that some *maintain* such views – at least they claim to – and there are determined questions of what to do about *that*. I.e., the question might not just be noticing minor differences in norms. The problem might not just be a wink, a nudge and a "well, that's how it is" while we carry on. The problem may not be that each society has its "ways" or "beliefs." The problem may be that what the UN calls "national and regional particularities" and "various historical, cultural and religious backgrounds" regarding approaches to personal freedom and social

---

44   Ibid., article 7. See also UDHR, article 5.

45   See Fiona de Londras, *Detention in the "War on Terror": Can Human Rights Fight Back?* (Cambridge: Cambridge University Press, 2011).

46   See W. Cole Durham, Silvio Ferrari, Cristiana Cianitto and Donlu Thayer, eds., *Law, Religion, Constitution: Freedom of Religion, Equal Treatment, and the Law* (London: Routledge, 2013).

privilege are deeply *real*.[47] The problem might be that, out of cultural perspective, some may *not* see the world the same way and that there may be unwillingnesses to bend particularly far in specific directions *at all*. *Qua* problem, that's not confined to any specific religion or cultural ideal. Hinduism, Buddhism, Confucianism and any Abrahamic faith all have their fundamentalisms, and some interesting politics play out in the name of many gods. Regarding the Saudi situation, however, one commentator from the country has noted that "we are quintessentially old."[48] Come the modern era, the view has often been that there *hasn't* been a need to remake social practice or modes of juridical belief. "We've already had our '-ism,'" Saudi Arabia's Crown Prince Abdullah has maintained. "We've already had Islam."[49] From the Saudi perspective, the point hasn't been the compatibility of one set of beliefs with another – finding where Wahhabism and human rights might overlap, e.g. The point has rather been engaging a *particular* identity and dropping all other questions at that point. The global community should be reserved in offering commentary a society's right to act on what it believes is God's will.

This again creates a heavy tension between human rights and cultural life. It strains the relations between universalist ethics and identities in which a level of particularity is claimed with a particular level of intensity. It generates torsion between notions of universal justice and those claiming specific varieties of the self. Now, rights allow for difference. Religious freedom means religious freedom and inclusion means accepting not small levels of diversity on the global stage. Few would imagine to raise much of a stink about the segregation of women and men at Shabbat services for Orthodox Jews, for example, and, last I noted, no one was bringing many European states to the European Court of Human Rights because their national calendars are organized near-exclusively around *one* religion's holy days (Christianity's) with minimal to no recognition of anyone *else's* high holy occasions (in addition to a half billion or so Christians, Europe *does* have around 40 million Muslims, a million and half Jews and a million and a half each of Hindus and Buddhists – close to 50 million *non*-Christians who *might* be deserving of *some* level of institutionalized acknowledgement in terms of holidays and vacations in the states in which they live).[50] Is one set of cultural politics and practices organized around identity ok and others not? Do we not

---

47   United Nations, "Vienna Declaration and Programme of Action" (1993, section 1), available at http://www.ohchr.org/en/professionalinterest/pages/vienna.aspx.

48   El-Tahri, *House of Saud*.

49   Ibid.

50   Pew Research Center, "Europe Projected to Retain Its Christian Majority, But Religious Minorities Will Grow," April 15, 2015, available at http://www.pewresearch.org/

have to investigate *all* instances of potential marginalization and condemn them, *not* assuming that one culture is the obvious holder of the truth of liberal acceptance while others have yet to see the light?

Clearly, yes. The demand for multicultural acceptance extends everywhere – recognition and belonging should flow through every nation and all dimensions of social life. No one should get a free pass to *not* think about those around oneself as partners in the larger projects we all share. Again, it should be acknowledged that such universalist perspectives are *also* worldviews. The kind of inclusion in which many may be interested may *not* be automatic for all, and some societies may include both – those looking for cosmopolitan inclusion, and those seeking to be left alone. As with any churchgoer, rights believers have core ideals – ideals that may *not* be interesting to everyone and might feel like oppressive droning when those who hold them continue to insist. Believers from the church of rights need to be aware that not everyone wants to be part of the parish, and that not all are particularly glad when you preach at their front door.[51]

Now, it's important to support difference – that even when it's hard to understand or feels out of place. That's in the name of diversity, inclusiveness and attempted concord with those around us in any capacity in which they exist. It's a matter of recognition and assuring that we've done all we can to make sure everyone feels at home. Dictating to people how they must "be" is no rights behavior itself. Still, one has to decide. There *are* choices to make. Does one join a church in which "everyone is entitled to a social and international order in which [all] rights and freedoms can be enjoyed?"[52] Does one subscribe to mindsets in which non-discrimination is the watchword and *no* human being is to be held from "freedom of speech and belief and freedom from fear" – that at *all* levels of social life, one has the right to be who one is?[53] Does one sign up for general respect and acceptance, and the attempt to include all? Or does one sign oneself up for something else – something more judgmental and invasive to the person? Does one sign up for something harder and more exclusionary – violent, even? Regarding the latter, footage such as that presented in *Frontline's* recent work shows what can happen when international norms are left too far behind. Documentary work such as that recently broadcast on PBS illustrates the risks of closing

---

fact-tank/2015/04/15/europe-projected-to-retain-its-christian-majority-but-religious-minorities-will-grow/.

51 Stephen Hopgood, *The Endtimes of Human Rights* (Ithaca, NY: Cornell University Press, 2013).

52 UDHR, article 28.

53 Ibid., article 28; preamble.

ourselves off and insisting on particular identities to the exclusion of others. Our question – global society's question – is how to tackle this: how to invoke broader norms while allowing difference to breath; how to engage in collective morality while recognizing that not all ideas regarding social and legal practice easily interlock. *How* can we allow the existence of distinct culturo-religious views, yet *not* leave the dictates of *truly* non-discriminatory and non-violent applications of universal justice behind? How do we allow true cultural distinction yet unequivocally insist on everyone's full battery of rights and privileges, full stop? How do we say "yes, be who you are, but remember that there *are* standards"? As the Saudi situation seems to illustrate, those are real and abiding questions on today's international stage.

At it Again

North Korea and Those Pesky ICBMs
(April 13, 2016)

Abstract: *North Korea is fascinating in a macabre way – a reality of which we're reminded of every time the country becomes involved in one of its infamous missile tests. What does the state look like from a human rights perspective, however? Short answer: not good.*

On Saturday, Reuters reported that North Korea had taken another step towards successfully launching an ICBM. An ongoing project for the neo-Stalinist regime, it appears that, despite what's traditionally been a high level of skepticism towards the relative strength of the North Korean nuclear program, there's a chance – a chance, anyway – that, as the Korean Central News Agency put it, that one of the last remaining Cold War holdouts might be able to toss a rocket into the American/ Western imperialist "den."[1] One can almost hear the excitement with which it was announced. If one occasionally takes a gander at North Korea state television – which I do – one sees two pre-senters: a man and a woman; the man in a West-

"Flag of North Korea." © Miro Novak / Fotolia.com 114672323

ern-style suit, the woman in traditional Korean dress. Compared with the smooth presentations of the news in the hyper-capitalist West, there's a lot of yelling – as though the news becomes truer if one says it loud and fast. The proclamations, as they almost always did in communist worlds now belonging to another time, unswervingly affirm the party line. In North Korea, that means homages to the Stalinist/Maoist *Juche*, or the socialist "self-reliance" on which Kim Il-Sung, the country's founder, insisted. It also involves homages to the Kims themselves – the ruling communist family who, perhaps to degrees worse than anything seen in the Soviet Bloc or revolutionary China, has run the country based near-solely on a personality cult. That involves the right of a highly specific clique of people

---

1   Jack Kim, "North Korea Says Leader Kim Supervises Test of New Engine for Missile," *Reuters*, April 9, 2016, available at http://www.reuters.com/article/us-northkorea-nuclear-idUSKCN0X52K3.

to exercise total control in what in today's *post*-communist world is a decidedly outlier state.[2]

Of course, there's hardly anything new to this. Now, one *might* note – might – that the North Korean state didn't necessarily have a *totally* illegitimate start. For a time after the Korean War (1950–3), the country in fact *outstripped* its opposite number in the South in terms of modernization and economic growth. I.e., like Germany, the Korean peninsula was the site of a great deal of intrigue in the wake of the Second World War. Split between the Soviets above the 38th Parallel and the Americans below, the two world powers installed puppet regimes in the form of the communist-led government that became the Worker's Party of Korea in the North and strongman Syngman Rhee's authoritarian regime in Seoul, the capital of the South. Now, it wasn't without mischief-making from the North. However, the South was in a state of near-civil war in the late 1940s as massacres such as those connected to the Jeju Uprising in 1948, resisting anti-communist suppression by the Rhee government, demonstrated the democratic deficit of the American-backed regime. It's common to point to the Soviets as the party backing out of support for national elections through 1947 and 1948. The reality may be, however, that had those elections been held, economic conditions and skepticism towards U.S. presence in the region might have lifted leftist parties to victory anyway.[3] In the midst of all this, Stalin, ever the geopolitical puppet master, gave the Northern regime the go-ahead to invade the South. It did, touching off three years of violence and destruction in which somewhere in the area of half a million people perished.[4] Still, the suppression of left-wing parties attempting to exercise their right to democratic expression was real, and there's a concrete question as to if the socialist big brother from the North hadn't been willing to defend them, who in fact would.

In any case, what's been called the North Korean "Wonderland" (as in "this-looks-like-an-alternate-reality-and-in-fact-is") was quick to set in. Again, especially in view of the fact that the War wrought noticeably more destruction in the North than the South, the ability of the Democratic People's Republic of Korea, or DPRK, as the new state above the 38th Parallel was monikered, to put together something akin to a modern economy was impressive. Due partly

---

2   See Bradley K. Martin, *Under the Loving Care of the Fatherly Leader: North Korea and the Kim Dynasty* (New York: St. Martin's, 2006).

3   See Glyn Ford, *North Korea on the Brink: The Struggle for Survival* (London: Pluto, 2007), 28; Stanley Sandler, *The Korean War* (London: Routledge, 1999), 27.

4   See, e.g., Bruce Cummings, *The Korean War: A History* (New York: Modern Library, 2011).

to centralized planning – some of the most centralized in the world – levels of economic growth in the North in the late 1950s sometimes reached as high as 20% (the highest economic growth in by any country in 2015, for example, was Papua New Guinea at 19.6% [the U.S. had a number of 2.2; the UK 2.7]).[5] A country that had previously low literacy rates also radically reversed *that* trend as the number of North Koreans reading towards the end of the twentieth century neared 100%. The building blocks for the betterment of other aspects of peoples' lives, such as a national health system, were also put into place.[6] That's not *atypical* of communist states – successful early years before drifting into stagnation or even worse.[7] Still, it *was* progress under the strictest ideological control. In the name of ensuring that power would never slip from the "Great Leader" Kim Il-Sung's hands, there was an attempt to delineate North Korean communism from the communism of even the world's leading socialist lights – China and the Soviet Union most specifically. That again meant *Juche*: a concept promoting *DPRK* socialism as near-solely about the *Korean* people as opposed to more international visions of the working class. *Juche* also involved high levels of national isolation. Though receiving aid from first the Soviets and then the Chinese – though both in some form until the late '80s – the North Korean ideal was that it had to go it alone. Of course, when the Eastern Bloc collapsed and China inched more towards the global mainstream, that was increasingly the case. Yes, the Chinese have generally been supportive of the country, paying lip-service to notions of socialist "brotherhood" (the USSR obviously doesn't exist anymore, and Russia has not filled the gap). Recent lacks of enthusiasm in such areas, however, have helped sharpen North Korea's "military first" (*Songun*) policy and assisted in highlighting a set of stances that have led to near jaw-dropping realities such as the fact that, especially since

---

5   See Jinwung Kim, *A History of Korea* (Bloomington: Indiana University Press, 2012), 460; World Bank, "GDP Growth (Annual %)" (2016), available at http://data.worldbank.org/ indicator/NY.GDP.MKTP.KD.ZG.

6   See Ford, *North Korea*, 63.

7   It's impossible to provide a resume of every communist state. East Germany provides some typical examples, however. Historian Jürgen Kocka notes a radically heightened increase in participation in both government and education by many working-class Germans that simply wouldn't have been possible at earlier points. This generated some initial enthusiasm for the regime. That enthusiasm petered out, however, once the period of initial gains was left behind. See Kocka, *Civil Society and Dictatorship in Modern German History* (Lebanon: The University Press of New England, 2010).

the mid-'90s, though significant parts of the country have starved, the DPRK funds one of the largest militaries in the world.[8]

It's in this context that North Korea began firing off rockets and playing around with nuclear technology. Again, especially since the end of the Cold War, the regime has largely maintained that *not* upholding its borders could mean a vulnerability to both the South Korea and the West not unlike what happened with East Germany in the late '80s – slow collapse as too many outside influences were let in and too many external pressures became camped outside its door.[9] Indeed, *China* might *also* be a source of pressure as the world's largest state sought to advance its own *bona fides* as a key player on the international stage.[10] Generally, China seeks a "win-win" situation along its northeastern border. Despite the DPRK's massive rights abuses, the People's Republic of China has been willing to look the other way because as long as it's stable, the country needn't worry about picking up the pieces of a DPRK collapse. China also has little interest in shining lights on civil rights issues in *other* countries given its own questionable practices in the area.[11] Still, North Korea's nuclear policies trouble the *U.S.*, wherein, despite Sino-U.S. tensions, China has an extra impetus to keep half an arm's length away from its smaller neighbor (China's interests are "better served by [tacit] cooperation with the United States," it's been argued – that as opposed to "direct confrontation" [trade is a significant issue]).[12] Of course,

---

8   See Yongho Kim, *North Korean Foreign Policy: Security Dilemma and Succession* (Lanham: Lexington, 2011). It's estimated that the DPRK has upwards of a million troops on active duty; one of a half-dozen or so countries to maintain forces of that size. The army is notoriously equipped with outdated material. Still, that's a massive force for a country of 25 million. See Anthony H. Cordesman and Aaron Lin, *The Changing Military Balance in the Koreas and Northeast Asia* (Lanham: Rowman & Littlefield, 2015).

9   See Steven Pfaff, *Exit-Voice Dynamics and the Collapse of East Germany: The Crisis of Leninism and the Revolution of 1989* (Durham, NC: Duke University Press, 2006).

10 See C. Fred Bergsten, Charles Freeman, Nicholas R. Lardy, Derek J. Mitchell, *China's Rise: Challenges and Opportunities* (Washington, DC: Center for Strategic and International Studies, 2009).

11 See Suisheng Zhao, ed., *China and Democracy: Reconsidering the Prospects for a Democratic China* (London: Routledge, 2000).

12 Yufan Hao, "Introduction," in *Sino-American Relations: Challenges Ahead*, ed. Yufan Hao (Farnham: Ashgate, 2010), 2. See also Nina Hachigian, ed., *Debating China: The U.S.-China Relationship in Ten Conversations* (Oxford: Oxford University Press, 2014). China and the U.S. are among each other's largest trading partners – that again despite disputes in the area.

as many know, North Korean missile tests have often been near-comic failures. The less-than-a-minute-long 2006 flight of a Taepodong-2 rocket designed to threaten the U.S. gained ironic guffaws in much of the world press. It basically went up, and then came straight down.[13] An Unha-3 that plopped harmlessly into the East China Sea in 2012 became the object of similar ridicule (what *are* those North Koreans doing?).[14] In December 2012, however, the DPRK used ICBM technology to become the tenth nation to successfully put a satellite into space. Combined with a few more successful missile launches and a handful of fruitful nuclear tests (the most recent effort included), and the smiles became wiped off the faces more than a few in the international community. This caused China to side with Obama Administration calls for condemnation. Come April, the Chinese banned most imports of North Korean coal and iron ore – a ban a country with few exports and little economic vitality could ill-afford.[15]

Every time North Korea shoots off one of its long-range toys or blows up some part of a mountain as a part of underground atomic research, the world is faced with the same kinds of issues. What happens when nuclear weapons either are or *could be* in the hands of an unstable regime? What happens when a madman might place his finger on a noticeably powerful trigger? What happens when so *much* firepower is concentrated in the hands of a clique or individual with few checks or balances on his or her power (I obviously refer to the Kims here)? What happens when a regime that simply seems so *strange* gets its hands on what's clearly the world's ultimate destructive force?

Of course, one *can* make the argument that the Kims know, and have known, precisely what they're up to.[16] They've ruled the country for sixty-eight years now; no mean feat. The "Gang of Four" that inherited Mao's rule couldn't maintain

---

13 E.g., Suzanne Goldberg, "North Korean 'Fireworks' Display Irritates US but Falls Short of Target," *The Guardian*, July 5, 2006, available at http://www.theguardian.com/world/2006/jul/05/japan.northkorea.

14 BBC, "North Korea Rocket Launch Fails," April 13, 2012, available at http://www.bbc.com/news/world-asia-17698438.

15 See Joe McDonald, "China Has Banned Most Imports of North Korean Coal and Iron Ore in a Significant Increase in Pressure on the North under U.N. Sanctions over Its Nuclear and Missile Tests," *U.S. News and World Report*, April 5, 2016, available at http://www.usnews.com/news/business/articles/2016-04-05/china-restricts-trade-with-north-korea-over-nuclear-tests.

16 See, e.g., Young Whan Kihl and Hong Nack Kim, eds., *North Korea: The Politics of Regime Survival* (London: Routledge, 2015).

power for more than a month after the Great Helmsman's 1976 death.[17] The elder Kim, e.g., resisted attempts to depose him in the so-called 1956 "August Faction Incident" – an episode in which anti-Stalinist reformers attempted to undo Kimist rule and bring a degree of Khrushchevian thaw to the state. That was put down with brute force and a creative set of parliamentary maneuvers.[18] Kim Jong-Il, Kim Il-Sung's son, engaged in negotiations with the Clinton Administration in the late 1990s and 2000 – a move simultaneously placating the West while allowing the country to pursue its military goals.[19] Power struggles ensued when Jong-Il's son, Kim Jong-Un, took the helm in 2012. Jong-Un has nonetheless held any opposition at arm's length, going so far as to murder an uncle who apparently questioned his rule. The Kims are hardly rubes. If they *are* crazy, it's like foxes.[20]

Still, the shaky state of North Korean relations with the international community *can* make one concerned. If the country ever comes close to *using* the weapons it's trying to develop, e.g., who has the ability to talk them down from the edge? Who might ease the regime back from what could be a dicey situation given that nuclear arms aren't exactly something to fool around with? The country *is* still technically at war with the South – the Korean War ended with an armistice, not a peace treaty – and the DPRK seems buried in a kind of inferiority complex that makes one wonder if there might not be a point when saber rattling turns into an attempt to swing the sword. Two regional experts have noted there is a reason *why* the country's 2006 explosion of a nuclear device – its first – sent "shockwaves" through the international community.[21] The level of isolation with which the regime is involved comes off as dangerous as it's drastically unclear

---

17 See David Bonavia, *Verdict in Beijing: The Trial of the Gang of Four* (New York: Putnam, 1984).

18 See Young Chul Chung, "The Suryong System as the Center of Juche Institution: Politics of Development Strategy in Post-War North Korea," in *Origins of North Korea's Juche: Colonialism, War, and Development*, ed. Jae-Jung Suh (Lanham: Lexington, 2013), 89–118.

19 See Ramon Pacheco Pardo, *North Korea – US Relations Under Kim Jong II: The Quest for Normalization?* (London: Routledge, 2014).

20 Malcolm Moore, "'I Killed a Three-Star Commander': Bloody Power Struggle behind Kim Jong-Un's Rise to Power Revealed," *National Post*, April 10, 2013, available at http://news.nationalpost.com/news/warring-factions-of-north-korean-army-divided-over-accepting-kim-jong-uns-command-officer-reveals.

21 Tae-Hwan Kwak and Seung-Hoo Joo, "Introduction," in *North Korea's Second Nuclear Crisis and Northeast Asian Security*, ed. Tae-Hwan Kwak and Seung-Hoo Joo (Farnham: Ashgate, 2013), 1.

who has its ear. Political acumen is one thing. Political unpredictability to the umpteenth degree may be something else.[22]

Of course *that* might just be seen as another way of discussing *another* point that comes up whenever the DPRK explodes one of its atomic devices or fires off an ICBM: peace. I.e., what are the effects of the state's behaviors on *concord* and atmospheres of international relations we'd like to create? How can we avoid bringing the world not only to Cuban Missile Crisis-like edges, but what does it take to avoid even *approaching* such situations because we've fostered better environments in which states might relate? How can we make *truly* sure we don't let slip the dogs of war – that especially when the bite of the dog involved may be so deep and intense (again, I think of nuclear technology here)?

There are a number of ways to go about the business of peace. Now, I should mention that *my* definition of the idea is what seminal peace researcher Johan Galtung has called a "negative," or "minimal," approach. I.e., I'm simply concerned with getting the guns put down and halting the destructive effects of war. That's opposed to more elaborate notions of social development and cultural well-being (Galtung, e.g., suggests that peace isn't fully peace unless one fosters the productivity of social lives when war *isn't* on – a valid, but in my view, secondary, point).[23] In any case, *using* a more minimalistic approach, one *can* employ philosophies of "deterrence" – force or sanction to get someone to take a different tack than they otherwise would.[24] This was a part of Cold War face-offs: that one's Other either could or should be worried about firing their weapons first because (*a*) if you don't get along with us, *we* might fire first or (*b*) if *you* fire

---

22 E.g., Sungtae Jacky Park, "When a Collapsing, Paranoid North Korea Turns to Nukes…," *The National Interest*, February 13, 2016, available at http://www.nationalinterest.org/feature/when-collapsing-paranoid-north-korea-turns-nukes-15201.

23 See Johan Galtung, *Peace by Peaceful Means: Peace and Conflict, Development and Civilization* (London: Sage, 1996), 31.

24 See Colin S. Gray, "Deterrence and the Nature of Strategy," in *Deterrence in the 21ˢᵗ Century*, ed. Max G. Manwaring (London: Cass, 2001), 18. Of course, one could argue that in the world of mutually assured destruction, nuclear build up was more about maintaining balance than one-upmanship – parity as opposed to demonstrations of who had more. Still, nuclear buildups involved meeting strength with strength and the idea that one maintained at least *somewhere* near as much destructive force as the other – the idea, of course, being that force, or at least its threat, has effect. See Joachim Krause, "Threat Scenarios, Risk Assessments, and the Future of Nuclear Deterrence," in *The Future of Extended Deterrence: The United States, NATO, and Beyond*, ed. Stéfanie von Hlatky and Andreas Wenger (Washington, DC: Georgetown University Press, 2015), 27.

first, you'll get struck by a yet-bigger stick. It's a realist approach to international relations – one at least partly explaining the stockpiles of nuclear weapons developed by great powers over the 1950s, '60, '70s and '80s. It also explains why, despite the fact that the Cold War has ended, major powers continue to keep such stockpiles in place.[25]

Nonetheless, one *could* argue that achieving peace concerns not only how one manages the weapons one *has*, but the *attitudes* one maintains and the *existence* of the weapons of war *at all*. I.e., anytime *anyone* enters the international stage with increasingly large missiles or guns, or approaches international affairs with reference to the threat of war, one may have jeopardized amity's cause – the question then being how to avoid *that*. That's a more idealistic approach to international affairs – one suggesting that the way to peace is through "peaceful means" (Galtung's vocabulary). In any case, idealist or not, one *can* say that such concepts don't represent the North Korean approach. As long as the Kims stay in power, they seem unlikely to do so. I.e., the Kims not only maintain a frightening regime in terms of predictability, but in terms of approaching international affairs in ways explicitly undermining the values that many of us would at least *like* to hold. Those involve staying *away* from armed power plays and bellicosity as a negotiating tactic – things that can again be alarming when nuclear weapons are in play.[26]

That being said, I'd nonetheless suggest that a *last* issue that shines through with every North Korean missile launch or attempt to build a nuclear device is *human rights*. I.e., in addition to peace, what kind of *regime* do the North Koreans maintain? As it's pushed and shoved its way into global consciousness, how does the DPRK relate to problems of the basic freedoms and privileges that all people, everywhere, are supposed to have? Is there anything behind those rockets and missiles that the DPRK could really be trying to *defend*?

A few points might be relevant here. Firstly, it's supposed to be the case that communist governments are good at preserving socio-economic rights. Quoting the Universal Declaration of Human Rights (1948), "everyone has the right to a standard of living adequate for the health and well-being of himself and of his family." "Food, clothing, housing and medical care and necessary social services" are supposed to be available to all. One has "the right to security in the event of unemployment, sickness, disability, widowhood, old age or other lack

---

25 See Stephen J. Cimbala, *The Past and Future of Nuclear Deterrence* (Westport: Praeger, 1998).

26 See Paul French, *North Korea: The Paranoid Peninsula*, 2nd ed. (London: Zed, 2007); Robert Daniel Wallace, *North Korea and the Science of Provocation: Fifty Years of Conflict-Making* (Jefferson: McFarland & Co., 2016).

of livelihood in circumstances beyond his control."[27] All should be materially taken care of regardless of who they are. Now, the history of socialism is organized around such principles – if not the right to work, then at least the right to be taken care of when one can't take care of oneself.[28] In name, such things are provided for in the DPRK. The national constitution – as socialist constitutions traditionally do – notes that "the State shall provide all the working people...every condition for obtaining food, clothing and housing."[29] As opposed to capitalist worlds in which countries sometimes *don't* provide economic bills of rights, there should be no possibility that one starves, or in times of hardship, fewer resources are devoted to one person than another.[30] I.e., the DPRK explicitly invokes the ideas of economic equality and basic sustenance that are supposed to be the calling cards of communist states – and, at least in certain ways, are present in human rights themselves.[31]

---

27 United Nations, "The Universal Declaration of Human Rights" (1948, article 25 [hereafter UDHR]), available at http://www.un.org/en/universal-declaration-human-rights/index.html.

28 On the right to work, see ibid., article 23. See also United Nations, "International Covenant on Economic, Social and Cultural Rights" (1966, article 6 [hereafter ICESCR]), available at http://www.ohchr.org/EN/ProfessionalInterest/Pages/CESCR.aspx.

29 Democratic People's Republic of Korea, *Socialist Constitution of the Democratic People's Republic of North Korea* (Pyongyang: Foreign Languages Publishing House, 2014), article 25. See also Williams B. Simons, ed., *The Constitutions of the Communist World* (Alphen aan den Rijn: Sithjof and Noordhoff, 1980).

30 See UDHR, article 25; ICESCR, article 12; Democratic People's Republic of Korea, *Socialist Constitution*, article 72. To be sure, many Western capitalist states provide for social rights. However, those provisions can be surprisingly vague. Other than senses of one's right to property, e.g., they appear nowhere in the American Constitution. And, even in relatively social democratic Europe, European law, anyway, binds countries to civil and political rights while documents like the European Social Charter (1961) are not adjudicated upon by bodies like the European Court of Human Rights. Though there are oversight bodies (the European Committee on Social Rights specifically), essentially, that committee is reduced to making "recommendations" when socio-economic rights are violated; there's no "court" to hand down rulings and individuals in fact can't bring suit. See Rhoda Howard-Hassmann and Claude E. Welch, Jr., eds., *Economic Rights in the United States and Canada* (Philadelphia: University of Pennsylvania Press, 2006); David Harris, *The European Social Charter* (New York: Transnational, 2001).

31 See Donald F. Busky, *Communism in History and Theory: From Utopian Socialism to the Fall of the Soviet Union* (Westport: Praeger, 2002). It is true that human rights don't demand economic equality – the same economic status for all people. They do, however,

The simple reality is that the DPRK doesn't provide those things to anywhere near the degree it either says it does or should. For whatever reasons – and we should be clear the threat of invasion by the United States or South Korea is a phantom menace (it simply wouldn't be worth it) – the country spends by far the largest percentage of its national budget on the military while *also* maintaining one of the lowest living standards on earth. Statistics are hard to come by. However, it's estimated that North Korea uses *twice* as large a percentage of its national budget on its military as any other country – roughly a quarter of its GDP (the next largest percentage is the Saudis at 12%).[32] Now, there has been something of an economic recovery of late. North Korean agriculture has done well in recent years, wherein some of the pressure regarding foodstuffs has been relieved.[33] Still, famine was deadly in the '90s – hundreds of thousands died – and hunger continues to come and go within the populace.[34] Unfortunately, North Korea doesn't participate in the UN's Human Development Index – the most referred-to indicator for global living standards. The CIA's *World Factbook*, however, places the DPRK's GDP at 209th out of 230 rankings (North Korea's per capita GDP is about $1800 a year – roughly the same as Burkina Faso and Rwanda).[35] Simply put, in a state where the people are supposed to be "God" – the way the preamble to the to the North Korean constitution phrases it – spending so *much* on the military while hunger remains a problem seems a shabby way to treat a body politic that's supposed to be the ultimate source of sovereignty and in whose service the state is supposed to exist.[36]

---

demand people's economic sustenance. See Audrey Chapman and Sage Russell, *Core Obligations: Building a Framework for Economic, Social and Cultural Rights* (Antwerp: Intersentia, 2002).

32 Bernhard Seliger, "A Peace Dividend for North Korea?: The Political Economy of Military Spending, Conflict Resolution and Reform," in *Towards a Northeast Asian Security Community: Implications for Korea's Growth and Economic Development*, ed. Bernhard Seliger and Werner Pascha (Dordrecht: Springer, 2011), 135. See also International Institute of Strategic Studies, *The Military Balance 2015* (London: Routledge, 2015).

33 Andrei Lankov, "North Korea Farm Policy Changes Point to Better Harvests," *Radio Free Asia*, April 3, 2015, available at http://www.rfa.org/english/commentaries/parallelt-thoughts/lankov-farm-03042015120240.html.

34 Stephan Haggard and Marcus Noland, *Famine in North Korea: Markets, Aid, and Reform* (New York: Columbia University Press, 2007).

35 See Central Intelligence Agency, "Country Comparison – GDP: Per Capital" (2016), available at https://www.cia.gov/library/publications/the-world-factbook/rankorder/2004rank.html#kn.

36 Democratic People's Republic of Korea, *Socialist Constitution*, preamble.

Of course, one has to acknowledge that economic, social and cultural rights aren't there for themselves. States aren't supposed to feed and clothe their people only to have them march about as automatons or be jailed, censured or disciplined if their thoughts aren't in sync with those of the regime. One shouldn't keep people physically healthy only to offer *no* political choice – never mind freedom of the press and the free transfer of ideas. Human rights demand *both*. Rights-positive states attempt to help individuals realize the *all* the capabilities of their physical and mental being. Rights-positive states look to foster intellectually rewarding *as well as* physically healthy lives. Rights-positive countries recognize civil liberties and freedom of thought as much as anything else. *If* one claims to be interested in basic human rights – and via not only its own constitution but its membership in the UN, North Korea does – one should pursue *liberal* societies in addition to worlds where people are economically sustained and have enough to get by. Of course, that's if North Korea even were to do *that*.

Obviously, the kinds of rights we're discussing here – civil and political rights – are a massive problem in the DPRK. According to the Economist Intelligence Unit's 2015 Democracy Index – the Economist Intelligence Unit providing one of the oft-referred to measures of democratic practice – North Korea is the world's single least democratic state. No one comes in *under* the DPRK in terms of measures of political freedom.[37] That doesn't just manifest itself as a lack of political choice – that there's one party to vote for ("vote"), or that there's no difference between the party and the state. It means Orwellian stuff outdoing the worst of socialism's historical dictatorships. The first element of this is again a personality cult that would make even the world's worst dictators blush – unusual weather events, e.g., have been attributed to the birth and death of the Kims.[38] One has to bow before statues and pictures of the family when one enters virtually every public building, always demonstrating subservience to the communist monarchy. Of course, there's again the fact the Kimist cult *has* survived absent the denunciations or attempts at least at *some* modicum of reform that have generally come at *some* point in the history of socialist governments. Stalin's

---

37 The Economist Intelligence Unit, "Demo cracy Index 2015: Democracy in the Age of Anxiety," available at http://www.yabiladi.com/img/content/EIU-Democracy-Index-2015.pdf.

38 See, e.g., Theodor Tudoroiu, *The Revolutionary Totalitarian Personality: Hitler, Mao, Castro, and Chávez* (Dordrecht: Springer, 2017). See also NC News, "Red Skies and Stormy Seas Heralded Kim Jong Il's Death, State Media Says," December 22, 2012, available at http://www.nbcnews.com/id/45763055/ns/world_news-asia_pacific/t/red-skies-stormy-seas-heralded-kim-jong-ils-death-state-media-says/#.V-WWGvArLDc.

excesses were unmasked at the Twentieth Party Congress (1956) – an event at which Khrushchev suggested that Soviet life should *somehow* concern the people it claimed to represent and not just one person's political whim.[39] Deng Xiaoping stepped back from the worst excesses of Maoism, loosening both the financial and, to some degree, ideological strings – moves that helped to birth the more internationally-oriented China we know today.[40] Now, reform in Eastern Europe led to the end of regimes from Czechoslovakia to Poland and, eventually, the fall of the Soviet Bloc *in toto*. China is involved with some complex debates both within its own borders and with the world around it regarding the precise dimensions of its political and ideological path.[41] Those are situations the DPRK wants to avoid. Still, the sustenance of *such* a singular orthodoxy in North Korea *is* impressive. Discussion's not in question; it's *Juche* or bust in the DPRK.

This "monothinking" leads to some frightening realities. Beyond the lack of any diversity in the top echelons of power, North Korea maintains a gulag system that's estimated to hold around 100,000 people. That involves labor camps whose conditions resemble the "reeducation camps" of 1970s Cambodia or the worst of Stalin's gulags in the '30s. Think the wrong way and the consequences can be dire.[42] The war on civil rights also means near-sealed borders. When foreigners come – the few that can get in – the destination is the show capital Pyongyang, where only a choice selection of the citizenry is allowed to live (there's a clear class system in a society that's supposed to have none).[43] Of course, forget about getting out; unless one is a highly-placed official or in distinct in favor with the Kims, there's no exploring the world *outside* the DPRK. Legal due process is simply ignored. "Completely lacking" is how one expert has described the country's relationship with even its own laws.[44] Indeed, though a bit flip, one might note that if you're a North Korean man and you want a haircut, you'll be limited to

39 Polly Jones, ed., *The Dilemmas of De-Stalinization: Negotiating Social and Cultural Change in the Khrushchev Era* (London: Routledge, 2006).

40 See Michael Y. M. Kau and Susan Marsh, eds., *China in the Era of Deng Xiaoping: A Decade of Reform* (London: M.E. Sharpe, 1993).

41 See Cheng Li, ed., *China's Changing Political Landscape: Prospects for Democracy* (Washington, D.C.: The Brookings Institution, 2008).

42 See Lankov, *The Real North Korea: Life and Politics in the Failed Stalinist Utopia* (Oxford: Oxford University Press, 2013), 45–9.

43 Ibid.

44 Morse Tan, *North Korea, International Law and the Dual Crises: Narrative and Constructive Engagement* (London: Routledge, 2015), 181.

ten options; eighteen if you're a woman.[45] I've also heard – heard, anyway – that Pyongyang apartments feature radios that can be turned down, but not off. That's so official broadcasting can be piped through in ways one can't describe as anything except an explicit attempt to brainwash.[46] It's dystopianism beyond bounds of which most of us can imagine.

Now, it should be noted that there's no specific requirement that one like human rights. I.e., as with all political ideals, rights involve a specific worldview – a complicated vision to which not all may automatically accede. Does one emphasize economic equality or freedom of speech? Are liberal freedoms the most important problems societies face (questions of individual choice), or are *material* needs the primary questions nations should address? Are we looking for full bellies, or the right to vote? The Cold War, of which North Korea is a product, featured two models. The West emphasized civil and political rights: that one might participate in government, be recognized under the law and essentially think what one wants. Amero-Western interventions from Vietnam to Nicaragua to Angola (never mind in Korea itself) were theoretically made in defense of such ideals. An "empire of liberty," one historian has argued, was the concept behind mid-twentieth century American/Western *Realpolitik*.[47] Now, insisting that *only* Western democracies knew then and know now what's best for the world may not be a particularly democratic move *itself*. Supporting *any* political vision by arms might also be a dubious proposition – one leaving little room for those imagining their political *raison d'être* as based in something else (say, economic equality, or minor states' ability to determine their political destinies for themselves).[48] Still, the international community maintains *some* sense that rights concern democracy and modicums of personal freedom. Political liberty *has* been identified as a standard for which the global community of nations should reach. Legislating haircuts, to say nothing of running camps for those

---

45 Courtney Subramanian, "These Are North Korea's 28 State-Approved Hairstyles," *Time*, February 23, 2013, available http://newsfeed.time.com/2013/02/25/these-are-north-koreas-28-state-approved-hairstyles/.

46 Robert S. Boynton, "North Korea's Digital Underground," *The Atlantic*, April 2011, available at http://www.theatlantic.com/magazine/archive/2011/04/north-koreas-digital-underground/308414/.

47 Odd Arne Westad, *The Global Cold War: Third World Interventions and the Making of Our Times* (Cambridge: Cambridge University Press, 2007), 8–38.

48 Makau Matua, *Human Rights: A Political and Cultural Critique* (Philadelphia: University of Pennsylvania Press, 2002).

who don't think in "correct" terms, is not in any way, shape or form a part of the human rights' picture. Of course, prison camps aren't either.[49]

To that extent, even if countries like North Korea *were* to provide the rights they claim – even if they *truly* delivered health care to everyone, the right to work and protection of the "everyman" against material deprivation – they would need to grant free speech as well. The country would need to empty its gulags and release all detained political grounds. "Freedom from want," as the Universal Declaration puts it, *is* a baseline.[50] One should alleviate economic worry such that one has the opportunity to think (thought can be hard on an empty stomach). "Freedom from want," however, has little meaning without "freedom from fear." Sustenance offers little satisfaction if the government can simply abduct you or jail you for something you said.[51] Indeed, one shouldn't have to choose. Just states should trade in *all* varieties of rights. *If* one takes human rights seriously, one should tend to *all* sides of the human soul. Certainly, one doesn't try to make situations surrounding one or the other variety of rights *worse*.

It's thus that nearly all analysts agree that North Korea registers virtually no-where on any scale of human rights. Again, late-1940s geopolitics may have pro-vided *some* legitimacy for the regime. The world *was* bending itself into a lot of different shapes in the wake of the Second World War and it's hard to judge all the rights and wrongs of the period; there were multiple visions of the good society, and many pressures weighed on the actors involved. Still, the gains achieved in what were largely socio-economic areas were achieved a long time ago – the '50s and '60s, primarily. Now, that the rights situation in the DPRK might have stag-nated is a problem. It points to a lag that demands address – a level of political modernization in which the country needs to engage. Indeed, the UN recently issued a report on the DPRK indicting the country on precisely those grounds.[52] Still, such indictments may be overtures to the obvious. Such criticisms may point to things we already know. Very simply, the *largest* problem with North Korea – the *largest* issue with the DPRK, over and above potentially dangerous instability,

---

49 See Carol C. Gould, *Globalizing Democracy and Human Rights* (Cambridge: Cambridge University Press, 2004).

50 UDHR, preamble.

51 See Louis I. Shelley, "Human Rights as an International Issue," *The Annals of the Ameri-can Academy of Political and Social Science* 506 (1989): 42–56.

52 Office of the United Nations High Commissioner on Human Rights, "Report of the Commission of Inquiry on Human Rights in the Democratic People's Republic of Ko-rea" July 7, 2014, available at http://www.ohchr.org/EN/HRBodies/HRC/CoIDPRK/Pages/ReportoftheCommissionofInquiryDPRK.aspx.

negative contributions to peace and the material and intellectual deprivations had while the government develops cold fusion and various rockets – is that launching ICBMs and exploding nuclear devices may ultimately concern the defense of the *Kims*. Behind so *much* in the DPRK, from the rights abuses to the bizarre social atmosphere, seems to be the ruling family and its power. Now, I don't subscribe ideas that dictatorships are solely the result of "evil minds" – "dictatorial personalities," as such. Be it the Third Reich or the worst of Stalin's Russia, a lot goes into the cocktails that create totalitarian states.[53] Still, the situation in the DPRK *is* stunning. In the face of the country's problems, it's hard to see *what* might be at issue *except* a ruling family's need to preserve some personal "Wonderland." It's hard to tell *what* might be preserved *except* the Kims' sovereignty and *their* right to rule. No doubt: we need to hear Cold War legacies and recognize that countries may have *begun* certain practices out of notions of both ideological and national self-defense. There were times when what may have been legitimate interests in building alternative societies were in fact under threat.[54] Today, though, it's not only hard to see what that threat is, but, in the DPRK's case, the distance between the society claimed and the one in place is *so* great that the entire enterprise deserves to be fundamentally questioned. Is there *any* argument to be made that one is *in fact* defending a "the people" or the interests of the "working class" in the face of what we know about North Korean life? In a land where the people are supposed to "God," is there *any* indication that the Godhead is being served? Is there *any* realization of essential rights – from those listed in the national constitution to international ideals intended to hold good for all? As North Korea's most recent rocket launch did *not* plop harmlessly into the East China Sea, it appears we might need to look again at the powers of a dictatorial ruling family and its iron grip on an intellectually and sometimes materially starved nation.

---

53 See, e.g., Klaus Ziemer and Jerzy W. Borejsza, eds., *Totalitarian and Authoritarian Regimes in Europe: Legacies and Lessons from the Twentieth Century* (New York: Berghahn, 2006).

54 Stéphanie Roulin, Giles Scott-Smith and Luc van Dongen, *eds., Transnational Anti-Communism and the Cold War: Agents, Activities, and Networks* (New York: Palgrave Macmillan, 2014).

"Without Distinction of Any Kind"

LGBT Rights
(April 30, 2016)

Abstract: *Progress has been made on the front of LGBT rights in many national contexts – especially via Western states' increasing acceptance of gay marriage. Why, though, are there still heavy taboos around the issue of LGBT rights on an international basis? Some classic-yet-provocative work from the realm of queer theory might help us realize why there's still some serious distance to go on this human rights front.*

Lately, the struggle for gay rights seems to be gaining new profile. Perhaps a touch surprisingly, given the country's oft-conservative social politics, more than a small part of that concerns events in the United States. As of 2015, thirty-six states had decided to allow same-sex marriage. That's thirty-six more than in 2003, when it wasn't allowed at all. Massachusetts changed all that in 2004 when, on May 17 of that year, Tanya McCloskey and Marcia Kadish from Malden, just outside of Boston, tied the knot. They became America's first couple in a legally-recognized same-sex marriage. Of course, it's fair to say that the boom was *really* lowered in June of last year when the Supreme Court voted to allow same-sex marriage not just in some states, but anywhere in the lower forty-

"Gay Rainbow Flag on Concrete Wall Surface." © Syda Productions / Fotolia.com 87591410

eight and Alaska and Hawaii too. It was a seminal event – one perhaps creating an irreversible path forward for gay rights on the American political tableau.[1]

Of course, the U.S. wasn't the first country to allow gays and lesbians the right to marry. The Netherlands and Belgium granted the LGBT community the right to tie the knot as early as 2000 and 2003, and socially-progressive countries like Denmark maintained registered partnership – a civil-administrative union, of

---

1   See National Public Radio, "How it Happened. 10 Years of Gay Marriage," May 17, 2014, available at http://www.npr.org/2014/05/17/313457795/how-it-happened-10-years-of-gay-marriage; Adam Liptack, "Supreme Court Ruling Makes Same-Sex Marriage a Right Nationwide," *The New York Times*, June 26, 2015, available at http://www.nytimes.com/2015/06/27/us/supreme-court-same-sex-marriage.html?_r=0.

sorts – as early as 1989 (though it took until 2012 for gay *marriage* to be recognized in that small Scandinavian state).[2] Still, more than marriage rights have recently brought questions of justice for lesbians, gays, bisexuals and transsexuals to the fore. When the Universal Declaration of Human Rights was under negotiation in 1947 and 1948, e.g., the countries party to the proceedings understood that they had to navigate a range of conservative views on familial, sexual and private affairs; especially the freedom to marry across religions was subject to extensive debate.[3] Over the past couple of years, however, radically punitive laws concerning sexual self-expression in locales from Russia to Uganda have gained a great deal of attention. Russia's laws against LGBT "propaganda," for example, kept a range of international leaders away from the opening of the 2014 Sochi Winter Games. Barak Obama may not have said so; the issue nonetheless played into his decision not to attend.[4] Uganda's practice of convicting citizens who don't report (*report!*) homosexual activity has been absolutely slammed in significant parts of the international press, to say nothing of standing as the object of withering NGO critique (cultural particularity is one thing; cultural punitiveness something else).[5] In 1980 and 1984, the Soviets and Americans boycotted each other's Olympics based on questions of Soviet intervention in Afghanistan (1980, in the case of the Americans) and "anti-Soviet hysteria" (1984, in the case of the Soviets).[6]

---

2   CPH Post Online, "Gay Marriage Legalised," June 7, 2012, available at http://cphpost.dk/news14/national-news14/gay-marriage-legalised.html.

3   See Johannes Morsink, *The Universal Declaration of Human Rights: Origins, Drafting & Intent* (Philadelphia: University of Pennsylvania Press, 1999), 120–5.

4   See Tanya L. Domi, "Obama Rightly Joins Political Boycott of Winter Olympics." *Al-Jazeera*, December 18, 2013, available at http://america.aljazeera.com/opinions/2013/12/russia-gay-rightslgbtsochiwinterolympics.html; Matthew Chance, "Why Russia is So Hung Up on Homosexuality," *CNN*, December 16, 2014, available at http://edition.cnn.com/2014/12/16/world/europe/chance-russia-gay-rights/.

5   Alexis Okeowo, "Out in Africa: A Gay-Rights Struggle with Deadly Stakes," *The New Yorker*, December 24, 2012, available at http://www.newyorker.com/magazine/2012/12/24/out-in-africa; Okeowo, "A Rising Tide of Anti-Gay Sentiment in Africa," *The New Yorker*, February 28, 2014, available at http://www.newyorker.com/news/news-desk/a-rising-tide-of-anti-gay-sentiment-in-africa; Saskia Houttuin, "Gay Ugandans Face New Threat from Anti-Homosexuality Law," *The Guardian*, January 6, 2015, available http://www.theguardian.com/world/2015/jan/06/-sp-gay-ugandans-face-new-threat-from-anti-homosexuality-law.

6   Philip D'Agati, *The Cold War and the 1984 Olympic Games* (Houndmills: Palgrave, 1984); Christopher R. Hill, *Olympic Politics* (Manchester: Manchester University Press, 1996).

Those were early examples of turning international sporting events into matters of political statement. That such statements would involve *gay rights*, however, would have been near-incomprehensible in those waning years of the Cold War. The past few decades, if not the entire forty-seven years since the 1969 riots outside the tiny Stonewall Inn in New York's Greenwich Village that are usually taken as the start of the international LGBT rights movement, have been productive – highly productive – indeed.[7]

Still – as perhaps North Carolina's controversial (and particularly ugly) "bathroom laws" demonstrate – LGBT rights remain a complex area.[8] The UN's Universal Declaration of Human Rights (1948), as well as further rights covenants such as the International Covenant on Civil and Political Rights (1966) and the International Covenant on Economic, Social and Cultural Rights (1966), guarantee individual freedom "without distinction of any kind."[9] No one – absolutely no one – is supposed to be denied the full battery of basic international privileges. Of course, if one is uninterested in human rights, such things hardly matter. The universal equality of all human beings isn't the *only* politics to bring to social life.[10] Still, as documents like the Vienna Declaration and Programme of Action note, the "indivisib[ility], interdependen[ce] and interrelated[ness]" of all essential freedoms should never be ignored.[11] Fundamental freedoms should function like an eclipse blocking the sun: there should be no way around them. In theory, being human is all one should need to do to enjoy all the liberties and privileges accorded by international law.[12]

---

7   David Carter, *Stonewall: The Riots that Sparked the Gay Revolution* (New York: St. Martin's, 2009).

8   See Richard Socarides, "North Carolina and the Gay Rights Backlash," *The New Yorker*, March 28, 2016, available at http://www.newyorker.com/news/news-desk/north-carolina-and-the-gay-rights-backlash.

9   United Nations, "The Universal Declaration of Human Rights" (1948, preamble [hereafter UDHR]), available at http://www.un.org/en/documents/udhr.

10   This isn't only a matter of clearly anti-rights ideologies – e.g., fascism or totalitarianism. It also involves simple skepticism towards rights, or ideas of their supposed "impractibility." See Karl Klare, Karl, "Legal Theory and Democratic Reconstruction: Reflections on 1989," in *A Fourth Way?*, ed. G.S. Alexander and S. Shapska (New York: Routledge, 1994), 310–34.

11   United Nations, "Vienna Declaration and Programme of Action" (1993, section 1, article 5), available at http://www.ohchr.org/en/professionalinterest/pages/vienna.aspx.

12   Distinctions need to be made between rights declarations – e.g., the Universal Declaration or Vienna Declaration – and rights covenants like the covenants on civil and political rights and economic, social and cultural rights respectively. The latter, covenants,

It's funny with international rights, though: they *can* be surprisingly specific. I.e., while documents like the Universal Declaration and the International Covenants assert human rights' non-discriminatory nature, they *also* quickly begin to list *what* people, or social identities, have been seen as needing defense in the *most* specific sense. "Race, color, sex, language, religion, political or other opinion, national or social origin, property, birth or other status," argues the Universal Declaration, are the lines along which discrimination should *not* take place. The International Covenants mirror this vocabulary – that discrimination along lines of "race, color, sex, language, religion, political or other opinion, national or social origin, property, birth or other status" is simply not ok.[13] Such perspectives have consequences. Primary is that it's often the working class, women, ethnic and racial minorities and religious groups who are singled-out for special rights protection. I.e., women, the working class, at-risk racial groups and those whose freedom of conscience is in peril are those that universal rights *tend to* indicate as specific sites for rights vigilance.[14] This is for good reason. Both within the West and without, it's long been a struggle for ranges of ethnic groups to gain even basic social recognition. From the Civil Rights Movement in the U.S. to movements against Apartheid from South Africa to Zimbabwe, racial and ethnic equality has been one of the modern world's decided themes.[15] Of course, one *can* argue over whether the recognition of non-Euro/non-Whites or the decided oppression of half the earth's population in the form of gender discrimination has been the more disturbing trope of modern times. Regardless of one's answer, however, the struggle for women's equality is also clearly one of modern history's important

---

have decidedly more legal force (declarations, theoretically, have none). Still, the essential principles the UN lays out around human rights inform the precise dimensions of rights law, wherein principle and the letter of the law are not always easy to separate. See David Weissbrodt and Connie de la Vega, *International Human Rights Law: An Introduction* (Philadelphia: University of Pennsylvania Press, 2007).

13 UDHR, article 2; United Nations, "International Covenant on Civil and Political Rights" (1966, article 2), available at http://www.ohchr.org/en/professionalinterest/pages/ccpr. aspx; United Nations, "International Covenant on Economic, Social and Cultural Rights" (1966, article 2), available at http://www.ohchr.org/EN/ProfessionalInterest/Pages/CESCR.aspx.

14 See Tawhida Ahmed and Anastasia Vakulenko, "Minority Rights 60 Years after the UDHR: Limits on the Preservation of Identity?" in *International Human Rights Law: Six Decades after the UDHR and Beyond*, ed. Mashood Baderin and Manisuli Ssenyonjo (Farnham: Ashgate, 2010), 155–72.

15 See Theodore Koditschek, Sundiata Cha-Jua and Helen Neville, eds. *Race Struggles* (Urbana: University of Illinois Press, 2009).

narratives.[16] Of course, that's beyond religious pluralism's importance in light of the world's many faith-based conflicts – never mind events like the Holocaust – or the fact that workers' rights stand as one of the oldest domains of rights concern in the book. Very simply, problems of gender equality, religious freedom, ethnic liberation and labor rights represent a quartet of issues that no rights activist would imagine that rights thought can do without.[17]

Still, a funny thing happened on the way to the forum; a strange phenomenon unfolded while the women's movement, the fight for racial equality, the movement for labor rights and petitions for religious liberty were under way. While protestors against gender and racial discrimination didn't win the war, e.g., they at least took some battles. They floated a few boats even if the entire navy didn't get out to sea. This included *national* victories, yes – the franchise and various civil rights acts. It *also*, however, included notice in *international* documents, such as the Universal Declaration, the International Covenants as well as issue-, and identity-specific treaties like the International Convention on the Elimination of All Forms of Racial Discrimination (1965) and the Convention on the Elimination of All Forms of Discrimination against Women (1979). Clearly, one wants one's rights recognized by national states – the state being the site where concrete change often begins.[18] It's also nice, however, when one's rights are recognized by an *international* community, and *global* actors have lent legitimacy to one's cause (that as it sometimes helps engender national change itself).[19] Indeed, religious liberty has been the subject of similar levels of appeal. The issue appears in a range of *national* constitutions – especially those of a liberal ilk.[20] It's *also* an area of concern, however, in *international* documents – e.g., the Universal Declaration and the International Covenant on Civil and Political Rights (the same goes for labor rights – a central area in the Economic, Social

---

16 Sheila Rowbotham, *Hidden from History: 300 Years of Women's Oppression and the Fight against It* (London: Pluto, 1977).

17 John Witte, Jr. and Johan van der Vyver, eds., *Religious Human Rights in Global Perspective: Religious Perspectives* (The Hague: Martinus Nijhoff, 1996). See also Micheline R. Ishay, *The History of Human rights: From Ancient Times to the Globalization Era* (Berkeley: University of California Press, 2004), 117–72.

18 See Edward Weisband and Courtney Thomas, *Political Culture and the Making of Modern Nation-States* (London: Routledge, 2015).

19 See, e.g., Thomas Risse, Stephen C. Ropp and Kathryn Sikkink, eds., *The Power of Human Rights: International Norms and Domestic Change* (Cambridge: Cambridge University Press, 1999).

20 See Paul A. Marshall, *Religious Freedom in the World* (Lanham: Rowman & Littlefield, 2000).

and Cultural Covenant over and above national attention to labor protection).[21] It may state the obvious. However, nowhere *near* the same situation exists for the international queer community. LGBT brothers and sisters are mentioned virtually *nowhere* in the major documents of international human rights.[22] That's curious when, despite issues like North Carolina's apparent discomfort with queer liberties and privileges, countries like the U.S. and the nations of Western Europe appear on their way to becoming noticeably more LGBT-friendly. Why have our lesbian, gay, bisexual and transsexual friends been left out of such progressive thought on the international stage?

It's hard to say. Of course, one *can* always appeal to the bugaboo of age-old prejudice. Ranges of religions have long held negative attitudes towards homosexuality, and one could argue that it's hard to force taboos anchored in faith to simply disappear.[23] It long ago became lodged in our minds, one commentator has argued, that being gay is a "sin." The level of theological censure around the idea might be such that we *still* can't steer clear of the taboo in our heads. It might also be that belief happens as a "totality," as one sociologist has argued, wherein the multiple parts of "complex wholes" are less than easy to transform (i.e., there's an inertia to cultural change wherein there's an innate resistance when it comes to putting aside taboos).[24] Still, we've *overcome* conservatism in the past. Ideas of welfare, the right of women to non-discrimination and attempts to help the working poor *have* been institutionalized. We've sought *inclusion* for ranges of religions, and petitioned to *not* hold people out on the basis of the color of their skin. Such rights were countermanded and demanded significant protest to achieve. Still, we got *somewhere* with such causes – that on planes not only on national but *international* as well. I thus ask again: why the slow road for LGBT

---

21 See Judy Fudge, "The New Discourse of Labor Rights: From Social to Fundamental Rights," in *Human Rights in the World Community: Issues and Action*, ed., Burns H. Weston and Anna Grear (Philadelphia: University of Pennsylvania Press, 2016), 179–88. See also Heiner Bielefeldt, Nazila Ghanea and Michael Wiener, *Freedom of Religion or Belief: An International Law Commentary* (Oxford: Oxford University Press, 2016); Ishay, *The History*, 117–72.

22 The Charter of Fundamental Rights of the European Union is the major exception. See footnote 25.

23 See Yvette Taylor and Ria Snowdon, eds. *Queering Religion, Religious Queers* (London: Routledge, 2014).

24 Jürgen Habermas, *Moral Consciousness and Communicative Action*, trans. S. Lenhardt and S.W. Nicholson (Cambridge, MA: MIT Press, 1990), 177. See also John Boswell, *Same-Sex Unions in Premodern Europe* (New York: Vintage, 1994).

brothers and sisters? Where are *their* sets of international conventions or mention in the basic documents of international law?[25]

Again, it's hard to say. Still, in one of the seminal works of queer theory, gender philosopher Judith Butler argued that, through time, societies have become accustomed to using "binary" categories to discuss sex: "man/woman;" "natural/unnatural;" "feminine/masculine;" "strong/weak," "gay/straight," "dominant/submissive" and so on. For reasons sometimes religious, sometimes cultural and sometimes having to do with science ("science"), hundreds of years if not millennia of momentum have simply settled such groupings into place.[26] Fair enough; societies come to the agreements that they do, and they're often less than perfect. As Butler poses it, however, key to such groupings was that they are in fact that: groupings, or categories. We've been involved with *concepts* to which we've become *accustomed* – that as opposed to anything "organic" or "natural." In principle, Butler argued (or at least she thought *we* did), it should be easy to know what a man or woman is. "Woman" is the opposite of "man." She is defined by a biology distinct from men's and, due to an identity emerging from that biology, she is a figure maintaining a *history* opposite of men's as well. "Men" are then the opposite of "women." They maintain a *sex* opposite of women's and play the "dominant" role to the supposedly subsumed "female" part in the larger narrative of human time. Politically, the point becomes to equalize the two – to offer deeper levels of experience binding the "man/woman" dyad at the same time that each is allowed to be what it naturally "is" ("men" or "women"). For Butler, however, that was the point: we simply don't *know* what a man or a woman is, nor what "gays," "straights," "lesbians" nor "transsexuals" are – nor even what the "*human*" is – before we start to act the part. We have to *perform* identities and behaviors and *code* them as things to invest them with "reality." We have to *point* to elements of our social world and say "that's that"

---

25 It's noticeable that some *regional* rights regimes, such as that of the European Union, *have* begun to acknowledge the LGBT cause (non-discrimination based on sexual preference is addressed in article 21 of the Charter of Fundamental Rights of the European Union, e.g.). Still, such addresses are noticeably thin when compared with other areas of rights concern See Laura Palazzani, *Gender in Philosophy and Law* (Dordrecht: Springer, 2012), 63–5. See also European Commission, "Charter of Fundamental Rights of the European Union" (2000, article 21), available at http://www.europarl.europa.eu/charter/pdf/text_en.pdf.

26 Kenan Malik, *The Meaning of Race: Race, History, and Culture in Western Society* (New York: New York University Press, 1996).

before that thing becomes anything particular at all. I.e., as opposed to a biological view of sex, we largely make up gender as we go along.[27]

Now, that idea was revolutionary in itself – that gender and sex ("sex") have little to do one another and that both that are matters of symbolization and social agreement as much as anything else. Butler doubled-down on such theses, however, by arguing that we concretized such ideas through institutions, social norms and legal codes. We "substantialized" gender by ingraining "binaries" into bureaucracy, law and the mores of everyday life.[28] Every arrest under sodomy laws, Butler argued, stamped gay life as outside the norm – a "no-no" under any social circumstance. Every denial in the company of others that one had affection for a person of the same sex reinforced the forbidden nature of queer life and insistences on its "deviance." Every exclusion from "good society" because of rumors concerning whom one might like or whom one might not represented a stigmatization from which it was hard to recover. Every instance of feeling uncomfortable in one's body yet having no way to change it was a way of locking down senses of the self and limiting relations with even one's own being.[29] Part of Butler's argument – a provocative part – was that such ideas damned traditional approaches to feminism: approaches embodied in documents such as the Universal Declaration, the International Covenants and the conventions on gender and race (Butler's concepts had consequences for race too).[30] Using the words of one of Butler's influences, such approaches relied on the "old dream of symmetry" – that society *could* be broken into binary groups and that we might declare one side or the other "liberated" or "not."[31] Now, that wasn't wrong – all identities,

---

27 We generally regard nature, Butler argues, as a matter of "mute facticity" – that it's simply there. That fully ignores the idea, she argues, that we have to bring nature into being as a *concept.* Judith Butler, *Gender Trouble: Feminism and the Subversion of Identity* (New York: Routledge, 1990), 176.

28 Ibid., 31. It's worth noting that Butler takes inspiration from Michel Foucault on this point. A major point of Foucault's was our "disciplining" into norms concerning sexuality. See Michel Foucault, *The History of Sexuality*, 3 vols., trans. Robert Hurley (New York: Vintage, 1990–2012).

29 See Lisa Keen and Suzanne B. Goldberg, *Strangers to the Law: Gay People on Trial* (Ann Arbor: University of Michigan Press, 2000).

30 See Malini Johar Schueller, *Locating Race: Global Sites of Post-Colonial Citizenship* (Albany: SUNY, 2009).

31 See Luce Irigaray, *Speculum of the Other Woman*, trans. Gillian C. Gill (Ithaca, NY: Cornell University Press, 1985). This was also very much the point of earlier feminist philosophers like Simon de Beauvoir: that though women had been constructed as the "Other" of men, the point was women finding their full personhood, which was,

"man," "woman," "white," "black," "brown" or otherwise, deserve liberation. Everyone should be allowed to be who they feel they are. Such divisions nonetheless left out anyone *not* fitting into neatly into one side or the other of such bifurcated ideals or, more to the point, the presumptions they often entail (straightness, largely). Simply put, LGBT life faced and faces us with the possibility of having to reconstruct categories it took centuries, if not millennia, to make. For many, that's simply a proposition too revolutionary to bear.[32]

Today, Butler's ideas are twenty-five years old. Among academics, anyway, they're now *doxa* as much as anything else. Few in the contemporary humanities or social sciences would pigeonhole gender or sex in such obviously bifurcated ways.[33] That doesn't preclude the relevance of theses like Butler's, however; it doesn't hold them back from being germane to our times. Again, both national and international communities appear willing to go to bat for, or at least pay lip service to, women's rights, the rights of ethnic minorities, the rights of the working class and the importance of religious liberty. The international community seems willing to take "pleasure" in at least *some* differences, as one critic has put it, suggesting that those who labor, women "traditionally-conceived" (read "straight"), religious minorities and people of color shouldn't socially be left out.[34] Now, it's true: even in the world's most gender-equal states – Scandinavian countries, e.g. – full pay equality has yet to be reached. Denmark, Sweden and Norway all pay women at least 7% less than men for precisely the same work.[35] We *don't* live in gender equal worlds – that without getting into the multiple issues surrounding present-day race relations (look at events in Ferguson or Baltimore, e.g.), the fact that workers' rights continue to demand vigilance or the reality that the persecution of religious minorities remains a global concern. No one would say that the world is absent torsion along the lines of the identities that rights

---

in essence, a deeper humanity. See Simone de Beauvoir, *The Second Sex*, trans. H.M. Parshley (New York: Vintage, 1989).

32 See also Mary K. Bloodsworth-Lugo, *In-Between Bodies: Sexual Difference, Race, and Sexuality* (Albany: SUNY Press, 2007).

33 Sonja K. Foss, Mary E. Domenico and Karen A. Foss, *Gender Stories: Negotiating Identity in a Binary World* (Long Grove: Waveland, 2013).

34 See Bell Hooks, *Black Looks: Race and Representation* (Boston: South End, 1992), 17. See also Steven Wheatley, *Democracy, Minorities, and International Law* (Cambridge: Cambridge University Press, 2005).

35 OECD, "Gender Equality" (2015), available at https://www.oecd.org/gender/data/genderwagegap.htm.

traditionally address. Historically-noted identity categories within human rights demand continued tending to as much as anything else.[36]

Again, though, there's been a will to *do something*. Not only *national* but *international* rights conventions *exist*. There's rough – rough – consensus that discrimination and prejudice towards women, workers, religious minorities and racial minorities should be on their way *out*. It's been fifty-one years since the Convention on Racial Discrimination was passed and thirty-seven since the Convention on Discrimination against Women cleared UN General Assembly hurdles. It's *fifty* years since the International Covenant addressing economic and labor rights passed muster, and since the *eighteenth century* that we've been addressing religious liberty as a matter of basic civico-legal concern.[37] Such rights are *popular* points of appeal. They represent areas in which there's a willingness to acknowledge who's at risk – to recognize pasts of discrimination and ask that they be fundamentally changed as global society moves towards the future.[38]

It's time we bring home such commitments to LGBT rights. I.e., it's time to make queer freedoms and liberties subject to not only national law but *international* justice as well. There should be mention of sexual preference and gender self-identification in the Universal Declaration and the International Covenants similar to discussions concerning women's rights, the rights of racial minorities, problems of religious liberty and the realization of working class rights as well. Indeed, from my perspective, LGBT rights deserve an international convention of their *own* – a Convention against All Forms of Discrimination Based on Sexual Preference and Gender Self-Identification, as it were. Small – small – steps in such directions have been taken. UN Secretary General Ban Ki-Moon has to date made forty-four speeches on non-discrimination concerning sexual orientation

---

36 See again Ahmed and Vakulenko, "Minority Rights 60 Years after the UDHR." See also Matthias Koenig and Paul De Guchteneire, eds., *Democracy and Human Rights in Multicultural Societies* (London: Routledge, 2007).

37 I refer here largely to The Enlightenment ear democratic revolutions in places like the U.S. and France – though there are differences, as the French Revolution had a sharper anti-clerical side that sometime brought religion in general under suspicion. Still, notions of free thought largely helped projects of free religious conscience. See, e.g., Samuel Walker, *The Rights Revolution: Rights and Community in Modern America* (Oxford: Oxford University Press, 1998).

38 See Michael Ignatieff, *The Rights Revolution* (Toronto: House of Anansi Press, 2000), 1–27.

and the right to occupy the gender that one wants – nothing to sneeze at at all.[39] The UN issued its first report on LGBT concerns in 2011, positing identity based on sexual orientation as a matter of "critical" rights concern – also meaningful.[40] Still, virtually *all* UN statements on LGBT issues have come since 2009. There are *few* resources devoted to the issue of sexual preference and gender self-identity when compared with minority issues of a similar ilk.[41] LGBT identities are *not* noted as on par with other identities in terms of the notation of those who maintain historically oppressed statuses. Again, such omissions may be a product of our "binary" modes of thought. They may concern concepts hard to dismiss because knowledge's social nature means that it's hard to recognize knowledge as social at all (we're socialized into thinking that knowledge concerns immutable truths, wherein we can't see that truth is something we *learn*).[42] Still, theses like Butler's help. Theses about our conceptual dyads make us aware of fundamental mechanisms that, despite progress, may continue to play-out. That involves our *in*ability to recognize certain identities because they don't fit into certain pre-prescribed boxes, and that there are identities we haven't conjoined to concepts other than the "outside," the "upsetting," the "different" or "off." I.e, there are "re-associations" we have yet to make – ranges of identities we have yet to join to concepts of "deserving of liberation," "needing to be freed" or perhaps bolted to the terms that are politically-determinant above all: the "human" and its "rights." Of course, there's only so far we can be cognizant of *all* the social agreements we make; even as we move to include more, some may continue to be left out.

---

39 United Nations, "Combatting Discrimination Based on Sexual Orientation and Gender Identity – Speeches and Statements" (2015), available at http://www.ohchr.org/EN/Issues/Discrimination/Pages/LGBTSpeechesandstatements.aspx.

40 United Nations, "Discriminatory Laws and Practices and Acts of Sexual Violence against Individuals Based on Their Sexual Orientation and Gender Identity" (2011), available at http://www2.ohchr.org/english/bodies/hrcouncil/docs/19session/A.HRC.19.41_English.pdf.

41 There are fourteen committees, offices, special rapporteurs and the like working on issues of gender and race; there's more than twenty if one throws in issues of class, labor and religious freedom. There's one on sexual orientation and gender identity. See United Nations Office of the High Commissioner for Human Rights, "List of Human Rights Issues" (2016), available at http://www.ohchr.org/EN/Issues/Pages/ListofIssues.aspx. See also Palazzani, *Gender in Philosophy and Law*, 63.

42 I simply point here to the fact that epistemologies like Butler's imply the idea that the social nature of knowledge often happens unconscious of it – that being partly what allows social truths to be perceived as "true." See Birgit Schippers, *The Political Philosophy of Judith Butler* (London: Routledge, 2014).

Any conceptual "reassociations" also won't be more "natural" than anything else; socially-constructed knowledge remains precisely that.[43] Still, if we're concerned to *truly* realize rights "without distinction of any kind," such reassociative work needs to begin. That's at the risk of continuing to leave some outside humanity's circle – something that no activist for fundamental rights could possibly accept.[44]

---

43 This is, for better or worse, a part of Butler's thesis: that gender *is* "culturally con-structed," and it never *won't* be a matter of perception and social norms. See Butler, *Gender Trouble*, 8.

44 It *is* worth noting the existence of the "Yogyakarta Principles" – a series of outlines made by a range of international lawyers with a view towards applying rights principles to areas of gender identity and sexual orientation. The Yogyakarta Principles don't fall within the UN mandate, however, and are not part of bodies of international law. See Palazzani, *Gender in Philosophy and Law*, 62–3.

The Clash of Civilizations

Sub-Continent Style
(May 2, 2016)

Abstract: *We hear a lot about the "clash of civilizations" from the perspective of the "War on Terror" and concerning relations between Islam and the "West." That's not the only faultline as concerns global cultural clash, however. What happens when we don't always put the "West" at the center of our international cultural analyses?*

Over the past year or so, two issues have brought the so-called "Indian Sub-Continent" to the fore – issues over and above well-recognized problems of development and modernization in the country oft-referred to as the "world's largest democracy" (India), as well as similar problems in neighboring and also geopolitically important states such as Pakistan and Bangladesh. The first concerns the murder of bloggers Avijit Roy and Nazimuddin Samad – Roy being a dual Bangladeshi-American citizen, secularist and free speech advocate killed in 2015 on his way home from a book fair, and Samad a Bang-

"India Globe." © marcyano79 / Fotolia.com 65295635

ladeshi rights activist who, just weeks ago, was hacked by attackers with machetes and then shot while returning from a university class. An arrest has been made in the Roy case: conservative blogger Farabi Shafiur Rahman, who apparently took revenge on Roy for "defaming" Islam.[1] An arrest has yet to be made in the Samad case; it's simply too fresh. Reports nonetheless point to multiple attackers first hacking the twenty-eight-year-old to inflict pain, then shooting him after he'd long lain prone on the ground, suffering.[2]

---

1   See Saad Hammadi and Mark Tran, "Bangladesh Authorities Arrest Man over Atheist Blogger's Murder," *The Guardian*, March 2, 2015, available at http://www.theguardian.com/world/2015/mar/02/bangladesh-authorities-arrest-man-atheist-bloggers-murder-avijit-roy.
2   See Serajul Quadir, "Liberal Bangladeshi Blogger Killed by Machete-Wielding Attackers," *Reuters*, April 7, 2016, available at http://www.reuters.com/article/us-bangladesh-blogger-idUSKCN0X40FZ.

The second issue concerns religious reconversion, and that's largely to Hinduism from Christianity and Islam – an issue playing out in India along resurgent lines of religious conflict. In recent years, Christianity's made relatively serious inroads into the country – Christianity of a missionary, evangelical type – and a society long marked by tensions between Muslims and Hindus (Sikhs as well) has yet another angle to contend with.[3] "Modern Hinduism" – Hinduism with a systematic theological foundation like Western monotheisms – is a controversial concept. Scholars have marked it as everything from a gentrification of the religion to a rallying point for oppressed masses to a product of "Orientalist" (read "imperialist") mentalities to, perhaps like Zionism, an offshoot of European-style nationalism when adopted in political form.[4] It also overlaps with issues of class – the division between Dalits, Sudra, Vaishya, Kshatriya and Brahman long woven into the base of Indian life.[5] Now, it appears that especially Dalits ("untouchables") – a concept some say was accented by the British – have long been protected under something called the system of Scheduled Castes. For outsiders like myself, "Scheduled Castes" aren't easy to explain. The example of affirmative action, however, might suffice. Generally, subsidies, non-discriminatory social practices, progressive education policies and proactive employment politics have been attached to a wide range of groups since India's 1947 breakaway from the British Empire – in some cases, before.[6] The focus has largely been on those sitting at the bottom of the Hindu social ranks (again, Dalits, primarily). In February 2015, the Supreme Court of India decided that if you convert *back* to Hinduism after having converted to, say, Christianity or Islam (the major competitors), you can get back your benefits as a member of a Scheduled Caste.[7] Some took this as a win. The British, it's often been said, brought little more than the Bible and the toothbrush and, in view of the legacies of colonialism,

---

3   See Goldie Osuri, *Religious Freedom in India: Sovereignty and (anti) Conversion* (London: Routledge, 2013); Sebastian Kim, *In Search of Identity: Debates on Religious Conversion in India* (Oxford: Oxford University Press, 2005).

4   See Brian A. Hatcher, *Bourgeois Hinduism, or the Faith of the Modern Vedantists* (Oxford: Oxford University Press, 2008); Brian K. Pennington, *Was Hinduism Invented?: Britons, Indians and the Colonial Construction of Religion* (Oxford: Oxford University Press, 2005). On Orientalism, see Edward Said, *Orientalism* (New York: Vintage, 1978).

5   See Ekta Singh, *Caste System in India: A Historical Perspective* (Delhi: Kalpaz, 2005).

6   See Makhan Jha, ed., *Scheduled Castes Today* (New Delhi: MD Publications, 1997).

7   Tarique Anwar, "SC Ruling on Reconversion: It's a Stamp of Approval for Ghar Wapsi, says VHP," *First Post*, February 28, 2015, available at http://www.firstpost.com/india/sc-ruling-on-reconversion-its-a-stamp-of-approval-for-ghar-wapsi-says-vhp-2126461.html.

Christianity has sometimes been posited as a phenomenon the country could do without.[8] It's also long been a debate as to whether India is a specifically Hindu nation or a *de facto* multicultural state (evidence would seem to indicate the latter as, in terms of religious distribution, the country is 80% Hindu, 15% Muslim, 2% Christian and 2% Sikh).[9] Still, not everyone embraced the high court's decision. Some viewed it is as encouraging the practice of *ghar wapsi*: a term which, though literally meaning "homecoming," has been taken as but scant cover for aggressively zealous reconversion programs. This has been seen to challenge the right to religious freedom enshrined in not only the Indian constitution but a range of international rights conventions as well.[10]

In many ways, it's tempting to think of the Roy and Samad incidents as "*Charlie Hebdo* sub-continent style": overly-zealous fundamentalists making stands in worlds they see as secularizing and Westernizing whether everyone wants them to or not. The deaths are not the first of Enlightenment-style free speech advocates either in Bangladesh or throughout the region, nor are they the only controversies concerning clashes between religion and free speech. Secular blogger Rajib Haider, e.g., was killed in 2013 for his criticism of Islamic fundamentalism by a supporter of an offshoot of one of the country's leading Islamist parties (Jamaat-e-Islami) – that though some of the party's branches, especially in India, have recently taken more secular and ecumenical turns.[11] A similar attack was directed in

---

8   See Saurav Datta, "India's Mass Conversion Problem," Al-Jazeera, January 4, 2015, available at http://www.aljazeera.com/indepth/opinion/2015/01/india-mass-conversion-problem-20151274531627294.html.

9   See Central Intelligence Agency World Factbook, "India" (2015), available at https://www.cia.gov/library/publications/the-world-factbook/geos/in.html. See also D.N. Jha, *Rethinking Hindu Identity* (London: Routledge, 2009).

10 See T.M. Krishna, "As I See It: In the Name of Ghar Wapsi," *The Hindu*, January 17, 2015, available at http://www.thehindu.com/opinion/columns/t_m_krishna/as-i-see-it-in-the-name-of-ghar-wapsi/article6788990.ece; Government of India, "The Constitution of India" (1949), available at http://india.gov.in/sites/upload_files/npi/files/coi_part_full.pdf; United Nations, "International Covenant on Civil and Political Rights" (1966 [hereafter ICCPR]), available at http://www.ohchr.org/en/professionalinterest/pages/ccpr.aspx; United Nations, "The Universal Declaration of Human Rights" (1948), available at http://www.un.org/en/documents/udhr/.

11 See Jim Yardley, "Vast Throng in Bangladesh Protests Killing of Activist," *The New York Times*, February 16, 2013, available at http://www.nytimes.com/2013/02/17/world/asia/vast-throng-in-bangladesh-protests-killing-of-activist.htm; Ifran Ahmad, *Islam and Democracy in India: The Transformation of Jamaat-e-Islami* (Princeton: Princeton University Press, 2009).

2004 against Humayun Azad, a Bangladeshi intellectual and social progressivist who authored what many consider the country's first work of feminist literature (*Naari*, 1992) and who made waves with his book *Pak Sar Jamin Sad Bad* (*The Blessed Sacred Land*, 2003) – a text deconstructing the role of Islamic fundamentalist in national life.[12] For its part, India recently witnessed the *de facto* censoring of University of Chicago professor Wendy Doniger's book *The Hindus: An Alternative History* (2009) – a work in which the author sexed-up the religion beyond what was apparently acceptable taste, and the kibosh was put on further publication after a popular initial run.[13] In Pakistan, Rashid Rehman, a human rights lawyer and regional rights commissioner, was killed in 2014 in the city of Multan, in the Pakistani Punjab, for his advocacy of religion-blind free speech.[14] Of course, that's without touching on the 2012 attack on Malala Yousafzai, or ongoing questions as to whether Pakistan's really an ally of the West or a hideout for militant Talibanis – that above and beyond the mystery surrounding how the state became home to Osama bin Laden over the course of his final year.[15]

There may be something to the *Hebdo* analogy. India, Bangladesh and Pakistan all maintain well-educated, secular middle classes – unsurprising in states with populations of over a billion, 190 and 150 million apiece – and those middle classes have often been derived from Western-educated cores. Regional analyst Shahid Shahidullah, e.g., has argued that development on economic and political scales has often been guided by "modernizing elites;" groups whose interests lay in cultivating cosmopolitan cultures and developed financial systems such that regional states might become more than marginal players on global political and economic scales.[16] Now, we have to be careful in making divisions between "authentic"

---

12 See Syed Al-Mahmood, "American Critic of Islamic Fundamentalism Hacked to Death in Bangladesh," *The Wall Street Journal*, February 27, 2015, available at http://www.wsj.com/articles/american-blogger-killed-in-bangladesh-1425026073.

13 Jonathan Shainin, "Why Free Speech Loses in India" *The New Yorker*, February 13, 2014, available at http://www.newyorker.com/news/news-desk/why-free-speech-loses-in-india.

14 BBC, "Pakistan Blasphemy Lawyer Shot Dead in Multan Office," May 7, 2014, available at http://www.bbc.com/news/world-asia-27319433.

15 Ayesha Jalal, *The Struggle for Pakistan: A Muslim Homeland and Global Politics* (Cambridge, MA: Harvard Belknap, 2014).

16 Shahid Shahidullah, "The Third World after the Cold War," in *At the Crossroads of Development: Transnational Challenges to Developed and Developing Societies*, ed. Alfred G. Cuzán (Leiden: Brill, 1997), 124; I.P. Desai, "Western Educated Elites and Social Change in India," *Economic and Political Weekly* 19, no. 15 (1984): 639–47; Rupal Oza, *The Making of Neoliberal India: Nationalism, Gender, and the Paradoxes of Globalization*

culture and things supposedly impregnated by the outside or, more specifically, the "West." Philosopher Martha Nussbaum, e.g., recently argued that it's overcooked to try to decide what's "native" to the Indian nation and what comes from "somewhere else." In a society as complex as India's, she maintains, it's simply patronizing to assert trends of "cultural domination" and that's it.[17] Still, *some* headway has been made in opposing the country's long-held, officially-instituted secular/multicultural politics – an opposition based partly on the charge that there *is* an indigenous India (it's Hindu), and that the swirl of global influences may have struck the nation on a false historico-cultural path.[18] Indeed, neighboring states like Pakistan have struggled with questions along similar lines: should the country (Pakistan) be an "Islamic state" ("Islamic Republic" is part of the country's official name ["The Islamic Republic of Pakistan"]), or is the country meant to be but a *sanctuary* for Muslims, wherein Islam has a clear home, but no particular social group is left out? Similar questions dog Bangladesh as the nation made secularism a cornerstone of its constitution upon gaining independence from Pakistan in 1971 – that though the country's Muslim-majority status was grounds for its initial inclusion in the bifurcated Pakistani state.[19] As Shahidullah puts it, many have felt "held from power."

(London: Routledge, 2006). See also Emma Tomalin, "Religion and Development in India and Pakistan: An Overview," in *The Routledge Handbook of Religions and Global Development*, ed. Emma Tomalin (London: Routledge, 2015), 183.

17 Martha Nussbaum, *The Clash Within: Democracy, Religious Violence, and India's Future* (Cambridge, MA: Harvard University Press, 2007). It should be noted that the "cultural domination" vocabulary is mine – not Nussbaum's. I'm rather pointing to the gist of her argument.

18 Kukum Sangari terms this an attempt to "re-authorise [traditional] norms through a discourse of anti-westernism" – that partly intended to counter-balance a "sycophantic capitulation to global capitalism." See Sangari, "Violent Acts: Cultures, Structures and Retraditionalisation," in *Women of India: Colonial and Post-Colonial Periods*, ed. Bharati Ray (New Delhi: Sage, 2005), 172. See also Bidyut Chakrabarty, *Coalition Politics in India* (Oxford: Oxford University Press, 2014).

19 See Srinath Raghavan *1971: A Global History of the Creation of Bangladesh* (Cambridge, MA: Harvard University Press, 2013).

It's worth noting that the Pakistani Constitution clearly denotes the country as an Islamic republic: the principles of "democracy, freedom, equality, tolerance [and] social justice," it argues, will be realized "as enunciated by Islam." Still – and perhaps predictably – article 18 of the first chapter of the constitution guarantees full freedom of religion and people of all faiths the right to practice their faiths. There seems to be an attempt to bridge concepts of a religiously and culturally-defined state with standards of international multiculturalism. See National Assembly of Pakistan, "The Constitution of the Islamic Republic of Pakistan" (2012), available at http://www.na.gov.pk/

Those *not* from "modernizing elites" may have grabbed onto claims of "cultural origins" to register modes of social resistance and lodge particular sets of political claims.[20] That's evinced by the wide range of recent electoral successes for conservative-culturalist parties over and above the violences unfortunately coloring large parts of regional cultural space.[21]

Regarding *ghar wapsi*, the crisscrossing of economic benefits with religion and class provides an issue one can interpret in multiple ways. Those interested in *resisting* conversion can reject the ruling out of hand – that based on the idea that reinstating benefits sullies "purer" senses of the faith (convert and one's belief somehow becomes "tainted").[22] Those *seeking* reconverts – a growing number – can use the ruling as a way of saying that "coming home" has sanction from the state; the "truth" of India's Hinduism has been given an official stamp of approval by way of government financial muscle.[23] Those *opposing* the organization of society so intensely around religion yet interested in helping the poor may have a hard time knowing *what* to do. Clearly, one wants all benefits to go to those who need them. 21.9% of Indians live in poverty – a hair under 275 million (a number that not long ago would have been roughly the population of the United States).[24]

---

uploads/documents/1333523681_951.pdf; Sumit Ganguly, "The Roots of Religious Violence in India, Pakistan, and Bangladesh," in *Religion and Conflict in South and Southeast Asia: Disrupting Violence*, ed. Linell E. Cady and Sheldon W. Simon (London: Routledge, 2007), 76; Farzana Shaikh, "From Islamisation to Shariatisation: Cultural Transnationalism in Pakistan," *Third World Quarterly* 29, no. 3 (2008): 593–609.

20 Shahidullah, "The Third World," 124.

21 Obviously, there's a difference between the rise of conservative religious parties – even highly conservative ones – and religious violence. Still, more than one commentator has noted the two as emerging from shared trends. See Rajdeep Sardesai, *2014: The Election that Changed India* (New York: Penguin, 2015); Philip Oldenburg, *India, Pakistan, and Democracy: Solving the Puzzle of Divergent Paths* (London: Routledge, 2010); Ali Riaz, *Islamist Militancy in Bangladesh: A Complex Web* (London: Routledge, 2012); Nussbaum, *The Clash Within*.

22 See The Express Tribune, "Indian Family Reverts to Islam after Adopting Hinduism under 'Ghar Wapsi' Campaign," *The Express Tribune*, May 2, 2015, available at http://tribune.com.pk/story/879808/indian-family-reverts-to-islam-months-after-adopting-hinduism-under-ghar-wapsi-campaign/; Peter Herriot, *Religious Fundamentalism: Global, Local and Personal* (London: Routledge, 2009).

23 See Sarbeswar Sahoo, *Civil Society and Democratization in India: Institutions, Ideologies and Interests* (London: Routledge, 2013), 152.

24 World Bank, "India," available at http://data.worldbank.org/country/india. The numbers in Bangladesh and Pakistan are 31.5 and 22.3%, respectively. Of course, the *ghar wapsi* issue concerns India.

That's while one doesn't want to encourage the many zealots that appear to increasingly dominate social life. "What is happening in this land of various belief systems," one commentator recently wrote in the moderate *The Hindu*? Are ecumenical, if not secular, ideas in danger of disappearing from the heart of Indian society?[25] For some, it appears that's precisely the case.

In 1996, the political scientist Samuel Huntington published the book *The Clash of Civilizations and the Remaking of the World Order*. In the post-Cold War world, Huntington argued, "the most important distinctions among peoples [would be] not ideological, political or economic. They [would be] cultural."[26] Now, Huntington hardly used the term; it came up but once in relation to another scholar's view of the concept (Immanuel Wallerstein's). Still, Huntington saw "culture" through the lenses of "worldview." He viewed culture via problems of identity; the meaning of "things;" at-large senses of who I "am."[27] Culture was life in its nuance: the "everyday" in its subtlety. It was faith, morality and history – all rolled into one.[28]

Now, today, cultural or "civilizational" conflict is often posited as a battle between the "West" the "rest." The "mainsprings of global power," one historian has written, are often seen to fall along the lines of those emerging from the traditions of the European Enlightenment and those who "don't" ("don't" [other cultures, of course, have their Enlightenments too]).[29] Indeed, *specific* focus often falls on *Islam* versus the West: "Jihad versus McWorld," as one scholar has phrased it, or the fight over Islam's "bloody borders," to use Huntington's words.[30] Such conflicts are clearly present on the sub-continent. Secularists like Roy, Samad and Haider use international norms to demand the unfettered transfer of information and the right challenge received truths when and where they want. They approach history from a "cosmopolitan point of view," as the philosopher Immanuel Kant put it, in

---

25 See Krishna, "As I See It."

26 Samuel Huntington, *The Clash of Civilizations and the Remaking of the World Order* (New York: Free Press, 1996), 21.

27 Ibid., 41.

28 It's not the most unusual definition of culture. Cultural theorist Raymond Williams, e.g., defined culture as a "whole way of life" – the kind of intuitive completeness referred to by Huntington. See Williams, *Culture & Society: 1780–1950* (New York: Columbia University Press, 1958), 43.

29 Niall Ferguson, *Civilization: The West and the Rest* (New York: Penguin, 2011), 12. See also S. Frederick Starr, *Lost Enlightenment: Central Asia's Golden Age from the Arab Conquest to Tamerlane* (Princeton: Princeton University Press, 2013).

30 Benjamin Barber, *Jihad versus McWorld: How Globalism and Tribalism Are Reshaping the World* (New York: Ballantine, 1995); Huntington, *The Clash*, 254.

which there are few natural limits regarding senses of what one might do.[31] Activists such as Yousafzai insist on the right to education for all, broadening access to civic institutions and widening opportunities for political participation in addition to one's ability participate in economic life. Lawyers like Rehman petition for the right to articulate oneself without worry about reprimand from the "pious" while figures like Azad advocate self-expression's benefits and the amelioratory powers of a relatively free reign for the arts. That's at the same time that "unmodern men" roam the modern world and traditionalists ask that inheritance define the person – that the mores of the present aren't deployed at the expense of those of the past.[32] In such contexts, "sub-continental" clash feels like part of a global squall – confrontations of science and faith, reason and revelation and the upholders of those who get the "message" versus those insisting it's possible to find values relevant for all (advocates of universal rights). It makes for a contentious mix indeed.[33]

Still, as opposed to just combatting "Westernization," "the cosmopolitan" or "secularism," the forces of fundamentalism also face off against the forces of *fundamentalism*. Faith crosses swords with faith, religion with religion, and the upholders of tradition seem to clash with *different* upholders of the same. In India, e.g., Islamists gained a great deal of attention when they took to the streets after the 2014 election of Narendra Modi, India's Hindu nationalist prime minister – that out of concern with marginalization by the country's Hindu majority (an ongoing theme since the partition of India and Pakistan in 1947).[34] That's while

31 Immanuel Kant, "Idea for a Universal History from a Cosmopolitan Perspective," in *Towards Perpetual Peace and Other Writings on Politics, Peace, and History*, ed. Pauline Kleingeld (New Haven: Yale University Press, 2006), 3–16. Now, Kant didn't argue for people's ability to simply do *anything*. Kant's general maxim involved the categorical imperative, or the demand that one's actions be able to be turned into universalizable law. Still, Kant famously asked the individual to "have the courage to use your own intellect" and posited such freedom of mind as history's teleological end. See Kant, "An Answer to the Question: What is Enlightenment?" in *Towards Perpetual Peace*, 17.

32 Michael J. Mazarr, *Unmodern Men in the Modern World: Radical Islam, Terrorism, and the War on Modernity* (Cambridge: Cambridge University Press, 2007).

33 By the notion of "values relevant for all," I simply point to the supposed universal applicability of rights ideas – that they're at least theoretically *not* about one's connection to a religious, cultural or social tradition. See, e.g., Johannes Morsink, *Inherent Human Rights: Philosophical Foundations of the Universal Declaration* (Philadelphia: University of Pennsylvania Press, 2009).

34 See Ashutosh Varshney, *Ethnic Conflict and Civic Life: Hindus and Muslims in India* (New Haven: Yale University Press, 2003); Nisid Hajari, *Midnight's Furies: The Deadly Legacy of India's Partition* (Boston: Houghton Mifflin, 2015).

Hindu aggression towards Muslims is a well-documented theme: massacres in 1964 in Kolkata, 1992 in Mumbai and 2002 in Gujarat State – the latter being an event with whose incitement Modi himself has been charged.[35] The perception of *Modi's* involvement in events in Gujarat, however, may have led *Muslim* resistance to take a yet more serious tone; *The Guardian*, e.g., reports that the backlash against India's Hindu nationalist swing has included even a bombing attempt against Mr. Modi himself – a serious charge indeed.[36] That comes against the backdrop of yet *further* problems, such as the states of Orissa, Madhya Pradesh, Chhattisgarh, Gujarat and Himachal Pradesh virtually outlawing religious conversion – a move almost all take as an attempt to indicate that India *is* in fact Hindu, and that debates over the nation's cultural nature should end.[37] That's while *Deutsche Welle* reports 1500 dead in Sunni-Shi'a violence in Pakistan since 2007 (an under-reported trend), and Bangladesh has seen more than one scene like that in 2012, when a mob of three thousand strong attacked the home of a Hindu resident in the southwest corner of the state. Again, intercultural and faith on faith violence isn't new to the region. They've been features of the area since independence, if not before. Still, a revitalized intensity to such violence is a worrying trend indeed.[38]

To me, this says two things. First, events on the Indian "sub-content" ask us to both widen and narrow our sense of international conflict. Especially if one sits in the middle of Western media and information streams, as do I, standards of normality can so often be dominated by those parts of the world commanding

---

35 See Parvis Ghassem-Fachandi, *Pogrom in Gujarat: Hindu Nationalism and Anti-Muslim Violence in India* (Princeton: Princeton University Press, 2012); Jason Burke, "Islamic Militants Incite anti-India Attacks after Narendra Modi's Victory," *The Guardian*, May 20, 2014, available http://www.theguardian.com/world/2014/may/20/islamic-militants-anti-india-attacks-narendra-modi; Ashutosh Varshney, *Ethnic Conflict and Civic Life: Hindus and Muslims in India* (New Haven: Yale University Press, 2003).

36 See again Burke, "Islamic Militants."

37 See Saurav Datta, "India's Mass Conversion Problem," *Al-Jazeera*, January 4, 2015, available at http://www.aljazeera.com/indepth/opinion/2015/01/india-mass-conversion-problem-20151274531627294.html.

38 Deutsche Welle, "Examining Pakistan's Growing Sectarian Violence," February 18, 2015, available at http://www.dw.com/en/examining-pakistans-growing-sectarian-violence/a-18265815; Saif Khalid, "Bangladesh Minorities Bear Brunt of Violence," *Al-Jazeera*, March 24, 2013, available at http://www.aljazeera.com/indepth/features/2013/03/201332472510585942.html; See Saurav Datta, "India's Mass Conversion Problem," *Al-Jazeera*, January 4, 2015, available at http://www.aljazeera.com/indepth/opinion/2015/01/india-mass-conversion-problem-20151274531627294.html.

the larger part of global political and economic power that it's not always easy to see that conflict isn't only between the "West" and the "rest," or "Jihad" versus "McWorld," but that there's a richer texture at play. Now, I wouldn't for a moment say that events like those surrounding *Charlie Hebdo*, the bombings in Brussels, London or Madrid, the fall of the Twin Towers in New York or recent events such as those at the Bataclan and Stade de France aren't of the highest global importance. They are. They illustrate faultlines that will produce continuing violence unless we provide them with fundamental redress. Still, more *is* happening out there. *Foreign Policy* magazine, e.g., recently listed its ten conflicts to keep an eye for 2016-7. Many were connected to "jihad versus McWorld" – Syria, Yemen, fighting in Iraq and continuing issues in Afghanistan (places where there *are* intense face-offs between fundamentalist groups and at least *partly* Western-based and -backed powers and forces).[39] Others, however, were in a slightly different orbit. Conflicts in Burundi and South Sudan, e.g., have dynamics concerning those states in and of *themselves*. They're at least *partly* organized around regional and national issues and *not* necessarily invasive powers attempting to impose some variety of external "will."[40] Meta-trends are clearly present – sectarianism perhaps chief among them.[41] Still, it's the *multitude* of sectarianisms at work that impresses; it's the *multiplicity* of identities attempting to reformulate, undermine and sometimes legitimize the form and function of states.[42] Of course, that's without pointing to the fact that the faultlines in what's supposed to be the contemporary world's preeminent conflict, Syria, are *also* complex, and that one can't understand *that* country's civil war (nor conflicts in Yemen, Afghanistan and Iraq) unless local issues, national factors and regional variables are taken into account.[43] The world of international strife is *not* just "Islamic State versus the U.S." It's *more* than just the legacies of al-Qaeda playing out in

---

39 See, e.g., Anne Aldis and Graeme Herd, eds., *The Ideological War on Terror: Worldwide Strategies for Counter-Terrorism* (London: Routledge, 2007). This is not to say that "West-non-West" or "Islam versus the West" issues are the only factors at play in these conflicts – they're not. It is to say that ideologically on both sides, elements of such issues *have* play in the conflicts in question (again, Iraq, Syria and Afghanistan – all of which have genealogical connections to 9/11).

40 Jean-Marei Guéhenno, "10 Conflicts to Watch in 2016," January 3, 2016, available at http://foreignpolicy.com/2016/01/03/10-conflicts-to-watch-in-2016/.

41 E.g., Frederic M. Wehrey, *Sectarian Politics in the Gulf: From the Iraq War to the Arab Uprisings* (New York: Columbia University Press, 2014).

42 See Guéhenno, "10 Conflicts."

43 Ibid. See also Reese Erlich, *Inside Syria: The Backstory of Their Civil War and What the World Can Expect* (Amherst: Prometheus, 2014).

ways we perhaps should have, but didn't, predict. It's a *panoply* of forces with asymmetrical lines and shifting natures about which we might need to make ourselves aware.

Still, what's happening "out there" is also happening "*in* there." I.e., it's not just the breadth of the *types* of conflict of which we need to be aware; it's also the specific *questions* conflicts raise concerning narratives sometimes demanding specialized knowledges to even *begin* to comprehend – senses of particularity we need to maintain to ask questions based in cultural specificity *at all*. For outsiders – one of which I am – "sub-continental" conflict present a dizzying maze. With the election of Modi, e.g., have Hindus taken an irrevocably fundamentalist turn? With their electoral successes, have Hindu nationalists opened levels of culturo-political intransigence from which it might be hard, if not impossible, to retreat?[44] Perhaps. However, maybe *Muslims* have upped the ante. Perhaps in reacting so vociferously to *Modi's* nationalism, *they've* established patterns of resistance from which might be difficult to pull back.[45] Indeed, how does one deal with *other* regional identities, from Buddhists to Sikhs to Christians to Jains? Can *they* feel safe in the crosshairs of local anger and culturally-based assertions of belief? What happens when we *do* add secularism to the mix – the kind of religion- and culture-blind ideals advocated by figures like Roy and Samad; ideas based on *internationalist* readings of basic rights and civil law? It's an intense politico-cultural cocktail playing out on the Indian "sub-continent" – one that asks us to delve into the nitty-gritty of societies' disjunctural splits and discover the role of, yes, the world's dominant powers, yet also senses of the self wending their *own* way through modernity and existing in proximity to identities that may or may not have anything to do with what one or the other European or North American state may have done.

Now, again, the dominance of reading world history exclusively through Western optics can lead to a hazy ignorance of world affairs. Western- and Eurocentric sensibilities can dismantle sensitivities helping us to encounter events

---

44 For an excellent discussion of this issue, see Mandikini Garlot (director), *Hindu Fundamentalists* (Qatar: Al-Jazeera, 2010). See also Sunny Hundal, "Hindu Nationalists are Gaining Power in India – And Silencing Opponents along the Way," *The Independent*, February 26, 2014, available at http://www.independent.co.uk/news/world/asia/hindu-nationalists-are-gaining-power-in-india-and-silencing-enemies-along-the-way-9155591.html.

45 See Dingwaney Needham and Rajeswari Sunder Rajan, eds., *The Crisis of Secularism in India* (Durham, NC: Duke University Press, 2007).

in their particularity – on the more micro level at which history plays out.[46] Comprehending situatedness not only in terms of the roles *we* play in world events but the places from which we *view* those events challenges us to look beyond headlines in search of issues that some of us might nominally ignore. Breaking through such barriers is a rote obligation; a potential baseline for global citizenship, as such. Still, such investigations need to be connected to *doing* something about the issues we find. Gaining finer senses of international and intercultural conflict must be connected to *action* concerning issues like the murders of Roy and Samad; they need to be joined to *opinions* about controversies like *ghar wapsi* and calls to *prevent* attacks like those on Rehman or Yousafzai. Free speech advocates should *not* be killed with impunity; blogging *shouldn't* be a death wish. Advocating basic rights should *not* mean taking one's life into one's hands, and global citizenries should pose *questions* about the state sanction of religion, noting that religious minorities shouldn't feel threatened for the act of being who they are. Looking more closely at global affairs means gaining perspective, yes. It means moving beyond certain presumptions. It doesn't, however, mean forgetting to ensure that violences aren't repeated and that we attempt to minimize the locales to which violence might spread. We have to find global standards we might invoke to establish at least *minimal* levels of coexistence. We need ideals suggesting that people have the right to occupy the identities they want. We have to look for norms proposing that *no* one's dignity be denied and that *all* should feel welcome to participate in civic and public life.[47]

Of course, we *know* the standards of which I speak. We're aware such standards exist. Those are the standards of international human rights. They're the standards to which nearly all the world's states sign up when they join the UN – standards proposing that *all* societies should be inclusive and that no government or social body should leave people out. They're the standards encouraging cultural acceptance and paths towards broad-based senses of social membership.[48] Now,

---

46 See William A. Green, "Periodization in European and World History," *Journal of World History* 3, no. 1 (1992): 13–53.

47 "Tolerance," Kofi Annan once argued, along with the ability to participate in political and social systems, is the gold standard of rights. See Annan, "Message by the United Nations Secretary-General," in *Reflections on the Universal Declaration of Human Rights: A Fiftieth Anniversary Anthology*, ed. Barend van der Heijden and Bahia Tahzib-Lie (The Hague: Martinus Nijhoff, 1998), 18.

48 Signing onto the UN means signing onto the UN Charter – a document affirming "faith in fundamental human rights [and] in the dignity and worth of the human person." This opens member states to further dimensions of the UN human rights regime. See

I don't insist on secularity as opposed to religiosity as a necessary norm. I don't want to boot out tradition and say that neither culture nor heritage have a place. Be it "ancient" or "modern," *all* deserve to be who they are. *No one* deserves to experience intimidation of any kind, and all should be encouraged to embrace the personalities they have.[49] Still, identities should *coexist*. One worldview shouldn't be prioritized over others. It's important to insist on *alleviating* discrimination and preventing violences which are clearly taking place. Of course, in societies as massive as those on the Indian sub-continent – a part of the world encompassing nearly one in five people on earth – that may not be easy. One *is* dealing with intensely large political structures, enormous bureaucracies and histories whose complexity extends well-beyond anything presented here. At issue *are* ancient cultures with pasts totally of their own. Still, for those of us trying to acquaint ourselves with the region's dynamics as well as those already in the know, efforts at both knowledge-dissemination and activism appear necessary. That's to the extent that, if one includes Nepal, Bhutan, Sri Lanka and the Maldives, the so-called Indian "sub-continent" in fact totals *23%* of the world's population: 4% more than China and 8% more than the combined populations of the North America and Europe. That's a situation in which the "sub-content" isn't "sub-" *anything*. It's rather a focal point that demands the attention and engagement of global society as a whole.

United Nations, "Charter of the United Nations" (1945, preamble), available at http://www.un.org/en/sections/un-charter/preamble/index.html. See also Manfred Nowak, *Introduction to the International Human Rights Regime* (Leiden: Brill, 2003).

49 See, e.g., Donald Clark and Robert Williamson, eds., *Self-Determination: International Perspectives* (New York: Macmillan, 1996).

Grappling with the Phenomenon
Donald Trump and Human Rights
(May 4, 2016)

Abstract: *Donald Trump is now the presidential nominee of one of America's two major political parties. If one is concerned about international human rights, that's a dangerous situation indeed.*

It happened last night. The Indiana primary was held and, despite the fact that Ted Cruz and John Kasich, Donald Trump's primary challengers in the contest for the Republican nomination, made a vague deal to "get out of each other's ways" in selected states in order to, if not to win themselves, then at least block the path for Trump, the strategy went nowhere. Indiana was Cruz's Alamo – a last stand he absolutely had to win (Cruz at least had a chance; Kasich did not) – and he didn't. Cruz was in fact crushed: 53-36%. It was the last barrier to preventing one of the most controversial presidential candidates in modern times –

"Presidential Election USA 11-08-16 – Ticket." © sulupress / Fotolia. com 124348789

the most controversial, in my estimation – from winning the nomination of one of America's two major political parties. That's the party of Abraham Lincoln, no less.

Of course, there's much one can say about Donald Trump. That's as both a candidate and a man. The first is that it's hard to tell if he's at all a serious politician, or if for him, the election registers as a kind of vague reality show. Indeed, with Trump, it's hard to know in *any* context exactly *where* to begin. Emerging on the New York real estate scene in the 1980s, Trump, among other things, built one of mid-town Manhattan's architectural fixtures: Trump Towers – the rather gaudy, golden-faced structure on New York's Fifth Avenue that's become something of a mid-range tourist attraction. Along with investments in places like Atlantic City – Trump took over the New Jersey gambling mecca's version of the Taj Mahal in the 1980s – the mogul became a playboy fixture on the Big Apple's social scene, often appearing as something of a gossip-page *bon vivant*. Trump's "brand," as it's sometimes put, was simply him; what he "did," be that "doing" erecting "facilities," running beauty pageants, insinuating affairs or finding new models or celebrities to pursue. Raking in money through his real estate investments, Trump gained a pop-culture reputation as the master of the "deal" – the latter word featuring centrally in the title of his 1987 bestselling book.[1] Now, as a number of commentators have noted, Trump has hardly always been a constant and unmitigated success. While he's made his pile, Trump, or at least his businesses, spent a large part of the end of the 1980s and early '90s hundreds of millions of dollars in debt; he played extensively with bankruptcy rules to keep himself at the center of the big-time real estate game. Trump's also had to close two *massively* expensive properties: Atlantic City's Trump Plaza and the Trump Taj Mahal – that relatively recently, in fact.[2] Indeed, it's also interesting that Trump was once a sports club owner. In 1983, he bought the New Jersey Generals – one of the premier clubs in what at the time was an upstart football league (the USFL). A massive venture – so it always is with American sports – Trump pushed for the league to ditch its approach of playing games in the spring (American football is traditionally an autumn and winter sport) and looked for the league to compete directly with the NFL – the latter being one of the most lucrative sports leagues in the world. It was a disaster. By 1985, the USFL had closed, and thousands of jobs were lost as league teams folded. It registers as a bizarre chapter tucked in an out-of-the-way corner within the larger Trump mystique.[3] Again, Trump has clearly bathed himself in the kind of wealth about which most of us can only dream. A constant and only howling success, however, he has not exclusively been.

In any case, the financial problems in the late '80s and early '90s knocked Trump, at least for a while, off the celebrity map. He was around. For a decade or so, however, Trump wasn't *quite* at the center of the maw of American celebrity goings-on. That changed, however, come the new century as, mounting something of a comeback, "The Donald" traded on his "mogul" mystique to gain the lead in *The Apprentice* – a reality show airing from 2004 to 2015. It was schlock: voyeurism in the vein of *Survivor* or *Big Brother*, only with business as the theme. Trump's outsized personality nonetheless somehow made it work. *The Apprentice*

---

1   Donald J. Trump and Tony Schwartz, *The Art of the Deal* (New York: Ballantine, 1987).
2   See, e.g., Roger Yu, "Trump Taj Mahal Closes after Years of Losses," *USA Today*, October 10, 2016, available at http://www.usatoday.com/story/money/2016/10/10/trump-taj-mahal-closes-after-years-losses/91845566/.
3   See Drew Jubera, "How Donald Trump Destroyed a Football League," *Esquire*, January 13, 2016, available at http://www.esquire.com/news-politics/a41135/donald-trump-usfl/.

was never the most-watched program on American TV. Still, it was for some years solidly ranked. Trump was well-paid to be the program's host.[4]

Indeed, it's precisely that sort of mishmash – the persona, the Hollywood spotlight, the media cult – that makes it difficult, indeed, *very* difficult, to say precisely *what* Trump's Presidential campaign is about. Over the course of his adult life, it appears Trump has switched parties a number of times, and the crux of his appeal seems to come largely from attitude: the idea that Trump speaks without a script, is a Washington "outsider" and without premeditation, simply says what he "thinks." Now, the latter may or may not be true. There's a debate over whether Trump says what he "thinks" or, if in reality, he but megaphones what he imagines at least a certain sector of people want to hear (how many want to hear it is difficult to say).[5] Still, that Trump talks about events not as a "wonk," but in a manner resembling the "average Joe," is an important – highly important – dimension of his style. It's been effective. We can note that Trump has *not* won the Republican nomination because of the party elite; he's had little support from the Republican Party establishment, and many fixtures from the Reagan and various Bush administrations have shown Trump serious distaste.[6] No; Trump's gained the nomination because voters – regular folks – put him in a position to win. That's while it's fair to recognize that few of us have the resources to privately fund campaigns and that, contrary to most, Trump's existence has been lived largely through a celebrity status that *has* allowed him to hobnob with the rich and powerful and keep himself strategically in the public eye. "Average

---

4   See Dylan Byers, "Trump Claims \$213M Payout for 'Apprentice,'" *Politico*, July 15, 2015, available at http://www.politico.com/blogs/media/2015/07/trump-claims-213m-payout-for-apprentice-210595.

5   Peggy Drexler, "What Does Donald Trump Really Think?" *CNN*, April 1, 2016, available at http://edition.cnn.com/2016/04/01/opinions/trump-changing-views-drexler/; NPR, "Show's Over? Trump Pledges to Be 'So Presidential You Will Be So Bored,'" April 21, 2016, available at http://www.npr.org/2016/04/21/475126907/shows-over-trump-pledges-to-be-so-presidential-you-will-be-so-bored; Kate Linthicum, "Donald Trump and His Supporters Wonder How Much Being 'Presidential' Matters," *Los Angeles Times*, May 4, 2016, available at http://www.latimes.com/nation/la-na-donald-trump-presidential-20160428-snap-story.html; Jeremy Diamond, "Who Is Donald Trump?" *CNN*, February 29, 2016, available at http://edition.cnn.com/2016/02/10/politics/who-is-donald-trump/.

6   See, e.g., Erik Sherman, "These 9 Republicans Say They Won't Vote for Donald Trump, Even Against Clinton," *Fortune*, March 1, 2016, available at http://fortune.com/2016/03/01/republicans-oppose-trump/.

Joes" might identify with Trump. Any claim that he is one himself, however, would be more than a stretch.[7]

In any case, throughout the campaign, Trump has said some controversial, if not frightening, things. Indeed, it should be noted that Trump's initial foray into the political arena came through questioning the first Black President's citizenship – a move that was shocking in and of itself.[8] Recently, however, Trump has accused his upcoming general election opponent, Hillary Clinton, of playing what he's called the "woman card." I.e., Clinton sometimes makes reference to the fact that were she elected, she'd be the first female President – an indubitable fact given that all forty-four presidents *have been* men (including the sixteen since American women first gained the vote in 1920).[9] Now, I find the "woman card" idea mystifying. While there's no doubt that there are gains to be made on gender equality fronts, in this day and age, it's hardly *non*-standard fare to talk about some modicum of equality between the sexes as a socio-political goal. Outside a limited number of subcultures, it seems that Phyllis Schlafly-like ideas that it's somehow natural for women to "stay in the kitchen" represents the view of increasingly few. Now, I totally agree: the United States Congress never passed the Equal Rights Amendment – a move that would more clearly have marked the U.S. as supportive of women's rights.[10] Still, it seems that more than a few Americans think it not *irr*elevant to put women's issues on the table as, look at the table, and you'll see it littered with the cards of men. Trump's come close to dismissing the whole project by apparently not understanding that women's identities aren't "cards." Again, especially as conservative politicians *also* sometimes speak the vocabulary of women's empowerment – an example would be earlier Trump

---

7   Connor Friedersdorf, "When Donald Trump Became a Celebrity," *The Atlantic*, January 6, 2016, available at http://www.theatlantic.com/politics/archive/2016/01/the-decade-when-donald-trump-became-a-celebrity/422838/.

8   See Meghan Keneally, "Trumps History of Raising Birther Questions about President Obama," *ABC News*, September 18, 2015, available at http://abcnews.go.com/Politics/donald-trumps-history-raising-birther-questions-president-obama/story?id=33861832.

9   For sticklers about such details, I refer here to the Nineteenth Amendment of the American constitution. Individual states allowed women's franchise previous to that. See Eleanor Flexner and Ellen Frances Fitzpatrick, *Century of Struggle: The Woman's Rights Movement in the United States* (Cambridge, MA: Harvard Belknap, 1996).

10 See Mary Francis Berry, *Why ERA Failed: Politics, Women's Rights, and the Amending Process of the Constitution* (Bloomington: Indiana University Press, 1988).

primary opponent, Carly Fiorina – I'm surprised that Trump's invocation of this line attack didn't do more damage. It didn't, however, as, again, here we are.[11]

Indeed, staying on the gender theme, Trump has *also* suggested that there should be punishment for women who decide to have an abortion. That's to say that there should be penalties – *penalties* (what would they be?) – for terminating a pregnancy. Now, in today's parlance, that's a statement Trump later "walked back" ("retracted" is the easier word). Indeed, in the context of his retraction, Trump *also* claimed, and he's right, that the question to which he was responding in which that vocabulary came out – posed by MSNBC journalist and former Carter Administration speechwriter Chris Matthews – was so convoluted that he (Trump) wasn't 100% sure what he was being asked. I've watched the interview, and Trump's got a point: it *was* hard to discern what Matthews had in mind.[12] Still, in an attempt to cozy up to the Republican Party's ultra-conservative base, Trump has posed himself as more Christian fundamentalist/fire-and-brimstone than many suspect he actually is (Trump has defended the right to abortion in the past) and, when conjoined with the "woman card" comment, the whole scenario projects the sense that Trump is simply willing to throw women's autonomy under the bus – that in the name of a political appeal (to the evangelical right, I guess).[13] Yet again, despite a media outcry, the whole affair had zero effect on Trump's electoral results.[14]

Of course, we all know that Trump *began* his campaign with a massive assault on immigrants and the culture of America's neighbor to the south (Mexico – though by association, all of Latin America) – that in addition to, of course, his

---

11 See Amy Chozick and Ashley Parker, "Donald Trump's Gender-Based Attacks on Hillary Clinton Have Calculated Risk," *The New York Times*, April 28, 2016, available at http://www.nytimes.com/2016/04/29/us/politics/hillary-clinton-donald-trump-women.html?_r=0. See also Tessa Berenson, "Here's How Carly Fiorina Wants to Redefine Feminism," *Time*, June 11, 2015, available at http://time.com/3918014/carly-fiorina-feminism/.

12 MSNBC, "FULL TRANSCRIPT: MSNBC Town Hall with Donald Trump Moderated by Chris Matthews," March 30, 2016, available at http://info.msnbc.com/_news/2016/03/30/35330907-full-transcript-msnbc-town-hall-with-donald-trump-moderated-by-chris-matthews?lite.

13 Megan Keneally, "Donald Trump's Evolving Stance on Abortion," *ABC News*, March 31, 2016, available at http://abcnews.go.com/Politics/donald-trumps-evolving-stance-abortion/story?id=38057176.

14 Rebecca Ballhaus and Beth Reinhard, "Donald Trump's Abortion Comments Spark Furor from Both Sides," *The Wall Street Journal*, April 4, 2016, available at http://www.wsj.com/articles/trumps-abortion-comments-spark-furor-from-both-sides-1459371715.

famous "Muslim ban." I.e., Trump's *first* campaign proclamation was that Mexico was "sending" drug dealers and rapists with the intention of loosing mayhem on American streets. In Trump's (verbatim) terms, these were people with "lots of problems." They were "bringing drugs, they [were] bringing crime; they are rapists" – and some, Trump demurred, might be "good people." Trump *then* pointed to the entire world of Islam – roughly one and a half billion people – and proclaimed they weren't welcome in his United States ("I, Donald J. Trump, am calling for a total and complete shutdown of Muslims entering the United States" – that until we can figure out "what's going on" [a vague reference to terror attacks such as those in Paris or San Bernardino]).[15] Again, many recoiled in horror – there was an outcry in the media, immigrant communities and among the many segments of American society valuing diversity and seeking intercultural and multi-faith outreach.[16] Again, though, in what can only be termed a stunning development, the outcry had virtually no effect. It was but the beginning of the march towards what today is a decided Trump win.[17]

For my money, anyway, there are many reasons to worry about a potential Trump presidency. Indeed, that should be said with the caveat that a Trump general election win is an event most consider unlikely. Triumph in presidential contests is based on the votes of the Electoral College (one wins electors by state), and the topography of the elector distribution simply doesn't look good for Donald J. Trump. He'd have to win everything Mitt Romney won in 2012, plus a handful of states more (Romney came up a Florida and a couple of medium-sized Midwestern states short). That may be tough as it's not clear Trump will even get enough *conservative* support to match Romney's totals; a range of moderate Republicans find Trump's statements as offensive as anyone else. Still, when the primary season started, pundits said the same about Trump's chances against his Republican opponents ("no way"). Again, we stand where we do. In a complex world, one has to be awfully careful about what one predicts.[18]

---

15 Time, "Here's Donald Trump's Presidential Announcement Speech," June 16, 2015, available at http://time.com/3923128/donald-trump-announcement-speech/.

16 See, e.g., Rebecca Kaplan, "Reactions to Donald Trump's Muslim Ban Range from 'Disqualified' to 'Nazi,'" *ABC News*, December 8, 2015, available at http://www.cbsnews.com/media/no-love-for-donald-trump-after-proposed-muslim-ban/.

17 Molly Ball, "Why Donald Trump, Though?" *The Atlantic*, March 25, 2016, available at http://www.theatlantic.com/politics/archive/2016/03/why-donald-trump/475386/.

18 E.g., Peter Fenn, "No Filter and No Chance," *US News & World Report*, July 20, 2015, available at http://www.usnews.com/opinion/blogs/peter-fenn/2015/07/20/donald-trump-has-no-filter-and-no-chance-in-2016.

In any case, one reason to worry about a Trump presidency is the politics of emotion over reason. I.e., the entire basis for Trump's success – at least a significant part of it – appears to be a particular emotive appeal. Trump plays heavily to the idea that there's a culture war underway, that, in the context of that culture war, many feel condescended to, and that those who *feel* condescended to (whether the condescension is real or not) have been looking for an opportunity – one Trump provides – to publicly say what's on their minds. Trump plays to an environment in which "average Joes" want to tell the eggheads where to stick it, expressing their discontent with how things "work." Now, such sentiment isn't wrong. Large countries can generate extensive bureaucracies which can in turn can create senses of significant distance on the part of a country's citizens from their politicians and decision-making bodies. Alienation from the halls of power *is* a comprehensible idea, again especially in a nation numbering over 300 million (nearly four times the size of the largest state in Europe, for example).[19] It's moreover the case that, for all the notions that modern democracies maintain about civic education and enlightened citizenries, "enlightenment" may not be the *only* thing that democracy is about. At root, democracies concern the *demos*, and that's the *demos*, or the people, as they are. One doesn't get to idealize people into forms one wishes they had (i.e., if the people want to tell the eggheads to "stick it," "sticking it" is what the eggheads may well have to do).[20] Still, when one *is* a major party candidate in the most powerful country on earth, one *might* ask whether one *totally* dismisses the idea of at *some* point explaining, or providing the rationale for, the general approach or philosophy behind one's political beliefs. I.e., the people one *represents* might be interested in participating in some level of public unpacking of what are supposed to be their ideas, and, anti "egghead" or not, they might be curious, beyond sloganeering, how one unpacks those ideas *oneself*. I know: Trump is playing the release valve for a massive, screaming id. He's channeling what many claim are high levels of frustration. Still, if one *really* values the "common man" or "common woman," one *might* see him or her as worthy of having a *discussion* with as opposed to standing as but an opportunity to capture emotions with little or no explication

---

19 See Kevin D. Williamson, "Chaos in the Family, Chaos in the State: The White Working Class's Dysfunction," *National Review*, March 17, 2016, available at http://www. nationalreview.com/article/432876/donald-trump-white-working-class-dysfunction-real-opportunity-needed-not-trump.

20 This was the basis for Plato's critique of democracy, e.g.: that it wasn't clear if the people would always take societies to the most well-considered place. See Plato, *The Republic*, ed. Robin Waterfield (Oxford: Oxford University Press, 2008), 70–114.

of what they're about. Beyond a sort of anger, I have yet to hear precisely what the Trump "philosophy" in fact is.[21]

Another point concerning Trump, however, is what the popular voice he claims to speak for in fact *says*. I.e., while there's no doubt that democracy involves accepting people as they are as opposed to how they "should be," one might also ask if it's ok to channel certain ideas into the world around one, and whether one might consider if one is helping to sustain ideas that may be damaging to civic life and democracy at-large. Now, certain of the numbers regarding Trump supporters *can* be startling. 31% of those who voted for Trump in South Carolina, e.g., think that Whites, as opposed to Blacks, are the demonstrably superior race. *Superior race* – as in African-American society is somehow genetically defect. 20% of Trump's South Carolina voters disagreed – as if it's a matter of opinion – with Abraham Lincoln's 1863 Emancipation Proclamation: the Civil War declaration freeing the American slaves.[22] True: South Carolina isn't every state. The Gallup polling organization ranks it as one of the U.S.' most conservative.[23] Still, regardless of how much of a popularity contest politics might be, one *could* suggest that in addition to a conversation with voters who deserve a chance to hear deeper iterations of the ideas one claims to represent, it's *also* incumbent on candidates to reflect on whether their invectives release varieties of racism and bigotry into the society as a whole. Clearly, Trump can't control who supports him. That doesn't stop *us* from noticing, however, that some of the opinions of his supporters are troublesome indeed.[24]

Then there's the manner in which Trump ducks talking about such issues. I.e., over and above the question of whether Trump bears *any* responsibility for the jingoistic atmosphere that seems to follow his campaign, there's the intense level of bobbing and weaving in which he engages when someone *does* ask him about the type of support he sometimes gains. An example of this is the case of

---

21 See, e.g., James Bohman and William Rehg, eds., *Deliberative Democracy: Essays in Reason and Politics* (Cambridge, MA: MIT Press, 1997).

22 Lynn Vavreck, "Measuring Donald Trump's Supporters for Intolerance," *The New York Times*, February 23, 2016, available at http://www.nytimes.com/2016/02/25/upshot/measuring-donald-trumps-supporters-for-intolerance.html?_r=0.

23 Frank Newport, "Mississippi, Alabama and Louisiana Most Conservative States," *Gallup*, February 6, 2015, available at http://www.gallup.com/poll/181505/mississippi-alabama-louisiana-conservative-states.aspx.

24 See, e.g., Daniel W. Drenzer, "The Ethic of Advising Donald Trump," *The Washington Post*, February 10, 2016, available at https://www.washingtonpost.com/posteverything/wp/2016/02/10/the-ethics-of-advising-donald-trump/?utm_term=.d1b880378644.

David Duke – a vocal Trump fan. When asked what he made of support from a former Ku Klux Klan Imperial Wizard (which Duke is), Trump asserted that he didn't know who Duke was. Confronted with the idea that *any* American should know about groups like the Klan (Duke was long among the group's most well-known figures in the '80s), Trump offered a distancing from the KKK so minimal and brief that hardly anyone took it as such (he offered a quick statement to a reporter while appearing exasperated that he even had to address the question).[25] *That* then became twisted into an odd set of claims about the policies of his upcoming opponent. Deploying notions that we need be worried about migrants and terrorists "flooding" into the country, Trump claimed that Clinton wants "totally open borders" – that, somehow, his prospective Democratic opponent wants to let "anyone…in." Now, Clinton hasn't advocated for "totally open borders." Largely, she seeks to keep current screening practices in place – that though she has advocated a path to citizenship for migrants in the country on long-term bases whose status is illegal; a policy supported by the Bush, Jr. administration as well. Indeed, Trump *also* likes to point out that Clinton seeks to increase the number of Syrian refugees the country takes in by 550%. Of course, 550% of anything seems like a lot. What goes *totally* unsaid, however, is that increasing migration from the Syrian conflict to the degree Clinton suggests might mean allowing something in the area of 60,000 Syrian refugees into the country in 2017. Sweden, a country with a population of about 9.5 million (3% of the population of the U.S.), accepted a hair over 64,000 last year.[26] Simply put – and with all acknowledgment that politics is politics – Trump is playing a rhetorical game that bounces between the ridiculous and patently uninformed.

Now, that is what it is. I.e., the points made so far may be damaging: the appeal to raw emotion, the unwillingness to discuss the views of at least *some* of his supporters, the insults and refusal to engage even those *supporting* one's campaign in terms of the larger lines of one's concepts – that to say nothing of the out-of-touch-with-reality senses of what his coming opponent has said. Perhaps the crux of all this, though, is what a Trump presidency might mean for *human rights*. I.e., how does the Trump "milieu," if it might be called that – the entire Trump "presentation" – relate to what are supposed to be humanity's "highest

---

25 See Evan Osnos, "Donald Trump and the Ku Klux Klan: A History," *The New Yorker*, February 29, 2016, available at http://www.newyorker.com/news/news-desk/donald-trump-and-the-ku-klux-klan-a-history.

26 Michael Martinez, "Syrian Refugees: Which Countries Welcome Them, Which Don't," *CNN*, September 10, 2015, available at http://www.cnn.com/2015/09/09/world/welcome-syrian-refugees-countries/.

moral precepts and political ideals"?[27] How does Trump relate to senses of how we *claim*, anyway, that all human beings are supposed to be treated – standards supposedly available to everyone no matter where they live? How does Trump relate to *global* standards of justice – deeper ideas of fairness to which all should be able to appeal? Indeed, one might specifically ask such questions in relation to the "letter of the law" and the general concept, or "spirit," of human rights. I.e., how does Trump relate to what are theoretically the most fundamental terms of human justice in the context of both *specifics* as well as what one might identify as the general *atmosphere* that rights are intended to create?[28]

Regarding point one – the "letter of the law" – the verdict seems mixed. One primary right, for example, is that "everyone has the right to freedom of opinion and expression." As the Universal Declaration of Human Rights (1948) phrases it, all are supposed to be able to hold opinions without "interference."[29] Freedom of conscience should be a universal privilege, and there's supposed to be *some* notion that people should have liberty of speech and intellectual choice. As such, there's no indication Trump is opposed to *this* – a right of which he and his supporters seem to liberally avail. Of course, one *might* like expression to respond to reason or truth. One *might* argue that fact and consideration help provide free expression meaning (are Mexicans *really* "rapists;" does a "550%" increase in immigration from conflict zones have any significance at all?). Still, there's no requirement that's how things be. Freedom of speech is a bedrock liberty whether one's speech is well-considered or not. The right to "take part in the government of [one's] country, directly or through freely chosen representatives," as the Universal Declaration expresses it, is contingent upon the ability to formulate one's own ideas and share them with others. It's not necessarily a matter of whether one's thoughts have been deemed "intelligent" (there are still a large number of Americans, e.g., who wonder at Barak Obama's citizenship; should they *not* be

27 Samuel Moyn, *The Last Utopia: Human Rights in History* (Cambridge, MA: Harvard Belknap, 2010), 1.

28 See, e.g., Kirsten Hastrup, ed., *Human Rights on Common Grounds: The Quest for Universality* (The Hague: Kluwer, 2001).

29 United Nations, "The Universal Declaration of Human Rights" (1948, article 19 [hereafter UDHR]), available at http://www.un.org/en/universal-declaration-human-rights/index.html. See also United Nations, "International Covenant on Civil and Political Rights" (1966, article 1 [hereafter ICCPR]), available at http://www.ohchr.org/en/professionalinterest/pages/ccpr.aspx.

allowed to vote?).[30] Though we may not agree with their statements, Trump and his supporters are at least *utilizing* a form of human right.[31]

Other areas in the Trumpian worldview, however, are decidedly grayer. While it's not an issue I've addressed up to this point, a number of times – the most recent being the March 3 Republican debate – Trump has advocated the use of torture as part of the fight against international terror. Trump would apparently look to inflict pain on captured individuals as part of his approach to international affairs. Because, as he put it, groups like Islamic State are "chopping off the heads of Christians [hyperbole at its best; IS violence targets other Muslims as much if not more])," it's supposedly only fair to bring back waterboarding or methods supposedly "worse" ("tougher" was Trump's exact vocabulary; one can only imagine what medieval practices he had in mind).[32] Here, there's no equivocation. Torture *is* a rights violation. That's not just a matter of the Universal Declaration or more general articulations of rights ideas (the Universal Declaration addresses international law at the level of the broadest of strokes).[33] It's a matter of *specific* rights conventions such as the UN Convention against Torture and Other Cruel, Inhuman or Degrading Treatment or Punishment (1984) – a treaty to which the U.S. is party. According to that agreement, severe "pain or suffering" for the purposes of "obtaining information or a confession" should never be used. The punitive employment of distress is something in which one should not engage. Hurting people for a political purpose falls outside the bounds of the proper conduct of international relations. Those are *concrete* dimensions of global norms. Indeed, because the U.S. signed and ratified the Torture Convention, they're supposed

---

30 UDHR, article 21. Of course, there are libel laws and hate speech crimes. One has to run awfully far afoul of free speech norms to enter into such territories, however. See Eric Barendt, *Freedom of Speech*, 2nd ed. (Oxford: Oxford University Press, 2005).

31 See Ross Barkan, "Donald Trump's Democratic Revolt," *The Observer*, February 29, 2016, available at http://observer.com/2016/02/donald-trumps-democratic-revolt/.

32 Tessa Berenson, "Donald Trump Defends Torture at Republican Debate," *Time*, March 3, 2016, available at http://time.com/4247397/donald-trump-waterboarding-torture/.

33 The Universal Declaration is technically not a legally binding document. It's a statement of principles on which much international law, especially grounded in the UN, is based. Nonetheless, the Universal Declaration stands as the most referred to international rights document – largely because of its elucidation of basic rights principles. Herein, principle and law become linked. See David Weissbrodt and Connie de la Vega, *International Human Rights Law: An Introduction* (Philadelphia: University of Pennsylvania Press, 2007).

to be part of *American* norms as well.[34] In fact, by most politicians *other* than Trump, those are norms that are relatively well-accepted and received.[35]

Now, the torture issue then jives with *other* elements of "Trumpist" foreign policy. I.e., beyond the vague ethnic and religious indictments and the overtures towards torture, specific Trump proposals on international relations have in fact been few and far between. Generally, there's been a lot of "let's bomb the crap out of ISIS" and suggestions that the Mid-East situation would have been better if we'd "taken the oil" (an idea that someone would have to help me understand).[36] On April 27, however, at the Center for National Interest, Trump held what was supposed to be his first in-depth foreign policy speech. At least *some* of the theory we had been lacking for Trump's ideas was supposed to come out. In essence, Trump's speech offered two takeaways. The first was that international relations consists of "deals" – that there are apparently overarching agreements outlining countries' relations with the U.S. (certainly, countries make deals – treaties, agreements and the like; that's about specific issues, however – *not* comprehensive listings of two nations' business). Point two was that, in terms of *evaluating* "deals," the baseline would be "America First": national interest above everything else. Never mind that there might be places desperate for American help. Never mind that stability elsewhere in the world could be *good* for the United States. Never mind humanitarian principle or philosophical commitments to the good. The point wasn't philosophy or the long game. It was an *immediate* sense of whether, out of a base calculus of the now, situations felt like they benefitted American interest – that, in Trump's vocabulary, "forthwith."[37]

---

34 See United Nations, "Convention against Torture and Other Cruel, Inhuman or Degrading Treatment or Punishment" (1984, part I, article 1), available at http://www.ohchr.org/EN/ProfessionalInterest/Pages/CAT.aspx.

35 See Tessa Berenson, "Donald Trump Defends Torture at Republican Debate," *Time*, March 4, 2016, available at http://time.com/4247397/donald-trump-waterboarding-torture/. Of course, in the wake of the Bush years, it took some debate for the American political establishment to be clear that it's waterboarding and rendition practices didn't represent the better side of American foreign policy. There's very few left, however – none that I'm aware of – who would continue to advocate such practices.

36 See Jim Geraghty, "Donald Trump's Odd Fixation with Seizing Middle Eastern Oil Fields," *National Review*, July 30, 2015, available at http://www.nationalreview.com/article/421825/donald-trumps-odd-fixation-seizing-middle-eastern-oil-fields-jim-geraghty.

37 See Ryan Teague Beckwith, "Read Donald Trump's 'America First' Foreign Policy Speech," *Time*, April 27, 2016, available at http://time.com/4309786/read-donald-trumps-america-first-foreign-policy-speech/.

Now, aside from the "deals" concept (again, there's no file cabinet with the "Mexican Deal," the "Chinese Deal," the "Russian Deal," etc.) – national sovereignty *is* complex. Two of the most significant international rights covenants, e.g. – the International Covenant on Civil and Political Rights (1966) and the International Covenant on Economic, Social and Cultural Rights (1966) – note that "all peoples have the right to self-determination." They assert that peoples' "political status[es]" lie directly in their hands.[38] It's not fully clear at what point the international community has the concrete authority to point to particular states and insist they do *anything* – from enacting specific social policies to participating in foreign aid programs to assisting in the solution of international crises to contributing to development projects in countries that need them. One can *criticize* nations. The *behavior* of other states can nonetheless be tough to compel.[39]

Still, human rights involve *some* principles. Human rights have *some* standards to which they expect we be held. "Everyone is entitled to a social and international order in which [their] rights and freedoms" can be realized, rights documents assert. "Freedom, justice and peace in the world" *should* be the goals of the international community. Though concepts of self-determination need be heeded, any self-determination has to be accomplished in view of basic social, civil and political rights.[40] Yes, respecting the rights of other national communities might sometimes involve leaving them alone. One has to be careful with the politics of rights intervention, e.g.[41] Still, rights ask us to reflect on whether what's good for the world is *only* "us" and "ours." They ask if we can find *broader* visions of community – visions in which what's "ours" is taken as part of a larger whole (the "ours" of everyone). Indeed, rights ask us to remember that principle is not to be automatically sacrificed on the altar of security, "peoples" or "nations." As he's laid it out so far, such concepts don't seem to be much on the mind of candidate Trump. Trump seems rather more interested in droning chants of "USA, USA," or developing mass catcalls at rallies that the U.S. will build a wall

---

38 ICCPR, article 1; United Nations, "International Covenant on Economic, Social and Cultural Rights" (1966, article 1), available at http://www.ohchr.org/EN/ProfessionalInterest/Pages/CESCR.aspx.

39 See Erika De Wet, Jure Vidmar, eds., *Hierarchy in International Law: The Place of Human Rights* (Oxford: Oxford University Press, 2012).

40 UDHR, preamble, article 29.

41 See Julie Mertus, *Bait and Switch: Human Rights and U.S. Foreign Policy* (London: Routledge, 2004); Aleksandar Jokic, *Humanitarian Intervention: Moral and Philosophical Issues* (Peterborough: Broadview, 2003).

along the Mexican border, and that the Mexican government will somehow "pay for it" – whatever, precisely, that means.[42]

Such issues, however, are really modes of addressing the *general* attitude that rights suggest – the "spirit" of justice that rights law should promote and the atmospheres rights might create. I.e., in addition to *specific* points like prohibiting torture and allowing free speech, how *does* Trump relate to the "gut" level of international justice – how does he relate to the *intuitive* connections we might have with fundamental rights? Again, rights are specific. Rights note liberal expression and political participation as points with which we need to be concerned. Rights point on *detailed* levels to the need to handle international conflict justly and avoid cruelty towards the actors involved.[43] Still, rights ask for *bonhomie*. Rights speak of "brotherhood" – the idea that human behavior should be governed by "conscience and reason."[44] Rights address "dignity," and request that, at some level, humanity concern itself with defending the unique yet universal spirit marking all human beings as who and what they are. Rights ask us to be sympathetic with and compassionate towards our fellow men and women.[45]

It's simply hard to reconcile such concepts with the attitudes Trump promotes. Whether it's he or his supporters, pointing fingers at entire religious groups – groups *already* part of the national polity (there's between 2 and 3 million Muslims in the U.S.) – or indicting ethnic communities that are among a nation's largest (Hispanics [roughly 16% of the U.S. population]), is about as far as one can get from the "brotherhood" human rights seek to achieve. The derisive and exclusionary vocabularies aimed at minorities is the *opposite* of treating people "without distinction of any kind," as rights ask that we do.[46] The Trumpist approach seems to involve knee-jerk reactions in which it's hard to see where "conscience and reason" enter the picture at all. As far as I can tell, discussions of Mexican "rapists" and the indictment of an entire religion has nothing to do with *bonhomie*

---

42 See Tim Haines, "Crowd in Michigan Erupts into 'Build the Wall!' Chant When Donald Trump Brings Up Trade, Auto Industry," *Real Clear Politics*, March 4, 2016, available at http://www.realclearpolitics.com/video/2016/03/04/donald_trump_crowd_in_michigan_chants_build_the_wall_build_the_wall.html.

43 See Amos Nascimento and Matthias Lutz-Bachmann, eds., *Human Rights, Human Dignity, and Cosmopolitan Ideals: Essays on Critical and Human Rights* (Farnham: Ashgate, 2014).

44 UDHR, preamble, article 1.

45 Ibid. See also Peter Baehr, *Human Rights: Universality in Practice* (New York: Palgrave, 2002).

46 UDHR, article 2.

or "dignity;" it has little to do with respect for the human spirit. Yes, one can talk about international or American law via specifics; one can invoke paragraphs and clauses in rights conventions and documents. In terms of the deepest, most *baseline* senses of human privilege, however – the *most* fundamental principles that should extend to every person – one wonders if we're on a conceptual territory of which Donald Trump is even aware. Of course, that's above and beyond questions of whether it's a territory Trump maintains an interest to *defend*.

Now, no doubt: Trump isn't the only politician to invoke hyper-nationalistic sentiment or engage in rightist controversialism. Italy's Silvio Berlusconi had his moments with such things, and many among Europe's far-right parties – from the French *Front National* to the Danish People's Party to Germany's *Alternative für Deutschland* – have gone some distance towards stirring up anger towards people it appears they don't like. The father of the *Front National*, Jean-Marie Le Pen, e.g., has not only decried Europe's "Islamicization" (whatever that means) but was fined multiple times for diminishing the importance of the Holocaust – about as low as one can go in terms of hurtful statements in the context of cultural life on either European or global scales. The Danish People's Party features vocabulary on its website suggesting that "72 million Turks are awaiting free entry into Europe" – an idea designed to strike fear of the non-European Other into the heart of every Dane. *Alternative für Deutschland's* Frauke Petry recently made headlines by proclaiming that Germany's border patrol should fire on migrants entering the country without legal papers: a Wild West approach to border control in supposedly rational Central Europe.[47] Casting blame on outsiders and suggesting drastic measures to keep foreigners away has been long a part of modern politics. That's even in states with democratic cultures and governed by the rule of law.[48]

Still, that's no excuse. Donald Trump is attempting to win the Presidency of the United States: the single most powerful office in the world. He's attempting to lead a country which *should* be a global example of democratic practice and

---

47 See Angelique Chrisafis, "Jean-Marie Le Pen Fined Again for Dismissing the Holocaust as 'Detail,'" *The Guardian*, April 6, 2016, available at http://www.theguardian. com/world/2016/apr/06/jean-marie-le-pen-fined-again-dismissing-holocaust-detail; Dansk Folkeparti, "EU-Politik," available at http://www.danskfolkeparti. dk/M%C3%A6rkesag-EU; Tony Paterson, "Alternative for Germany: Party Behind Germany's 'Shoot at Migrants' Politician is Attracting Unprecedented Support," *The Independent*, February 1, 2016, available at http://www.independent.co.uk/news/world/ europe/frauke-petry-and-alternative-for-germany-party-behind-germanys-shoot-at-migrants-politician-is-a6845861.html.

48 See Lynn Hunt, *Inventing Human Rights: A History* (New York: W.W. Norton, 2007).

which should point societies towards more *liberal* futures – not exclusionary, divisive ones. There are deep uglinesses in the American past; segregation, slavery, Red-baiting, worker's oppression, sexism and a myriad of other hatreds large and small. The United States is and has been far from perfect; it can sometimes make a heck of a mess. Still, the country *is* intended to appeal to the better side of humanity. The nation was founded on *Enlightenment* ideals – notions that all deserve "life, liberty, and the pursuit of happiness," and that we're marked by our possibilities and inherent equality as much as anything else; ideas from American founding documents that had decided influence on *international* rights.[49] If Trump sticks to his guns and continues to use the ammunition he's so far deployed, such concepts appear in danger. Politics in the world's most powerful state risks turning into a Freudian scream. In terms of the thumbprint the 320 million strong American plurality puts on the world, the next opportunity comes in November. Based on what's happened so far, any rights supporter can only hope that the results break one way and decidedly not another.

---

49 Declaration of Independence, in Mary Beth Norton, et al., *A People and a Nation, Volume II: Since 1865* (Boston: Wadsworth, 2011), A-1.

"Reason and Conscience"

The Arts and Politics in Denmark
(May 5, 2016)

Abstract: *All isn't just Lego and H.C. Andersen in the small Scandinavian state of Denmark. The country is also in the middle of Europe's right-leaning, immigration-skeptical trends. In passing laws allowing the seizure of refugees' goods at the border, the country angered the well-known artist Ai Weiwei.*

A strange set of buses seems to have collided at the start of 2016: the Kingdom of Denmark, culturally conservative political ideologies, the European migration crisis and the work of one of the world's most famous artists, sculptor and installation virtuoso Ai Weiwei. The origins of the situation apparently lay with Denmark's Eurosceptic turn – something that some say may have in begun *before* the country's 1973 membership in the EU kicked off. I.e., for some experts, it's the case that Denmark has *long* been a blend of professed internationalism yet practiced nationalism via which the inhabitants of the small northern European state have kept half an arm's length away from a fully open approach to cultural identity and global affairs.[1] From this writer's perspective,

"Flag of Denmark." © *Miro Novak / Fotolia.com 132441983*

however, the situation appears not to have been *that* bad until Danish membership in the EU (or EC as it was at the time) became official. When the country held its 1972 referendum on joining the bloc, e.g., 63.3% of Danes said "yes" – that with 90% of eligible voters turning out (a typical Scandinavian polling day).[2] That's a pretty hefty, let's-join-the-larger-community-immediately-around-us sentiment (if an American Presidential election were won with 63% of the

---

1   Richard Jenkins, *Being Danish: Paradoxes of Identity in Everyday Life* (Copenhagen: Museum Tusculanum, 2012), 145.

2   See Morten Kellstrup, "Denmark's Relation to the European Union: A History of Dualism and Pragmatism," in *Denmark and the European Union*, ed. Lee Miles and Anders Wivel (London: Routledge, 2014), 14–29.

popular vote, it would be the largest landslide in history).[3] After some years of relative calm around the idea, however, problems arose in the '90s with the referendum on the Maastricht Treaty – the treaty that made the EU the EU and organized the bloc as much around political as economic affairs.[4] In a surprising turn of events, 50.7% of Danes voted *against* Maastricht – a result that sent shockwaves through European political society.[5] Now, the Danes *did* sign up for Maastricht via a new vote in 1993. That was only after some pretty heavy opt-outs, however: no Euro and self-control over justice and home affairs (immigration most noticeably). Such sentiment appeared again when in 2000, asked to vote on specifically on participation in the common currency, the Danes *again* turned the Euro down – 53.6 to 46.4%.[6] I'm not expert enough to say precisely why those results played out in the way they did. Having lived in the country for some time, however, I'd simply say that I'm compelled by an argument made in a paper released by the Danish Institute for International Studies in which its author, Catharina Sørensen, notes that time after the time as regards participation in larger Europe, "close to half of the Danish population has voted contrary to the recommendation of more than two-thirds of the Danish Parliament."[7] I.e., politicians have tended to say "yes" to the European project while ordinary Danes have said "no." Especially when one considers that the Danish Crown (the national currency) is pegged to the Euro (there's hardly fluctuation between the two), and that, nestled on top of Germany and a stone's throw away from Sweden, Norway, the UK, the Netherlands and Poland, Denmark is centrally located in European geography, the issue seems to concern cultural identity and national symbolism as much as anything else. Danes often strike me like Americans: they want to be that, and aren't much interested in being anything else.[8]

---

3 See Mary Beth Norton, et al., *A People and a Nation, Volume II: Since 1856*, 9th ed. (Boston: Wadsworth, 2008), A-16–A-20.

4 Very roughly, Maastricht opened the door for greatly expanded common political regulation and policy-making, including the notion of European citizenship. See Martin Dedman, *The Origins and Development of the European Union 1945–2008* (London: Routledge, 2010).

5 Kellstrup, "Denmark's Relation to the European Union."

6 Ibid.

7 Catharina Sørensen, "Danish and British Popular Euroscepticism Compared: A Sceptical Assessment of the Concept," *DIIS Working Paper* 25 (2014): 4.

8 Jenkins, *Being Danish*, 83–5.

Now, all of this would be but curiosities except that also perhaps not unlike the U.S., a significant amount of Danish politics over the last two decades has concerned who gets in and who gets out – immigration, basically. Now as, the country is hard to mark as anything but progressive – concerned with humanitarian ideals and basic rights. Denmark protects civil liberties and, though it's clearly capitalist, it spreads enough of the national wealth around to guarantee health care for all, access to basic social services, generous retirement benefits and high-quality education – approaches that mark it high on scales of international justice.[9] Still, there seems to be an appetite for something else. One of the noticeable events in the country over recent years has been the rise of the Danish People's Party (*Dansk Folkeparti*) – a movement coming out of the Eurosceptical '90s and which has won some stunning electoral victories of late. On par with groups like the *Front National* in France, the group explicitly imagines keeping "Denmark for the Danes," arguing for justice via the "nation" as opposed to necessary subscription to global institutions or international norms. Indeed, some of the party's vocabularies are stunning. I quote from the party platform: "Denmark is not an immigrant country and never has been. Thus we will not accept transformation to a multiethnic society…Denmark belongs to the Danes."[10] Come the general election in 2015, the People's Party gained the second largest number of representatives in the national Parliament. Many maintain that it's now the country's most influential.[11]

All of this has had some interesting results. Clearly, the *Folkeparti* doesn't represent all Danes – far from it. There's thirteen parties in the nation's Parliament (a lot [though some have to do with representing Danish protectorates like

---

9   The Cingranelli and Richards (CIRI) Human Rights Data Project puts Denmark among the top ten most human rights compliant states – obviously, a massive feather in Denmark's cap. In large part, however, that concerns the state's treatment of its own citizens. The index is noticeably less oriented towards the question of international outlook, the consequences of focus on the nation or how one should deal with asylum. See David L. Cingranelli and David L. Richards, "The Cingranelli and Richards (CIRI) Human Rights Data Project," *Human Rights Quarterly* 32, no. 4 (2010): 401–24; see also CIRI Human Rights Data Project, "Human Rights in 2010: The CIRI Report," December 9, 2011, available at http://www.humanrightsdata.com/2011/12/human-rights-in-2010-ciri-report.html.

10   Dansk Folkeparti, "The Party Program of the Danish People's Party" (2002), available at https://www.danskfolkeparti.dk/The_Party_Program_of_the_Danish_Peoples_Party.

11   Per Bang Thomsen, "Valgets Store Vinder: Vores Succes Skal Bestemt Omdannes til Indflydelse," *DR*, June 19, 2015, available at https://www.dr.dk/nyheder/politik/valg2015/valgets-store-vinder-vores-succes-skal-bestemt-omdannes-til-indflydelse.

Greenland or the Faroe Islands]), and many are supportive of internationalist
ideals via which the country of Frederik Bajer (the 1908 Nobel Peace Prize lau-
reate) and Bodil Begtrup (an early UN rights activist) remains precisely that –
humanitarian-internationalist. The country gives a significant portion of its
national budget to foreign aid – though it's cut back recently – and it runs its
military affairs almost exclusively through coalition-based organizations like
NATO and the UN.[12] The nation is also party to all UN rights conventions and
is completely supportive of international humanitarian organizations from Doctors without Borders to the International Red Cross.[13] Still, since 2001, the country's been turning the screws to restrict the flow of foreigners. The first move
was the "24-Year-Old Rule" of 2002, stating that non-resident spouses must be
twenty-four years of age to join spouses already living in the country – a move
that gained heavy international criticism (one usually sticks with the age of majority, or perhaps twenty-one, and that's it). *That* was then attached to the denial
of spousal reunification if the resident spouse received social assistance within
the year previous to application – another issue sparking off consternation on
the international stage.[14] Last year, however, in reaction to the heightened flow of
refugees from North Africa and the Middle East, the proverbial doo-doo really
really hit the fan. As millions flowed across European borders from locales like
Syria and Iraq, Denmark fought tooth and nail with countries like Germany and
Italy to resist European-wide quotas for dealing with asylum seekers – something
to which it *did* have a right to given its EU opt-outs. In a striking move, however,
the country also resurrected border controls with its neighbors (that in contra-
diction of the general EU spirit of free movement between member states), and it

---

12 Through 2015, Denmark had been one of a few dozen countries spending more than
0.7% of its national budget on foreign aid. That compares to about 0.2% from the United States – though the U.S. is the largest net donor. See Naomi Larsson, "Foreign Aid:
Which Countries Are the Most Generous," *The Guardian*, September 9, 2015, available at http://www.theguardian.com/global-development-professionals-network/2015/
sep/09/foreign-aid-which-countries-are-the-most-generous. On the Danish military,
see Bertel Heurlin, "Denationalisaton of Danish Armed Forces and Militarising of
Danish Foreign Policy," in *Denationalisation of Defence: Convergence and Diversity*,
ed. Janne Haaland Matlary and Øyvind Østerud (London: Routledge, 2016), 113–34.
13 See Norbert Götz and Heidi Haggrén, eds., *Regional Cooperation and International
Organizations: The Nordic Model in Transnational Alignment* (London: Routledge,
2009).
14 See Chris Bowlby, "Do Denmark's Immigration Laws Breach Human Rights?" *BBC*,
February 10, 2011, available at http://www.bbc.com/news/world-europe-12366676.
This article also picks-up on the issue of the 24-Year Rule.

increased the wait time for refugee family reunification from one year to three.[15] Most noticeably, however, the country enacted a law allowing police to seize valuables from refugees entering the country – valuables assessed at over roughly 1300 Euros. That's right. Denmark. Seizing valuables. At the border. From people on the run. For sale by the state – a state with one of the highest living standards on earth.[16]

Now, the Danish government has defended this action by noting that other European states have begun considering the same. That's in fact correct. Germany has begun to institute similar laws, as has Switzerland (of course, Switzerland isn't an EU member).[17] The Danish government has *also* noted that it's technically not asking anything of asylum seekers not asked of Danish citizens who go on social support (one is only allowed to have only so many assets before state help kicks in). Also true. Danes aren't supposed to have much left before going on welfare, and the amount *is* the same as the "confiscation limit" for immigrants. Still, I have a hard time imagining Danish authorities stopping Danes in the street to take their goods to ensure that they've conformed with welfare laws. I can't imagine the cops barging into Danish families' homes to check the size of their bank accounts or demand that they sell their stereos or kitchen appliances because they have too much to qualify for social help. I can't imagine anything but a civil rights outcry if government buildings were used to pat people down to see if they "have something" that might be used to pay their way. Very simply, the confiscation idea is hard to imagine without the "Denmark for the Danes"

---

15 Most noticeable is that Sweden has also resurrected border controls in relation to Denmark. That, however, concerns the massively higher level of asylum seekers and migrants with which the Swedes were dealing, however. That point is discussed further on in the essay.

16 United Nations Development Program, "Human Development Report: Statistical Annex" (2015), available at http://hdr.undp.org/sites/default/files/ranking.pdf. See also Lizzie Dearden, "Denmark Refugee Law: Concern over 'Inhumane' Family Reunification Delays That Could Cause More Deaths," *The Independent*, January 27, 2016, available at http://www.independent.co.uk/news/world/europe/denmark-refugee-law-concern-over-inhumane-family-reunification-delays-that-could-cause-more-deaths-a6836511.html; Reuters, "Denmark Says it Will Not Join EU Refugee Quotas, Has Taken its Share," September 11, 2015, available at http://www.reuters.com/article/us-europe-migrants-eu-denmark-idUSKCN0RB0TJ20150911.

17 Lizzie Dearden, "Germany Follows Switzerland and Denmark to Seize Cash and Valuables from Arriving Refugees," *The Independent*, January 23, 2016, available at http://www.independent.co.uk/news/world/europe/germany-follows-switzerland-and-denmark-to-seize-cash-and-valuables-from-arriving-refugees-a6828821.html.

mentality running in the background – and if one looks at advertisements the country has run in Middle East newspapers telling people not to come, it seems that's precisely the case.[18] It's a heavy social statement indeed.[19]

Now, the second "bus" in our "crash" is that Denmark maintains a thriving art scene. For such a small country, there's an impressive number of good galleries, high-quality museums and well-funded schools for design, music, dance and the visual arts. The nation punches well above its weight in intellectual innovation and artistic creativity on both European and global scales. A couple of those good museums – the Faurschou Foundation in Copenhagen and the ARoS Museum in Aarhus – managed to book some of Ai Weiwei's installations: room size pieces entitled "Ruptures."[20] Weiwei is known for many things. Though primarily an artist, it's his political activism that frequently takes the headlines. It's significant: exposing shoddy housing in the wake of China's 2008 Szechuan earthquake; protesting the Chinese state's arrest and censorship of dissidents like Liu Xiaobo (2010's Nobel Peace Prize Winner) and drawing attention to the shoving-out of Beijing residents from certain areas of the city when the Olympics were held there in 2008.[21] Indeed, such activities have landed the artist in police custody and resulted in the demolition of his Shanghai studio in 2011. Weiwei also had his passport suspended by the Chinese government for a handful of years.[22] Art-wise, it's fair to say that Weiwei is best-known for his contributions to the "Bird's Nest" stadium – the centerpiece of the 2008 Olympics of which he

---

18 See Adam Taylor, "Denmark Puts Ad in Lebanese Newspapers: Dear Refugees, Don't Come Here," *The Washington Post*, September 15, 2015, available at https://www.washingtonpost.com/news/worldviews/wp/2015/09/07/denmark-places-an-advertisement-in-lebanese-newspapers-dear-refugees-dont-come-here/.

19 See Edward Edelman, "How Not to Welcome Refugees," *The Atlantic*, January 27, 2016, available at http://www.theatlantic.com/international/archive/2016/01/denmark-refugees-immigration-law/431520/.

20 Christopher Shea, "Ai Weiwei Says He's Closing Danish Exhibition in Protest of Refugee Law," *The New York Times*, January 27, 2016, available at http://www.nytimes.com/2016/01/28/world/europe/ai-weiwei-faurschou-foundation-copenhagen.html?_r=0.

21 See Barnaby Martin, *Hanging Man: The Arrest of Ai Weiwei* (New York: Faber and Faber, 2013).

22 Austin Ramsey, "Ai Weiwei, Chinese Artist and Provocateur, Is Given Back His Passport," *The New York Times*, July 22, 2015, available at http://www.nytimes.com/2015/07/23/world/asia/ai-weiwei-chinese-artist-and-provocateur-is-given-back-his-passport.html?_r=0.

was ironically critical.[23] Still, Weiwei has a massive back catalog – much of which is housed in top museums – and his style is diverse. Playing between controversy and beauty, his *œuvre* spans everything from printing "Coca-Cola" on a Han Dynasty vase (surprisingly pretty, in fact) to some pleasing yet conceptual assemblages of bicycles and stools filling an entire room. He's also gotten significant press for a set of satirical sculptures depicting the atmosphere around his arrest. Weiwei's reputation is well-deserved. He's a serious craftsman with a varied pallet and an intriguing sense of material and design.[24]

Weiwei has an anti-authoritarian streak. Upon being informed of Denmark's laws concerning the confiscation of asylum seekers' goods, the artist canceled his Faurschou and ARoS shows. "This decision follows the Danish parliament's approval of the law proposal that allows seizing valuables and delaying family reunions for asylum seekers," Weiwei wrote – a level of violation of the rights to privacy and personal dignity of which he wanted no part.[25] The move touched off various reactions. The head of Faurschou expressed support. Hardly all Danes are fans of the country's shift to the right, and Jens Faurschou offered that he regretted the Danish Parliament's decision "to be in the forefront of symbolic and inhuman[e] politics of today's biggest humanitarian crisis." It was part of a larger outcry against the country's anti-immigration politics from the nation's humanitarian left.[26] The head of ARoS became snarky. He suggested that Weiwei was unfairly "punishing" the Danes for a political decision for which they may or may not have been responsible.[27] Now, it *does* occur to me that people are responsible for the governments they elect; is not people's responsibility for their

---

23 See Ai Weiwei, "China Excluded its People from the Olympics. London is Different." *The Guardian*, July 25, 2012, available at https://www.theguardian.com/artanddesign/2012/jul/25/china-olympics-london-ai-weiwei.

24 See Ai Weiwei and Anthony Pins, *Ai Weiwei: Spatial Matters: Art Architecture and Activism* (Cambridge, MA: MIT Press, 2014).

25 Shea, "Ai Weiwei Says He's Closing Danish Exhibition."

26 "You're contributing to the separation that war creates," the leader of one of the left-wing opposition parties claimed in parliamentary discussion – crystallizing the sentiment of the many Danes who do *not* want their country known for such policies. See Dan Bilefsky, "Danish Law Requires Asylum Seekers to Hand Over Valuables," *The New York Times*, January 26, 2016, available at http://www.nytimes.com/2016/01/27/world/europe/denmark-asks-refugees-for-valuables.html.

27 David Crouch, "Ai Weiwei Shuts Danish Show in Protest of Asylum-Seeker Law," *The Guardian*, January 27, 2016, available at http://www.theguardian.com/artanddesign/2016/jan/27/ai-weiwei-shuts-danish-show-in-protest-at-asylum-seeker-law; Jan M. Olsen and Karl Ritter, "Ai Weiwei Withdraws Work in Denmark Due to Immigration Law," *CBC*

governments at least *part* of what democracy is all about? In any case, counter-cultural sensibilities and centuries-long traditions tying liberation politics to the arts didn't much seem to count in the director of ARoS' mind.

Now, that's all meaty, and there's much one can say about it (indeed, I have to admit that my several-bus-crash really boils down to two: the arts and right-leaning immigration politics). The first point I'd make, however, concerns our sometimes-short memories and our ability to idealize particular states – quaint Scandic countries, e.g., that we just *know* are harmless and where things are simply done "right." Now, Weiwei hasn't been the only voice raising a stink about Denmark's confiscation policy or the country's at-large approach to immigration and asylum. Britain's *The Guardian* printed a well-publicized cartoon of the country's Prime Minister in Nazi garb – the idea being that the confiscation policy recalled the 1930s and '40s German practice of taking goods from Jews.[28] Council of Europe Commissioner for Human Rights Nils Muiznieks quickly wrote to the Danish government to indicate that "such measure[s] could amount to an infringement of the human dignity of the persons concerned" – a dressing-down from the most "local" international organization, if it might be put that way. Organizations from Amnesty International to Human Rights Watch to the UN absolutely slammed the country, reflecting the stances they've taken on nearly all the controversies surrounding Denmark and immigration over the last ten to fifteen years.[29] Indeed, it *has* been jarring. For a country usually associated with Lego, H.C. Andersen

---

News, January 27, 2016, available at http://www.cbc.ca/news/arts/ai-weiwei-denmark-migrants-1.3422346.

28 The Guardian, "Steve Bell on Denmark Seizing Refugees' Assets – Cartoon," January 26, 2016, available at http://www.theguardian.com/commentisfree/picture/2016/jan/26/steve-bell-on-denmark-seizing-refugees-assets-cartoon.

29 Al-Jazeera, "Denmark Urged to Reject 'Cruel' Refugee Laws," January 21, 2016, available at http://www.aljazeera.com/news/2016/01/denmark-urged-reject-cruel-refugee-laws-160121045329929.html; Gerry Simpson, "Dispatches: Denmark's Deterrence Tactics on Refugees," *Human Rights Watch*, March 3, 2016, available at https://www.hrw.org/news/2016/03/03/dispatches-denmarks-deterrence-tactics-refugees; Lizzie Dearden, "Denmark Refugee Bill: Everything You Need to Know about Law Allowing Police to Seize Asylum Seekers' Cash and Valuables," *The Independent*, January 26, 2016, available at http://www.independent.co.uk/news/world/europe/denmark-refugee-bill-politicians-to-vote-on-law-allowing-police-to-seize-asylum-seekers-cash-and-a6834276.html; Dearden, "Denmark Approves Controversial Refugee Bill Allowing Police to Seize Asylum Seekers' Cash and Valuables," *The Independent*, January 26, 2016, http://www.independent.co.uk/news/world/europe/denmark-approves-controversial-refugee-bill-allowing-police-to-seize-asylum-seekers-cash-and-a6834581.html.

and the Tivoli Gardens (and, again, more than a few international humanitarians), watching Denmark get tossed in with the range of countries moving to the reactionary right has felt strange. *The New York Times* has gone so far as to do an extensive piece of journalism based precisely on that sense of shock. It just doesn't jive with the idea that many have of what the nation is about.[30]

Still, as Europe's immigration crisis has worn on, the Danish situation has faded from view. More concern has focused on policy questions surrounding Europe's largest state – Germany – as well deals the EU has made with the Turkey for the purpose of keeping as many migrants away from European shores as possible. Focus has also fallen on the complications present at places where migrants tend to *enter* Europe: countries like Italy and Greece (they're simply unable to deal with the load coming to their shores).[31] That's while, in the U.S., Bernie Sanders has sung Denmark's praises as a humanitarian model, and Barak Obama has been preparing to host a dinner for Scandic Bloc countries without reference to the radically divergent paths between, say, Sweden and Denmark, on basic approaches to immigration and asylum rights.[32] To date, though a slightly larger country (a population of roughly 9.6 million versus the Danes' 5.6 million), Sweden has handled roughly 4.5 times the number of asylum applications per capita as Denmark. In large part, that's because the political momentum in Denmark is such that officials aren't' particularly keen to handle those applications in the first place.[33]

Now, Sanders again has a point. The cradle-to-grave welfare model of the Scandinavian countries – maintained as strongly in Denmark as anywhere else – *in fact* preserves rights in ways that are just and rare. The Scandinavian welfare

---

30 See David Zucchino, "'I've Become a Racist': Migrant Wave Unleashes Danish Tension over Identity," *The New York Times*, September 5, 2016, available at http://www.nytimes.com/2016/09/06/world/europe/denmark-migrants-refugees-racism.html. See also Katya Adler, "Is Europe Lurching to the Far Right?" *BBC*, April 28, 2016, available at http://www.bbc.com/news/world-europe-3615080.

31 See, e.g., Dearden, "Refugee Crisis: Concern over 'Unprecedented' Arrivals in Greece and Italy after 2016 total passes 100,000," *The Independent*, February 23, 2016, available at www.independent.co.uk/news/world/europe/refugee-migrant-crisis-concern-unprecedented-numbers-greece-italy-2016-passes-100000-a6891101.html.Racist.

32 Chris Moody, "Bernie Sanders' American Dream is in Denmark," *CNN*, February 17, 2016, available at http://edition.cnn.com/2016/02/17/politics/bernie-sanders-2016-denmark-democratic-socialism/; Gardiner Harris, "Obama Warms Up to Nordic Leaders," *The New York Times*, May 13, 2016, available at http://www.nytimes.com/2016/05/14/world/europe/obama-warms-to-nordic-heads-of-state.html.

33 BBC, "Migration Crisis: Migration to Europe Explained in Seven Charts," March 4, 2016, available at http://www.bbc.com/news/world-europe-34131911.

model generally assures dignified existences for all its citizens, and largely extends those privileges to permanent residents as well.[34] Again, that involves extensive welfare services and a large pool of public resources. That's on top of Denmark's democratic culture – an educated country with a free press and guaranteed freedom of mind. Especially in view of the country's historic support for rights agreements like the European Convention on Human Rights (1950) and the range of rights treaties sponsored by the UN, there's a way in which most Danes, including many on the right, would imagine themselves as staunch rights supporters.[35] In many ways, they'd be correct to do so. Danes participate in their country's democracy and, though they have been pared back, the essentials of the welfare state remain strong. It thus *does* come off like a needle scratching across a vinyl 33 when the UN High Commissioner for Refugees suggests Denmark's country's policies are "worrisome" and contribute to spreading "xenophobia" and "fear."[36] It feels weird when NGOs suggest that Denmark's immigration policies are discriminatory and analysts can't find any way around them except to connect them to the dramatic rise of a party looking for a monocultural state. It comes off like a self-inflicted black eye – one that, insofar as the country *maintains* such policies, it seems willing to live with; perhaps defiantly so.[37]

Again, that is what it is. States can do things counter to their reputations, and social critics deserve the right to call them out on that. It also strikes me, though, that the Denmark-Ai Weiwei "bus crash" asks us for a slightly more thematical reflection on *human rights*. I.e., in *terms* of international outrage – as well as, apparently, some local discontent too – what *are* the problems are with the Danish situation, and how might we put more meat on the bone in terms of *how*

---

34 See Eric S. Einhorn and John Logue, *Modern Welfare States: Scandinavian Politics and Policy in the Global Age* (Westport: Greenwood, 2003).

35 Ed Bates, *The Evolution of the European Convention of Human Rights: From Its Inception to the Creation of Permanent Court of Human Rights* (Oxford: Oxford University Press, 2010); Roger Normand and Sarah Zaidi, *Human Rights at the UN: The Political History of Universal Justice* (Bloomington: Indiana University Press, 2008); Johannes Morsink, *The Universal Declaration of Human Rights: Drafting, Origins & Intent* (Philadelphia: University of Pennsylvania Press, 1999).

36 Sabina Zawadzki, "Denmark, Under Fire, Ups Limits of Valuables that Refugees Can Keep," *Reuters*, January 8, 2016, available at http://www.reuters.com/article/us-europe-migrants-denmark-idUSKBN0UM26220160108.

37 South China Morning Post, "'Despicable and Vindictive': Human Rights Watch Boss Lashes Denmark for Passing Law that Allows Refugees' Valuables to be Confiscated," January 28, 2016, available at http://www.scmp.com/news/world/article/1906308/despicable-and-vindictive-human-rights-watch-boss-lashes-denmark-passing.

the country may have run afoul of essential principles of international justice? *Where* in terms of specific rights clauses do problems emerge, and how do the country's policies coincide, or not, with the spirit of rights – the *atmospheres* that overtures towards universal justice are intended to create? *Where* is Denmark cutting against the "letter" of rights law, and where does it run afoul of the general *idea* of fundamental privileges and freedoms – the *attitudes* that rights ask us to take towards one another, and the ethical treatments they expect? I admit I'm rather more a moralist than a lawyer (in fact, I'm not a lawyer at all). However, what, both legally and ethically, does it seem that Denmark has done?

Rights are complex. There are international covenants and declarations such as the International Bill of Human Rights, consisting of the Universal Declaration of Human Rights (1948) and the International Covenants on Civil and Political Rights and Economic, Social and Cultural Rights, respectively (both from 1966). There are international conventions on *specific* issues, like women's rights, children's rights and the rights of racial minorities.[38] There are also *regional* regimes, such as those based in the Council of Europe and the European Court of Human Rights (the European Convention is the most prominent agreement here [there are also various national rights acts; I'll leave those to the side for the moment]). Now, some within the Danish government *itself* have noted that the property seizure law runs afoul of article 8 of the European Convention – an article declaring one's right to "respect" for "private and family life" (the idea of the inviolability of the person and one's ability to maintain a private emotional space). It's a dubious proposition to simply "get into" people's belongings or their private personal affairs. Approaching someone to "find" things when, *prima facie*, they haven't done wrong, borders on the invasive – again, especially if people are on the run for reasons of escaping conflict or persecution.[39] *Those* points are then echoed in conventions like the Covenant on Civil and Political Rights, which wonders about "interference" with people's privacy, to say nothing of attacks against one's "honour and reputation."[40] I.e., specifically-focused border stops to the end of saying "pay up" seem to offer pretty heavy stigmatization. That's again when it

---

38 See United Nations, "Fact Sheet No. 2 (Rev.1), The International Bill of Human Rights" (1996), available at http://www.ohchr.org/Documents/Publications/FactSheet2Rev.1en. pdf. See also David Weissbrodt and Connie de la Vega, *International Human Rights Law: An Introduction* (Philadelphia: University of Pennsylvania Press, 2007).

39 Council of Europe, "European Convention on Human Rights" (article 8), available at http://www.echr.coe.int/Documents/Convention_ENG.pdf.

40 United Nations, "the International covenant on Civil and Political Rights" (1966, article 17), available at http://www.ohchr.org/en/professionalinterest/pages/ccpr.aspx.

seems clear *who* those border stops involve. I.e., one again has to notice that Denmark has run its "don't come here" advertisements in Middle East newspapers and that questions of "civilizational clash" lurk in the background of more than a small part of the politics with which Europe's migration crisis is involved.[41]

Indeed, critics have *also* pointed to the Convention on the Rights of the Child (1989) to indicate problems with raising the waiting time on family reunification to three years – again, another part in the recent ramp-up in immigration restrictions. I.e., states party to the Children's Convention pledge to "ensure that a child shall not be separated from his or her parents against their will, except when competent authorities subject to judicial review determine, in accordance with applicable law and procedures, that such separation is necessary for the best interests of the child."[42] That's to say that *if* families are to be kept apart, it has to be to be to the *child's* benefit – not some state's.[43] Indeed, the country was criticized on the basis of similar principles when the 24-Year-Old Rule emerged – though that based on more generalized conceptions of civil rights and the 1951 UN Convention and Relating to the Status of Refugees as well as the 1967 Protocol Relating to the Status of Refugees. You simply can't keep people who belong together apart because you're worried about "the economy" or "cultural integration." Private lives and private decisions can't be subject to coincidental whim.[44] In any case, those are at least *some* examples of nitty-gritty, letter-of-rights-law points of which Denmark *appears* to have run afoul.[45]

---

41 See Zucchino, "'I've Become a Racist.'"

42 United Nations, "Convention on the Rights of the Child" (1989, article 9), available at http://www.ohchr.org/EN/ProfessionalInterest/Pages/CRC.aspx. See also Lizzie Dearden, "Denmark Refugee Law: Concern over 'Inhumane' Family Reunification Delays That Could Cause More Deaths," *The Independent*, January 27, 2016, available at http://www.independent.co.uk/news/world/europe/denmark-refugee-law-concern-over-inhumane-family-reunification-delays-that-could-cause-more-deaths-a6836511.html.

43 See Commissioner for Human Rights, "CommHR/GC/sf 002-2016," January 12, 2016, available at https://www.altinget.dk/misc/CommDH(2016)4_EN.pdf; United Nations, "Daily Press Briefing by the Office of the Spokesperson for the Secretary-General," January 26, 2016, available at http://www.un.org/press/en/2016/db160126.doc.htm.

44 Andrew Osborne, "Denmark under Fire from UN for Tough Asylum Laws," *The Guardian*, April 9, 2002, available at https://www.theguardian.com/world/2002/apr/10/immigration.uk: United Nations, "Convention and Protocol Relating to the Status of Refugees" (1951/1967), available at http://www.unhcr.org/protection/basic/3b66c2aa10/convention-protocol-relating-status-refugees.html.

45 Griff Witte, "Denmark, a Social Welfare Utopia, Takes a Nasty Turn on Refugees," *The Washington Post*, April 11, 2016, available at https://www.washingtonpost.com/world/

Still, what I term the general "spirit" of rights – "extra-legal" senses of what rights might mean, or what they're intended to achieve – adds fuel to the fire. Indeed, that might be the more important point: what is the "spirit of the laws," as the Baron de Montesquieu once put it, and what are issues like the inviolability home and private space supposed to be *about*?[46]

For me, this is where rights *really* find their traction: that modern nations might stand for something *larger* than themselves and that there are standards to which *all* countries should be held – ideas suggesting that the question is building political systems in relation to *everyone's* humanity and ridding ourselves of notions that human responsibility stops because one set of human beings comes from one place and others come from somewhere else (i.e., one can't simply close oneself behind a set of national borders and *not* worry about the fate of one's fellow women and men). The most referred to international rights document, e.g., the Universal Declaration (1948), is explicit on this point. The expectation of countries signing on to that document's principles, which one essentially does as a function of joining the UN (and Denmark has done that), is to create atmospheres of "peace." The goal for countries claiming *any* interest in human rights is undoing the "barbarous acts" which have "outraged the conscience of mankind." The goal of rights regimes is to "promote and develop friendly relations between nations" and the peoples they represent. Human rights ask us to act towards one another in a spirit of "brotherhood" and *not* say "here are *my* rights and, when things don't benefit me, damn the larger destiny of all." Rights are about being part of a *larger* world and *not* walling oneself off as – at the moment, Denmark seems at least somewhat wont to do.[47]

---

europe/denmark-a-social-welfare-utopia-takes-a-nasty-turn-on-refugees/2016/04/11/
a652e298-f5d1-11e5-958d-d038dac6e718_story.html.

46   Baron de Montesquieu, *The Spirit of the Laws*, ed. Anne M. Cohler, Basia Carolyn Miller
and Harold Samuel Stone (Cambridge: Cambridge University Press, 1989). See also
Bryan S. Turner, *Vulnerability and Human Rights* (University Park: The Pennsylvania
State University Press, 2006).

47   United Nations, "The Universal Declaration of Human Rights" (1948, preamble [here-
after UDHR]), available at http://www.un.org/en/universal-declaration-human-rights/
index.html. This is a slightly complex idea as it's really only the UN Charter by which
member states are bound upon entering the organization (though, of course, they may
accede to any number of conventions or treaties). However, the Charter notes the UN
as a human rights organization, and it's patently clear that the UDHR was intended
to stand as an articulation of what that means. It's thus not a stretch to suggest that
joining the UN means more or less committing oneself to the principles of the UDHR –
which is where the wordplays of creating "peace" and avoiding "barbarity" come from.

Now, yes: *literal* walls are going up in countries like Bulgaria and Hungary. Slovakia declared it will only take Christian refugees – *Christian refugees!* – and, again, Germany and Switzerland have begun something of a Danish-style policy of confiscation to make migrants "pay" for their stays. I can say little to defend Bulgaria and Hungary. The rise of Hungary's far-right *Jobbik*, which sometimes parades around in neo-fascist uniforms and whose members sometimes engage in less-than-subtle anti-Semitism, is disturbing in ways that exceed Denmark's People's Party. The People's Party, if not to my taste, generally stays within the bounds of parliamentary politics and doesn't present itself through paramilitary aesthetics.[48] Moreover, as much as one might recognize that south-central Eastern Europe *is* something of an immigration "frontline" – it's where many come through once having gotten through Turkey – raising massive sheets of razor-wire and barriers as in Bulgaria seems an awfully aggressive move.[49] One *can* defend Germany. For the better part of two years, the country maintained a nearly open-door policy in which it accepted around one and a half million refugees. That's a 1.8% addition to a population of about 81 million. It's also a move that brought Angela Merkel consideration for the 2015 Nobel Peace Prize.[50] Now, it's not that the Danes have done *nothing*. The country actually says "yes" to asylum applications it *does* get at a relatively high rate (85.2%; compare that to Poland, which grants asylum to around 15% of applicants). Denmark remains in the EU – despite clamoring from the right, it hasn't made any serious overtures to pulling out – and, though it's resurrected border controls, it hasn't built any border *walls*. That bespeaks a level of moderation. Still, look at countries of the kind with which Denmark would generally imagine to compare itself – the most developed states, like Sweden and Germany – and the atmosphere has been markedly different. Taking in a significant number of people per capital – about 16.9 per 100 residents – the Swedish government

See also Jussi M. Hanhimaki, *The United Nations: A Very Short Introduction* (Oxford: Oxford University Press, 2008).

48 Tony Paterson, "Hungary Election: Concerns as Neo-Nazi Jobbik Party Wins 20% of Vote," *The Independent*, April 7, 2014, available at http://www.independent.co.uk/news/world/europe/concerns-as-neo-nazi-jobbik-party-wins-20-of-hungary-vote-9244541.html.

49 See Rick Lyman, "Bulgaria Builds a New Wall, But This One Keeps People Out," *The New York Times*, April 5, 2015, available at http://www.nytimes.com/2015/04/06/world/europe/bulgaria-puts-up-a-new-wall-but-this-one-keeps-people-out.html?_r=0.

50 Julian Borger, "From Pope Francis to Angela Merkel: The Top Contenders for the 2015 Nobel Peace Prize," *The Guardian*, October 7, 2015, available at http://www.theguardian.com/world/2015/oct/06/nobel-peace-prize-top-contenders-for-2015-award.

has taken the position that there's a humanitarian crisis underway, people need help, and everyone has the duty to step up. "My Europe takes in people fleeing from war," Swedish Prime Minister Stefan Löfven said in September 2015; "my Europe does not build walls."[51] Again, Germany made a *massive* effort; one making Germany the preferred destination of the larger part of migrants on their way to Europe. At the moment, the simple fact is that such openness doesn't define the attitudes of the Danish political class nor certain sectors of the society as a whole.[52] Indeed, it creates an almost comical effect when one drives between Denmark and Germany and one has to stop at the border to get into the Danish Kingdom, yet there's free access on the highways to the much larger neighbor to the south. It's a day in the history of European politics I think few of us thought we'd ever see.[53]

The last point I'd like to make regarding the Denmark-Ai Weiwei situation, however, in fact concerns *Weiwei*, or the kind of figure *he* is. I.e., my last point concerns why an *artist's* sense of justice might be meaningful in discussions about international rights and ethics, and what makes us pay attention when questions concerning social justice become framed by someone who *paints* or *sculpts*; someone who is *prima facie* concerned with the boundaries of *aesthetic* expression, and *not* primarily politics. Why, with the not small amount of commentary that exists on Denmark's migration issues, if not migration in Europe generally, might *Weiwei's* actions gain attention? What would make us think that an *artist's* opinion is relevant, and what, if any, connection might there be between the *arts* and human rights?

---

51 See EuroNews, "Collective Responsibility Key to Addressing Refugee Crisis, Says Swedish Prime Minister," January 23, 2016, available at http://www.euronews.com/2016/01/23/collective-responsibility-in-europe-key-to-addressing-refugee-crisis-says/. See especially embedded video. See also Migration Policy Institute, "Asylum Applications in the EU/EFTA by Country, 2008–2015," available at http://www.migrationpolicy.org/programs/data-hub/charts/asylum-applications-euefta-country-2008-2015?width=1000&height=850&iframe=true.

52 PBD, "As Sweden Offers Shelter, Denmark Tries to Discourage Refugees," *PBS*, September 4, 2015, available at http://www.pbs.org/newshour/bb/sweden-offers-shelter-denmark-tries-discourage-refugees/.

53 In reference to a point raised earlier, Sweden has in fact also erected border controls with Denmark, most noticeably on connections from Copenhagen; that partly via pressure from the rise of its own right-wing party, the Sweden Democrats. Again, though, the context is quite different as Sweden made an explicit effort to take in a massive number of refugees, at least in relation to the size of its population. See BBC News, "Denmark Responds to Swedish Border Checks with its Own Controls," January 4, 2016, available at http://www.bbc.com/news/world-europe-35222015.

Here, the answers are direct. At root, rights organize themselves around ideas of "reason and conscience." At some level, rights concern *thought*, and the idea that, as human beings, we see things, react to them and have things we want to say as a function of our understandings of the world.[54] Now, material life is undoubtedly a part of rights' purview. There's a demand that both states and international society look after the physical human being and provide "standard[s] of living adequate for the health and well-being of [the individual] and his... family." Human rights should provide food, doctors, clothing and shelter; they should help put food in bellies.[55] Still, rights don't just keep people alive. They don't just keep us breathing. Rights encourage the "free and full development" of the human "personality."[56] They suggest that all should have the opportunity to cognitively and emotionally realize who they are. One has *truly* engaged human rights when at the end of the day, one has the freedom to say what one wants – to discuss one's sense of truth and debate with others the kinds of societies in which one would like to live. One should have the chance to reflect and say what sense one makes of what one has reflected upon.

Very simply, such things are also the task of art. I.e., whether visual, written, musically performed, danced or architectural in nature, art concerns perception. Art concerns understanding; it concerns comprehension: "views" of things and "ways of seeing," as it's been put.[57] Art concerns sensibilities involving things one feels either *need* to be said or, for whatever reason, one *wants* to say. Art is an act of mind – a putting out, if sometimes abstractly, of senses of understanding that one wishes to communicate to one's surrounding world. Now, there are huge – huge – debates to be had about the conditions under which art is made. Is the artist the product of his or her times, wherein there's always a vocabulary within which he or she has to work (a historically-inherited lexicon determining what he or she might say)? Perhaps. Maybe the artist's function is to *push* social boundaries, challenging conceptual possibilities such that we might think our lexicons anew. Also a possibility. Indeed, need art always be *so* intellectual – about theories or ideas, or the "painted word," as one writer has called it?[58] Maybe art should be spontaneous – a matter of impulse or how one intuitively "feels"?[59]

---

54 UDHR, article 1.
55 Ibid., article 25.
56 Ibid., article 29.
57 See John Berger, *Ways of Seeing* (New York: Penguin, 1972).
58 See Tom Wolfe, *The Painted Word* (New York: Bantam, 1975).
59 See David Cottington, *Modern Art: A Very Short Introduction* (Oxford: Oxford University Press, 2005), 53.

In part, the profusion of styles in the history of art has to do with answers to such questions – how one considers the task of the artist. Still, at some level, we're involved with problems of *how* one says what one wants and how one deploys the physical, intellectual and psychological tools available to do so. What *is* the expression one seeks to make, and what reflections and dialogues does one need to engage in to distil the essence of one's thoughts? Art represents the domains of reflection and expression in ways both elemental and pure.[60]

Now, I grant: art isn't always easy to understand. Certain pieces from figures like Weiwei – roomfuls of welded-together bicycles or bizarrely-stacked chairs, e.g. – are on the one hand simplistic, yet on the other hand complex and abstract.[61] They may induce some to ask "what's that all about?" and force some to shake their heads, arguing that there's little value in such things. That's art. Sometimes we like it, sometimes we don't. Still, what's *really* interesting is that we have reactions *at all* – that enthusiastically or not, we enter into *conversation* with and about the things we hear and see. We feel a *need* or *impulse* to say something *back*. We react to the *fact* of expression – that whether our reactions "well-formulated" or not. For my money, that's what gives art its cultural function. It's what explains our interest in music, painting, sculpture, architecture, dance, poetry or prose, be they "high" or "low" (Madonna or sculptures of *the* Madonna). By engaging in expression, art explicitly does something common to us all. It leaves articulations and forms there for others to judge, inviting our *own* articulations and forms. It induces *us* to articulate ourselves, offering our own reflections – at which point we engage in a bit of art ourselves. "Human beings are artistic animals no less

---

60 The writer Tolstoy once argued that "art is that human activity which consists of one man consciously conveying to others, by certain external signs, the feelings he has experienced." Tolstoy, ever the Romantic, put a great deal of emphasis on feeling. My sense is that we're a bit more engaged in thought (the American painter Edward Hopper once claimed that "great art is the outward expression of an inner life in the artist;" that bears a bit more on the notion of contemplation to the extent that one would see contemplation as key to "inner life"). In any case, there seems to be something to the idea of an external representation, through material, of some mode of consideration, perspective and conceptualization. See Leo N. Tolstoy, "Art as Communication of Feeling," in *The Nature of Art: An Anthology*, ed. Thomas Wartenburg (Boston: Wadsworth, 2012), 104; Henry Peacock, *Art as Expression* (Washington, DC: Whalesback, 1995), xv. See also Robert Stecker, *Aesthetics and the Philosophy of Art: An Introduction* (Lanham: Roman & Littlefield, 2010).

61 See Weiwei and Pins, *Ai Weiwei*.

than political ones," one set of critics has claimed; we think and make because it's hard to do otherwise.[62] We are art, and art is us.

I'd thus end my observations as follows. *If* Denmark is involved in human rights violations either in spirit or as concerns the letter of the law, we're in a certain way on the most normal of terrain. Look at Denmark's major NATO ally, e.g., and we know of U.S. soldiers stacking prisoners naked in an Iraqi prison and the legacies of Guantanamo Bay – ugly incidents that are clearly beyond the pale. The U.S. has refused to ratify the Economic, Social and Cultural Rights Covenant, excepting itself from international standards concerning basic socio-economic justice. Indeed, the U.S. has not even ratified the Convention on *children's* rights – something that boggles the mind.[63] There's no *way* Denmark comes out worse in any general assessment of human rights than ranges of other modern states, including the world's most powerful.[64] Indeed, outside the country's difficulty with migrants and an interest in ethno-identity preservation, Denmark would generally have to be considered a highly rights-friendly state. Still – still – what acts like Weiwei's do is to ask us to look at what happens when senses of "peoples" and "nations" go too far. What Weiwei points to is the notion that especially in states that *are* wealthy and *have* roles in important institutions like NATO or the EU, the sustenance of not only the *legal* dimensions but also the *spirit* of human rights is a charge one shouldn't forget. It's dubious if not wrong to say we like rights ideas in one context and not another, and constant vigilance is needed lest rights projects become cracked. Indeed, *Weiwei's* criticisms gain particular force because of what *he* represents. That's an explicit symbolization of the processes of conscience, consciousness and communication that we all bring

---

62 Arthur M. Melzer, Jerry Weinberger and M. Richard Zinman, "Introduction," in *Democracy and the Arts*, ed. Arthur M. Melzer, Jerry Weinberger and M. Richard Zinman (Ithaca, NY: Cornell University Press, 1999), 1.

63 See Rhoda E. Howard-Hassmann and Claude E. Welch, Jr., eds., *Economic Rights in Canada and the United States* (Philadelphia: University of Pennsylvania Press, 2006). See also Yvonne Vissing, "Children's Rights in the United States: 25 Years Later and Counting," in *The United Nations Convention on the Rights of the Child: Taking Stock after 25 Years and Looking Ahead*, ed. Ton Liefaard and Julia Sloth-Nielsen (Leiden: Brill, 2017), 73–101.

64 Alfred W. McCoy, *Torture and Impunity: The U.S. Doctrine of Coercive Interrogation* (Madison: University of Wisconsin Press, 2012); Fiona de Londras *Detention in the "War on Terror": Can Human Rights Fight Back?* (Cambridge: Cambridge University Press, 2012); Michelle Alexander, *The New Jim Crow: Mass Incarceration in the Age of Colorblindness* (New York: New Press, 2012).

to the table: the reflection and expression that defines humanity itself. *Qua* artist, Weiwei represents the art that all of us have inside.

The question we have to answer, then, be it about Denmark or any place else, is whether the politics we support help or hinder our art; do they encourage or diminish our being? Do they contribute to or take away from the essential tasks of human existence? Do we liberate our reflective qualities or not? Indeed, are we looking for *all* to realize their potential and engage in self-realization and self-expression, or are we delineating such rights as pertinent to some, leaving others to their fate? As far as I can see, the hand Denmark is putting up – the strongest iteration of which is the confiscation policy – is hard to read as anything except willful myopia. It reads like a statement of disinterest in- if not the outright rejection of- millions upon millions of people's art. It's a way of saying "if you've got something to say, say it somewhere else – and if you didn't get the message, you'll be searched when you show up (thus you really *should* take your statement somewhere else)." To that extent, my guess is that we haven't heard the last from figures like Weiwei – those interested in bringing the reflective essence of human existence to an explicit fore and encouraging its growth and freedom. One *can* shut such things down in the name of national borders. One can claim the sovereignty of "folk." That doesn't mean one has helped human rights, however. Rather, one may have explicitly struck against them. One can only hope that the reason and conscience of art might help restore the reason and conscience that should be present in social and political life as well.

The Sound of Many and One
Bergen-Belsen
(May 7, 2016)

Abstract: *The Holocaust represents the nadir of both Western and world history; it's the worst of what humanity has to had offer. How, though, do we think about the Holocaust both in terms of the event itself and its relation to larger, global views of genocide? How do we grapple with our imaginations of the Holocaust in terms of the limitations and possibilities those imaginations provide? Indeed, how does the Holocaust connect to* human rights *in terms of rights history and philosophy? A visit to the Bergen-Belsen concentration camp in Lower Saxony drives such questions home – the meaning of histories of suffering and the rights that all human beings should maintain.*

I have to admit that I was surprised at Belsen's appearance. I had forgotten, at least from what I'd read, that large sections of the camp had been burned to the ground; part of an effort not long after the camp's liberation to hold back a ty-

Photo by author.

phus epidemic. Personally, I'd only been to Auschwitz – a locale where much more remains intact. The two are nonetheless connected. When the Red Army pressed in on Auschwitz at the start of 1945, Hitler's government ordered the camp in Polish Silesia (Auschwitz) evacuated. That resulted in massive death marches towards the west – one of which is portrayed in Elie Wiesel's well-known book *Night* (1960).
Wiesel's contingent ended up in Buchenwald, the concentration camp liberated by the Americans a handful of days before the British liberated Belsen. Somewhere around 20,000 Auschwitz evacuees made it to Belsen – that after, between 1943 and '44, some two to three thousand Belsen inmates had been sent to *Auschwitz*. Among other things, Belsen is known as the place where Anne Frank and her sister Margot met their final end. There are headstones – though no knows for sure exactly where the bodies lay.

Today, Belsen is what in German is called a *Gedenkstätte* – a site of remembrance. Approaching the site, the grounds include a range of memorials and burial mounds spread over the several square miles once constituting the main camp. That's accompanied by a long, austere museum dominating the east side of the grounds. The museum is impressive: a profound cement structure with a bunker-like feel telling the history of the camp from its initial construction around the start of the War to its use as a POW facility to its use as an "exchange" camp (holding Jews hostages to exchange for interned Germans) to a more directly-styled concentration camp from 1943 on.[1] The exhibitions are extensive: films of interviews with survivors (the Nazi regime's "undesirables"), vast displays of POW registration cards (largely from Soviet soldiers arriving after the start of Operation Barbarossa [the German invasion of the USSR]), film reels and photographs taken by the British soldiers who liberated the camp, documentation of prisoners' attempts to reconstruct their lives in the wake of the camp's liberation and coverage of the "Belsen Trials" – the first attempt to legally pin down at least *some* extent of Nazi madness. All of it's important – one can't put too much information about the Holocaust before the public eye. It is, however, taxing. Obviously, there's the mental taxation; the amount of anguish and suffering one has to countenance is not small indeed. There *is*, however, also physical taxation. The museum is constructed on a continual upward slope, where one has to exert bodily effort to take in the camp's history (one follows events in chronological order, from beginning to end). In part, Belsen's reputation was built on that fact that, upon liberation, roughly 13,000 unburied bodies were found by the British – the discovery of which more than one British soldier has described as the nadir of their life.[2] The center of the upward walk through the museum is a small theater with film reels of this discovery – films where bodies are noted and laid-out with bulldozers coming to plow emaciated corpses into mass graves and other bulldozers coming to cover them with dirt. Outside the museum, the graves of those dead mark the landscape: burial mounds headed by modernistic script noting "here rest 5000 dead," "here rest 2000 dead," "here rest 4000 dead" and so on. The graves are then punctuated by some startling monuments – most noticeably the Belsen Obelisk, attached to a wall of remembrance

---

1   See Eberhard Kolb, *Bergen-Belsen: vom "Aufenthaltslager" zum Konzentrationslager, 1943–1945* (Vandenhoeck and Ruprecht, 2002).

2   British cameraman Sergeant Michael Lewis, e.g., noted that "something had changed for me after I'd seen the camp." It was a lasting impression of large-scale death for which he was unprepared – a sentiment echoed by virtually every British soldier who entered the Belsen in its first days of liberation. See Imperial War Museums, "The Liberation of Bergen-Belsen," available at http://www.iwm.org.uk/history/the-liberation-of-bergen-belsen; Imperial War Museum, *The Relief of Belsen, April 1945: Eyewitness Accounts* (London: Imperial War Museum, 1991); Joanne Reilly, *Belsen: The Liberation of a Concentration Camp* (London: Routledge, 1998); Ben Shephard, *After Daybreak: The Liberation of Belsen, 1945* (London: Jonathan Cape, 2005).

featuring phrases of memorialization in the languages of all the interred. The wall is fronted by a broad stone plaza – though, as with much of the camp, the grass surrounding the plaza is simply left to grow, and the natural dimensions of the locale are generally permitted to speak for themselves.

Belsen wasn't a death camp. It's a macabre conversation to have. However, especially the reputation of especially *Auschwitz* has become so great that it can be easy to confuse extermination camps, largely located in Eastern Europe, with the entire punitive internment system run by the Nazis state. I.e., as opposed to the closely-measured calculus of death making places like Auschwitz, the killing in Belsen was largely a function of neglect. Roughly 52,000 died in the camp – a massive number, to be sure. It is a number that pales, however, in comparison to the more than one million murdered in Auschwitz-Birkenau, or the roughly 800,000 killed in places like Treblinka. Of course, it's hard to imagine anything other than that there must have been at least *some* summary executions; prisoners who got out of line, individuals capos no longer wanted alive or groups attempting to put up some kind of resistance or seeking to escape.[3] Still, disease, malnourishment, exhaustion, lack of sanitation and, yes, some medical experimentation, were Belsen's most significant killers. Indeed, when one visits the camp, that issue – the issue of death camps versus "other" camps – creates some hard-to-countenance scenes. If one looks closely at other visitors – especially the young – one can sometimes see people *looking* for the extermination camp. Many aren't sure *how* to process the overriding sense of death – the images of masses of corpses simply lying about in the open – with the absence of gas chambers or the massive unloading docks for box cars filled with "Untermenschen" that feature so prominently in the landscape at places like Auschwitz.[4] That's at the same time that Belsen underlines the fact that torture, death and the trial of the human soul – the obliteration, or *Vernichtung*, of people – can happen in any number of heart-wrenching and existentially rage-inducing ways. I.e., Belsen underlines the multiplicity of the modes through which the Holocaust played out.[5]

---

3   The exact number of these actions has been hard to detect. See, however, Abel J. Herzberg, *Between Two Streams: A Diary from Bergen-Belsen*, trans. Jack Santcross (London: I.B. Taurus, 1997).

4   It should be noted that Belsen did have its unloading sites and rail lines, though on a noticeably smaller in scale, and not in the immediate area of the main camp.

5   See, e.g., Omer Bartov, ed., *The Holocaust: Origins, Implementation, Aftermath* (London: Routledge, 2000); Michael Berenbaum, ed., *The Holocaust and History: The Known, the Unknown, the Disputed, and the Reexamined* (Bloomington: Indiana University Press,

In considering my time at the camp, I have to say that point has especially stuck with me – that, perhaps especially among the young, Auschwitz-style killing is often seen as the way that the Holocaust *must* have played-out; the notion that other experiences, as mind-boggling as they may have been, don't always fully register. *That* then becomes connected to the fact that, via broad knowledge of a supremely important yet also specific experience of mass murder (again, Auschwitz), there's often knowledge of the existence of the *Holocaust*, but far from automatic senses of other genocides.[6] Examples of genocide in modern times are rife. In 1994, in ninety days, Hutus put to death roughly 900,000 Tutsi and Tutsi sympathizers in Rwanda, the small central African state – an orgy of death in a drastically short period of time. That was preceded by the murder of roughly 25,000 *Tutsi's* in Burundi, Rwanda's neighbor, in 1993 – another dark chapter in the history of Central Africa's modern past. Many remember that Europe saw the murder of 8-9000 Bosniacs at Srebrenica in 1995 – perhaps the most disturbing event among many tragedies that mark the 1990s Yugoslav Wars.[7] In the 1980s, Saddam Hussein guided a murderous operation against the Kurds and other northern Iraqi non-Arabs, killing tens, if not hundreds, of thousands of civilians (the notorious Al-Anfal campaign).[8] Between 1975 and 1979, Pol Pot killed somewhere around 1.7 million individuals in his remake of Cambodia, deporting droves of "intellectuals" and "cosmopolitans" to the country's infamous killing fields. In the early '70s, tens of thousands of *Hutus* were murdered by a *Tutsi*-led government in *another* period of ethnic strife – that in Burundi again.[9] At the end of the '50s and start of the '60s, Mao Zedong's policies in the so-called "Great Leap Forward" contributed to the deaths of tens of millions of Chinese – that from overreporting agricultural production as farmers attempted to placate the demands of the state. It's hard to link the tens of millions who died at Stalin's

1998); Devon E. Hinton and Alexander L. Hinton, eds., *Genocide and Mass Violence: Memory, Symptom, and Recovery* (Cambridge: Cambridge University Press, 2015).

6   See Rebecca Jinks, *Representing Genocide: The Holocaust as Paradigm* (London: Bloomsbury Academics, 2016).

7   See David Rohde, *Endgame: The Betrayal and Fall of Srebrenica, Europe's Worst Massacre since World War II* (New York: Penguin, 1997).

8   See Martin van Bruinessen, "Genocide in Kurdistan?: The Suppression of the Dersim Rebellion in Turkey (1937–38) and the Chemical War Against the Iraqi Kurds (1988)," in *Genocide: Conceptual and Historical Dimensions*, ed. George J. Andreopoulos (Philadelphia: University of Pennsylvania Press, 1997) 141–70.

9   See Christian P. Scherrer, *Genocide and Crisis in Central Africa: Conflict Roots, Mass Violence, and Regional War* (Westport: Praeger, 2002).

hands in the USSR to a single event; does one focus on the hard-to-calculate number of political prisoners who disappeared into gulags and other varieties of prison camps, or does one underline the deaths resulting from the regime's own forced collectivization in the '30s and the famines that ran rampant through the Soviet countryside? Of course, a good three-quarters of Turkey's Armenian population were killed in the sinews of World War I – the annihilation of hundreds of thousands if not millions in the name of defending the then-Ottoman state. And that's just the twentieth century – and but a partial list of what many would count as acts of genocide in roughly the last one hundred years' time.[10]

Now, the idea that many know the Holocaust while there's often ignorance of other genocides and state- and socially-sponsored mass killings is a well-known phenomenon. So is the idea that Auschwitz looms perhaps decisively large over Holocaust consciousness in general. Regarding the first point, two education scholars have, for example, recently noted the tendency of even university-level classes to use terminologies such as "the Holocaust and 'other genocides,'" or "Genocide and Holocaust Studies" – potentially patronizing formulations when one is discussing an experience that has been characterized as "worse than war." Indeed, I admit to having used such vocabularies myself.[11] Now, there *are* rationales for the focus on the Holocaust. I.e., there *may be* a particular power to certain lines of Holocaust experience that make it hard to look away from, or *not* take center stage in humanity's theater of hate and destruction. I.e., at the center of the Holocaust lies the Shoah or, though there's debate about the proper use of terminology, what the Israeli Holocaust center Yad Vashem defines as the targeted killing of Europe's Jews.[12] The millennia – *millennia* – long persecution

---

10 See Ben Kiernan, *Blood and Soil: A World History of Genocide and Extermination from Sparta to Darfur* (New Haven: Yale University Press, 2007). There is, of course, an extensive debate on how to define genocide. Does it concern primarily ethnic groups? Must it be intentional? Can political identities be part of the picture? Who has to prosecute it? Roughly, I'm using a more expansive notion of the term in which all targeted killings on mass scales either by governments or societies qualify. See, e.g., George J. Andreopoulos, ed., *Genocide: Conceptual and Historical Dimensions* (Philadelphia: University of Pennsylvania Press, 1994).

11 Samuel Totten and Jon E. Pedersen, eds., *Educating about Social Issues in the 20th and 21st Centuries: A Critical Annotated Bibliography, Volume One* (Charlotte: Information Age Publishing, 2011). See also Daniel Godlhagen, *Worse than War: Genocide, Eliminationism, and the Ongoing Assault on Humanity* (New York: PublicAffairs, 2009).

12 The question of the precise terminology around the Holocaust is complicated. There's overlaps between the terms Shoah and Holocaust and debate about what pertains to whom and why. As linguist Anna-Vera Sullam Calimani notes, however, the growth in

of the Jews is one of Western history's most enduring themes, and the Shoah brings the entire history to its sordid head. I.e., the Holocaust demonstrates the power of "othering" when it runs centuries-long unchecked. It also gives one pause when one realizes that it's not just prejudice *at-large* one is talking about, but a *specifically-targeted* bigotry that appears over *so many* historical eras. Indeed, the history of prejudice towards the world's Jews is *so* extensive that the renowned Russian-French historian Léon Poliakov once dedicated four volumes of scholarly work to the issue, covering everything from pagan antiquity to the European twentieth century. As Poliakov notes, anti-Semitism has simply been a theme that the European past has been unable to shake, and the anti-Semitism of that continent has lapped over into other regions, such as North America and the Middle East. Simply put, nothing underlines this past like the Shoah – anti-Semitism's most complete and heart-wrenching result.[13]

Indeed, it's *also* the case that there are few times in history when an apparatus quite so *massive* been set in motion for such a monstrous purpose. I.e., the mechanisms put into place to kill Europe's Jews – yet many others as well – were simply vast. No, the Final Solution didn't take its *most* concrete shape until December 1942, at the Wannsee Conference – the meeting of Nazi head honchos led by Reinhard Heydrich intended to coordinate the efforts of multiple departments of the German government towards the realization of their anti-Semitic goals.[14] Still, one might characterize Nazi society *itself* as a machine in which the Holocaust and Shoah began in small-scale forms with the boycott of Jewish businesses and the disbarring of Jews and other "non-Aryans" from the civil service in 1933, the racial classifications of the 1935 Nuremberg Laws in which Jews were stripped of German citizenship and forbidden to "defile" German blood, and then events like *Kristallnacht* (1938), sanctioning the physical damage of Jewish property and

---

interest of the term "Shoah" is connected to searching for a means of best describing the attempt to exterminate Europe's Jews by the Nazis. That distinguishes itself from a wider extermination program oriented towards a noticeably larger range of ethnicities, religions and political persuasions. See Calimani, "A Name for Extermination," *The Modern Language Review* 94, no. 4 (1999): 978–99. See also Yad Vashem, "Shoah Victims' Names" (2016), available at http://www.yadvashem.org/archive/hall-of-names/shoah-victims-names.

13 See Léon Poliakov, *The History of Anti-Semitism*, 4 vols. (Philadelphia: University of Pennsylvania Press, 2003). See also Albert S. Lindemann, and Richard S. Levy, eds., *Anti-Semitism: A History* (Oxford: Oxford University Press, 2010).

14 Mark Roseman, *The Villa, the Lake, the Meeting: Wannsee and the Final Solution* (New York: Penguin, 2002).

rubber-stamping the physical intimidation of Jews, if not all minorities, by German society at-large (that to say nothing of the concentration camps that came into existence immediately upon Hitler's ascension to power and which took little time to start interning those not in the regime's favor). Indeed, the flabbergasting racism of Nazism follows the entire history of the movement, extending beyond even books like Hitler's *Mein Kampf* to the Nazi leader's time as a young man in Vienna under the city's anti-Semitic mayor, Karl Lueger, to perhaps the entire culture of Central European anti-Jewish attitudes that scholars like Poliakov have done so well to trace.[15] The Nazi view of humanity, if "view of humanity" is what it should be called, was simply that some were in and others were out. As more than one social psychologist has noted, it's infinitely easier to destroy others when they've been designated as "out" – if they've been reduced to the status of not being human at all.[16]

Indeed, it's also noticeable that the Holocaust's and Shoah's are attached to the Second World War – the most destructive event of modern times – and that event is then attached to the West's historical heart (again, Europe). I.e., many will have the sense that the "West" and Europe, especially in the years after the Renaissance and Scientific Revolution, provided global society with many of its progressive ideals: liberal democracy, universal franchise, inherent political equality, addresses to civil rights and ranges of theories concerning economic justice (varieties of socialist and liberal political-economics, largely). Indeed, though related to larger trends in the history of rationalist thought, those are brainchildren of the *Enlightenment* specifically: the event, as intellectual historian Anthony Pagden once put it, providing the "key terms" for almost every "modern conflict" and attempt to "understand and define 'humanity'" as well as improve its conditions.[17] Those are positives about European and Western legacies – concepts by which we often define their worth. Still, sitting smack in the middle of such ideals has been decidedly something else: enough nationalistic venom to produce two world wars, mountains of imperialist arrogance, pogroms, ethnocentrisms of more than a little intensity and multiple

---

15 See also Hajo Holborn, "Origins and Political Character of Nazi Ideology," *Political Science Quarterly* 79, no. 4 (1964): 542–54; Sebastian Hafner, *The Meaning of Hitler*, trans. Ewald Osers (Cambridge, MA: Harvard University Press, 1979).

16 See David Livingstone Smith, *Less Than Human: Why We Demean, Enslave, and Exterminate Others* (New York: St. Martin's, 2011); James Waller, *Becoming Evil: How Ordinary People Commit Genocide and Mass Killing* (Oxford: Oxford university Press, 2007).

17 Anthony Pagden, *The Enlightenment and Why It Still Matters* (Oxford: Oxford University Press, 2013), 5.

invocations of science in defense of hierarchies of race.[18] Now, as more than one historian has noted, *because* of its centuries-long centrality to global events (often because it's forced itself onto others), *world* history has for better or worse often been read through *European* lenses. I.e., though perhaps due to its colonial proclivities, the markers for the European past are often used as the historical makers for the world as a whole. As the nadir of *that* history – i.e., as Europe's worst moment – the Holocaust often becomes the nadir of the global historical narrative *in toto*.[19] Now, as Elie Wiesel remarked to Bill Clinton at the dedication of the U.S Holocaust Museum at a moment when it was becoming clear where the Yugoslav Wars were heading, important about Holocaust consciousness is that it neither doesn't nor shouldn't provide "minor lessons." The Holocaust doesn't offer "book learning" to which we should pay lip-service and then go about our daily lives. The power of knowing about the Holocaust is that it charges us to "stop the bloodshed" that comes with oppression – that wherever oppression is to be found. The Holocaust asks us to halt the identification of peoples as "unwanted" and resist the naked grabs for power that politics can sometimes bring.[20] The Holocaust asks humanity to *broaden* its knowledge in ways such that, as one historian put it, we can establish "unstinting concern with the tragedy and immorality of each and every [killing and unjust death]."[21] I.e., by standing as *everyone's* experience, the Holocaust *should* take us to *different* experiences – places where peoples and groups can say "we've had a tragedy of a similar kind, but here's how it either is or was for us."[22] Knowledge of the Holocaust should help engender broader, global sympathies and more cosmopolitan views of conflict – that though there are good reasons to take care that it doesn't drown out other events.

To that extent, it's appropriate to address the potential limitations of knowledge that can happen *within* consciousness of the Holocaust too. I.e., as one historian

---

18 See Mark Mazower, *Dark Continent: Europe's Twentieth Century* (New York: Vintage, 2000).

19 See, e.g., Amos Goldberg and Haim Hazan, eds., *Marking Evil: Holocaust Memory in the Global Age* (New York: Berghahn, 2015) – though Peter Novick's contribution to this volume offer nuance to the idea of "global" Holocaust memory. See also Martin L. Davies and Claus-Christian W. Szejnmann, eds., *How the Holocaust Looks Now: International Perspectives* (New York: Palgrave Macmillan, 2006).

20 C-Span, "Elie Wiesel Bosnia Remarks," April 22, 1993, available at http://www.c-span.org/video/?c3342709/elie-wiesel-bosnia-remarks.

21 Israel W. Charny, "Foreword," in *Is the Holocaust Unique?: Perspectives on Comparative Genocide*, ed. Alan S. Rosenbaum (Boulder: Westview, 2009), xi.

22 Ibid.

has noted, Auschwitz *specifically* can sometimes be "taken [as] an adequate or even final symbol" for the Holocaust *as such* – wherein images from the world's most famous camp ("Arbeit Macht Frei" above the Auschwitz I gates or the train tracks leading to the ominous port of Birkenau) are taken to suffice for a full understanding of what the Holocaust was and how it played out.[23] Again, visiting Belsen, it is clear that more than a few have senses of the Holocaust as *only* the rounding up and extermination of "undesirables," immediately, forthwith and without compunction. Now, the "without compunction" is clearly true. The numbers at Chełmno, Sobibór, Bełżec, Treblinka, Majdanek and Auschwitz – the primary death camps – are near-incomprehensible; around 3.5 million were murdered within their walls. Auschwitz *was* the worst of them as it again featured roughly 1.1 million put to death. Indeed, in addition to the killing, there was the slave labor provided for the industrial concern I.G. Farben at Monowitz, just outside the main part of the Auschwitz complex.[24] Those are experiences that are simply hard to calculate – that even upon visiting the sites themselves. Other factors play into Auschwitz's notoriety, however. As one expert has noted, the presence of a large number of Western European Jews in Auschwitz whose ability to communicate about their experiences *after* the war helped the camp's profile – that compared to camps with larger Eastern European populations that largely returned to what became the Eastern Bloc (i.e., the free speech strictures of Eastern Bloc regimes may have helped shade more diverse types of Holocaust memory).[25] Of course, it's also the case that, by hook or by crook, historical events simply accumulate their narrative symbology. We may naturally seek moments, locales, figures and images that speak to the "larger picture" of things – symbols that become shorthand for happenings as a whole (think Civil Rights, e.g., and the 1963 March on Washington quickly comes to mind; think of the French Revolution and one imagines the storming of the Bastille).[26] That's at the same time that the Holocaust *in fact* happened in more ways than we can count, and we *shouldn't* forget deaths from overcrowding in ghettos from Poland to Belarus, the sterilization of those the regime considered "feeble-minded," the spontaneous killings of Jews by locals in places like Lviv in the Ukraine, *Einsatzgruppen* marauding through the Nazi-conquered territory in the regime's *Drang nach Osten* or client states assisting in the round-ups, sometimes

---

23 In René Lemchard, "Introduction," in *Forgotten Holocausts: Oblivion, Denial, and Memory*, ed. René Lemchard (Philadelphia: University of Pennsylvania Press, 2011), 11.

24 See Laurence Rees, *Auschwitz: A New History* (New York: PublicAffairs, 2005).

25 Ibid.

26 See, e.g., Hayden White, "The Value of Narrativity in the Representation of Reality," *Critical Inquiry* 7, no. 1 (1980): 5–27.

with gusto, demanded by the Nazi state. As a concept or symbol, "Auschwitz" helps
us process events. "Auschwitz" provides a heading through which to organize our
view of Holocaust tragedy. That's while Nazi killing constituted a cacophonic mosaic: screaming bits of color one tries to arrange into tones one can understand –
that though the number of tiles and the hues involved are too chaotic to bring
under full control.[27]

All of that's useful. I.e., we again need to think about how to consider genocide
and the benefits and drawbacks of the kinds of memories we have. We need to
consider what we know about the Holocaust *as such*, and the kinds of conscious-
nesses and symbolisms that knowledge of that event involves. A last point that
comes, or at least *came*, to mind regarding Belsen, however, is the relationship
of the Holocaust to *human rights*. I.e., a particular *concept* comes to mind as one
moves through the museum and grounds of the concentration camp in Lower
Saxony – a concept we take to stand as the pinnacle of our international ethics
and modern ideals; a socio-political concept that though perhaps not gaining
total consensus on the international stage, may represent the closest to consensus
we get. That's the idea that there are sets of socio-ethical standards that all of us
might expect; that there are fundamental freedoms and liberties which should
be universal and never be undone. It's the idea that human value is inherent, and
that such inherent value should never be put under threat.[28] It's the notion that
"freedom, justice and peace" are the goals of the world community and that they
should be pursued persistently and at near-any price. It's the idea that justice and
recognition should be what human existence is fundamentally about.[29]

Now, on *historical* bases, it *is* the case that, for better or worse, some have made
the point that the Holocaust may have played *little* role in post-War formulations
of universal rights. I.e., human rights *qua* specific concept are often suggested as
something rounding into shape in the 1940s (the idea of larger, international- or

27 See David Crowe, *The Holocaust: Roots, History, and Aftermath* (Boulder: Westview,
    2008); Doris L. Bergen, *The Holocaust: A Concise History* (Lanham: Rowman & Lit-
    tlefield, 2009).

28 The intention of human rights, Eleanor Roosevelt claimed, was to be the "international
    Magna Carta" for all humankind. They were to be cross-border and wholly universal – a
    commitment to humankind *in toto*. In Micheline R. Ishay, *The History of Human Rights:
    From Ancient Time to the Globalization Era* (Berkeley: University of California Press,
    2004), 218.

29 The vocabulary of "freedom, justice and peace" comes from United Nations, "The
    Universal Declaration of Human Rights" (1948, preamble), available at http://www.
    un.org/en/universal-declaration-human-rights/index.html.

fully-universal privileges), and some argue that popular notions of the move to *articulate* those privileges after the Second World War as concerning places like Belsen and Auschwitz *in fact* concern a later, counterfactual memory in which we *want* that to be the case more than it actually is. A more accurate picture, some argue, is rights as something that interest groups and particular cliques of lawyers advocated at specific moments during the formation of the UN – points that were taken up almost incidentally and which were more "peripheral" than "central" to the formation of new internationalist regimes.[30] This isn't just historical nay-saying. There *are* interesting phenomena concerning rights and post-War relations with the Holocaust. Pointing to the films made by the British at Belsen, e.g. – including those of bulldozing bodies into mass graves – one historian has noted that many film reels were shelved for years out of concern with alienating the local population. I.e., the Allies had to win over ordinary Germans if they were to reconstruct the country, and one had to be careful with explosive material like the British film footage as Germany was too simply large and too central to the overall European reconstruction plan to risk delaying its rebuilding because German workers felt their noses were overly-rubbed in the worst of Nazi crimes. Some shaming was good. Too much, though, and one risked the success of after-War projects.[31] Indeed, pulling back a bit, it's *also* the case that, at least according to one of the more referred-to accounts of UN delegates as *they* debated the notion of human rights in the years immediately following the War, there's little on-record mention of the murder of the Jews or other minorities in any specific sense. I.e., in the major forum in which human rights were discussed and formulated, references by delegates were often to Nazi atrocities in broad-brush terms: the practices of "brutal totalitarian States," as the Ecuadorian representative put it, or decrying the general crimes of "fascism," as one often heard from Soviet Bloc states. That's as opposed to referencing *specific* acts of mass murder or the

---

30 Samuel Moyn, *The Last Utopia: Human Rights in History* (Cambridge, MA: Harvard Belknap, 2010), 68. Important here is a distinction between human rights – transborder, fully universal privileges – and rights as articulated by nations. The latter may have appealed to universal ideals. They were, however, largely meant for the citizens of states – not a *global* citizenry.

31 That's while it's well-acknowledged that there were also concrete attempts on the part of the Allies to have Germans look directly at sites like Belsen – though, again, the question is whether it was nearly as much as it should have been. See Yehuda Cohen, *The Germans: Absent Nationality and the Holocaust* (Brighton: Sussex, 2010), 107.

persecution of *particular* groups.[32] Moral outrage appears to have sometimes been a touch vague, and perhaps not as widespread as we might think.

It's hard to know what to say to this. On one hand, there *were* pragmatic dimensions to the way the Allies handled multiple post-War relations with the Holocaust. The Belsen Trials provide an example of this. Trials related to the camp were set up quickly after its liberation – already in the autumn of 1945. Indeed, the Belsen Trials included figures from *Auschwitz*, meaning that they were among the first prosecutions for the crimes committed in the most infamous of Holocaust camps.[33] This had significance for international law – that to the extent that such issues put questions of international ethics on the agenda and indicated that there was a need for deepened vocabularies of universal justice.[34] The Belsen Trials convicted a bit more than twenty people – about half of whom were sentenced to death and half to prison terms. Still, many sentenced to prison were released within a few years. Defendants were tried under the heading of war crimes – that as "crimes against humanity" mechanisms had not been fully worked-out.[35] In fact, the couple of dozen convictions that *did* occur might be posed against what the Belsen Memorial homepage notes as *two hundred* SS members at the camp who never stood trial *at all*. Very simply, it's been claimed, too much Bible-thumping would have been seen as "moralist regression" – something that the Allies, again faced with the challenge of reconstructing Europe, couldn't afford.[36] That's while "Bible-thumping" may have been precisely what was needed – i.e., that the Belsen Trials may have represented a lost opportunity to push for more basic standards of fundamental rights and universal justice.[37]

---

32 In Johannes Morsink, *The Universal Declaration of Human Rights: Origins, Drafting & Intent* (Philadelphia: University of Pennsylvania Press, 1999), 36.

33 This included particularly notorious criminals, such as Josef Kramer and Irma Grese. See, e.g., Donald Bloxham, *Genocide on Trial: War Crimes Trials and the Formation of Holocaust History and Memory* (Oxford: Oxford University Press, 2001), 100. Bloxham does note, though, supporting some of the arguments suggesting that the Holocaust wasn't understood in the ways that it perhaps should have been, that there was very little mention, even in the context of figures like Kramer and Grese, of Jews or any other specific identity group. This attaches itself to the idea that at the Belsen trials, war crimes were the focus as opposed to crimes against humanity.

34 See Yoram Dinstein, *The Defence of 'Obedience to Superior Orders' in International Law* (Oxford: Oxford University Press, 2012); William A. Schabas, *Genocide in International Law: The Crime of Crimes* (Cambridge: Cambridge University Press, 2009).

35 See Bloxham, *Genocide on Trial*.

36 Richard Falk, *Achieving Human Rights* (London: Routledge, 2009), 91.

37 See Bloxham, *Genocide on Trial*.

Again, there may be truth to this; not pushing immediately for justice on the grandest scale and *not* tying humanity's worst crimes immediately to an international regime intended to address them sounds unimaginable. It's hard to comprehend how the international community would not have been *ready* with a set of legal and ethical standards that would address not only the conduct of war, but ideas of crimes against humanity and the fundamental rights of humankind against which such crimes might be contextualized.[38] Still, that might not be the whole picture. It may not be the case that with events like the Belsen Trials, the ball was simply dropped. As some note, the Belsen Trials *did* strike a chord that subsequent trials like those at Nuremberg – better-known today – would amplify. Though not employed at the Belsen proceedings themselves, the trials related to Belsen *did* underline the need for a "crimes against humanity" mechanism – a concept the Nuremberg Trials *did* develop and deploy to no small effect. Some claim that Nuremberg didn't place the Holocaust as centrally as it might (that it was still too broad-brush in its address to mass murder).[39] Still, in invoking "crimes against humanity," the proceedings opened a conceptual ground within human rights' "ambit."[40] Indeed, while the UN was forming its initial principles during the same period, it's also not as though delegates *weren't* talking about the "barbarous doctrines of Nazism and fascism," as Charles Malik, a member of the Universal Declaration of Human Rights (1948) drafting committee, put it.[41] References to the despicability of Nazi ideas and practices came frequently and, given that knowledge of the Holocaust *was* emerging rapidly upon the end of the War, one has to wonder *what* statements like Malik's, or other indictments of "Nazi crimes" would have referenced if it wasn't at least *partly* the destruction of Jews, Roma, homosexuals, political opponents, "Slavs" and other "non-persons" persecuted by the Nazi state. I.e., could one think Nazi crimes *without* such events *somewhere* in the background – that again given that camps like Belsen and Auschwitz

---

38 Indeed, this is another complicated point regarding emerging human rights regimes. Allied powers were at work constituting the UN – what would become the world's primary rights organization – before the end of the war. Early approaches to the organization, however, much deprioritized human rights. It took a substantial effort to finally get rights recognized as part of the UN Charter (1945), to say nothing of beginning the process of composing documents like the Universal Declaration of Human Rights (1948). See Roger Normand and Sarah Zaidi, *Human Rights at the UN: The Political History of Universal Justice* (Bloomington: Indiana University Press, 2008).

39 See, e.g., Moyn, *The Last Utopia*, 82.

40 Falk, *Achieving Human Rights*, 92.

41 Morsink, *The Universal Declaration*, 36.

were hardly *un*known and were increasingly discussed? Hard to say. One never knows what's in historical actors' minds.[42] Still, it's clear that Nazi behaviors were identified as beyond the pale, and it seems that the international community was at least *attempting* to indict a doctrine that it was increasingly known had caused the death of millions. Nazi mass murder seems to have featured *somewhere* in the institutions and actors that would help create regimes of human rights.[43]

Now, historical linkages are important. That more than just the military aspects of events between 1939 and 1945 were *somehow* taken seriously and that the global community was considering Nazi transgressions while it considered the future of justice has meaning.[44] It's good to know that international institutions weren't *just* about pragmatics, and that there was an attempt to at least *formulate* principle. Still, the important point for the Holocaust as concerns human rights might be more than just facts. The key issue concerning the Holocaust and concepts of international justice might not only be only narratives and counter-narratives; history as it's best interpreted or not. The key issue for the Holocaust as regards human rights might be *philosophical*. The key issue might be the inviolability of the person that sits at the center of rights concepts and ideas of the "inalienability" of the human being which suggest that there's no room for transgressing the existence of people not only on the basis of who they are, but because they are *at all*. I.e., from a rights perspective, going after anyone for anyone reason stinks. Yes; one might sometimes discuss suspending rights in order to preserve them (e.g., one may need to contemplate killing as a necessary step to *stop* a genocide). In a general sense, though, undercutting the worth of others – never mind radical strikes against their *existence* – are dark paths on which humanity should never find itself.[45]

---

42 See, e.g., Michael Flemming, *Auschwitz, the Allies and Censorship of the Holocaust* (Cambridge: Cambridge University Press, 2014): Peter Novick, *The Holocaust in American Life* (Boston: Houghton Mifflin, 1999).

43 See Daniel Levy and Natan Sznaider, *The Holocaust and Memory in the Global Age*, trans. Assenka Oksiloff (Philadelphia: Temple University Press, 2006), 193. See also Michael Burleigh and Wolfgang Wippermann, *The Racial State: Germany 1933–1945* (Cambridge: Cambridge University Press, 1991).

44 See Ishay, 218.

45 The notion of suspending rights in order to preserve them relates to the notion of *jus cogens* – the idea of "inderogable" human rights that one might defend by force. Most would include genocide, or the right to avoid it, as among those. That's not uncomplex, though, as there is a question as to whether one takes concepts like the absoluteness of the right to life seriously – a right central to significant human rights documents. I.e., one has to very much be able to explain what one is doing with the use of force in

I'd put it this way. If – *if* – a world characterized by "freedom, justice and peace" is our goal; *if* we seek recognitions of essential humanity and worlds free from violence on both local and global scales, such things can be won in a number of ways. Victory might come on political fronts – that in terms of popular participation in government and people's ability to determine their civic lives. Victory might come on economic fronts – that in terms of the accordance of basic living standards and the insurance that basic needs as concerns food, housing and medical will be taken care of. Victory might come in terms of social justice – situations in which social groups achieve legal equality and are provided with generally equal concern by the body politic.[46] Still, the *basic* question rights ask – perhaps the basic question that *any* ethics asks – is what to do when we're confronted by the face of another. What we do when we have to calculate the fact we stand in each other's presence and have to negotiate the reality that we share a common space?[47]

Now, this "space sharing" might mean a number of things. It might mean "categorical imperatives," as the philosopher Immanuel Kant once suggested. It might mean considering the universalizability of one's moral actions, or whether one can one turn one's ethical decisions into general rules.[48] It might mean considering social contracts – finding modicums of agreement, as philosopher John Rawls has suggested, in terms of how we might live together without knowing the outcomes of the agreements that we make.[49] It might mean considering law and the institutions through which legal right is preserved. It might mean assuring that legal guarantees aren't winnowed down to legal philosophy.[50] Still, our presence around each other might have *existential* consequences. Our presence around each other might mean that I primarily find myself in encountering you. I.e., lest I desire nihilism, my ethical substance may rely on my ability to transcend myself

---

the furtherance of rights – that while it from time to time may well be acceptable. See, e.g., Robert Kolb, *Peremptory International Law – Jus Cogens: An Inventory* (Oxford: Hart, 2015); Elizabeth Wicks, *The Right to Life and Conflicting Interests* (Oxford: Oxford University Press, 2010).

46 This simply gets at the basic purpose of rights. See, e.g., A. Reis Monteiro, *Ethics of Human Rights* (Dordrecht: Springer, 2016).

47 Emmanuel Levinas, *Totality and Infinity: An Essay on Exteriority*, trans. Alphonso Lingis (Pittsburgh: Duquesne University Press, 1969), 198–9, 304. The "face" vocabulary is Levinas' most famous phrase.

48 See Immanuel Kant, *Grounding for the Metaphysics of Morals*, trans. James W. Ellington (Indianapolis: Hackett, 1981).

49 See John Rawls, *A Theory of Justice* (Cambridge, MA: Harvard University Press, 1971).

50 See David Earl Childress III, ed., *The Role of Ethics in International Law* (Cambridge: Cambridge University Press, 2012).

and embrace not just *my* life, but life *as such* – the baseline of any human community (there's simply no social philosophy without social *life*). Now, one *can* take Zarathustrian approaches and suggest that one should escape humanity in order to find one's own power – that one need to go into solitude to find the strength to establish one's *own* values and think without distraction. Perhaps. Authenticity and individuality – to say nothing of clarity of thought – have meaning. They can help us discover what we'd like to say.[51] To what end, however? What does isolated meditation *mean* unless its results are applied to a world in which one *lives*? What does solitary reflection accomplish unless it accomplishes something one might *use*? The philosopher Emmanuel Levinas once suggested that such questions are the reason why ethics is "first philosophy." Such questions are why right and wrong are our *ultimate* problems. There's little meaning in human existence without questions of how we might relate to the others by which we find ourselves surrounded – that, of course, in addition to the question of how we want others to deal with *us*.[52]

Visiting Bergen-Belsen, one finds oneself confronted by many faces – individuals who looked on others, individuals who were looked on by others themselves, and the individuals who looked upon them too. The souls attached to those many faces are spread out over a clearing several miles long and wide, sixty miles south of Hamburg. They lie amidst rough, untended grass in the midst of a North German forest – a one-time site of internment, segregation, marginalization, the limitation of possibility, disease, the corruption of things human and death upon death. One can draw physical lines to the locales where ethics, coexistence and basic engagements in so many parts of the human project were relinquished. Five hundred miles to Auschwitz. Eight hundred miles to Bełżec. Three hundred miles to Nuremberg. Two hundred to the seat of the government that allowed *Kristallnacht* and organized the conference at Wannsee (Berlin). We see and hear in many lives of many kinds effected by those many locales both the request and possibility that comes with any face – the desire to be treated well, but also the desire to simply *be*; the wish to have *any* kind of possibility, and the hope that we'll embrace and acknowledge the fact that we affect those around us. Annihilate you and I silence myself. I narrow down the space for my ethics as I eliminate ethics' space for play

---

51 See Nietzsche, *Thus Spoke Zarathustra*, trans. Graham Parkes (Oxford: Oxford University Press, 2009). In *Zarathustra*, the main character (Zarathustra) does precisely this – goes into extended retreat to find his own ethics and path. Again, one can sympathize with that move to the extent that society's conformities can be stultifying. Not deploying the resulting reflections for progressive purposes nonetheless seems a dubious proposition.

52 Levinas, *Totality and Infinity*, 304.

(others). Hurt me and you hurt *yourself*. You reduce your existence by condemning yourself to loneliness and the company of but the sound of your own voice (that as you limit the possibilities of those who might keep you company). Allow each other to *live*, however, and we might revitalize the meaning of *both* our lives. Not only accept but *promote* each other's existences and we might *expand* the space of humanity by expanding the space of the chance to act ethically: the meaning of human life itself.[53] *That's* what emerges at Belsen. *That's* what we get as we contemplate a camp's grounds and encounter its artifacts. That's what we gain when we travel not only to Auschwitz or Treblinka, but the many sites of the multiple experiences had within history's nadir. There are so *many* ways to close down existence. There are so *many* ways to bring life to an end and limit who we are. There are so many ways to reduce ourselves and pull the rug out from under the value all human life should have. Without negating any headline memory, we *have to* engage the multilayeredness of our most dismaying stories to gain a sense of how badly the screws can come loose – the multiple ways in which humanity's boat can spring a leak when it enters dangerous waters. *All* the tiles in the mosaic of human tragedy need to be known such that we might better understand the meaning of the freedoms for which many of us fight: participation in universal humanity and the chance to contribute to our collective existence by engaging it in the multiple ways that we do. Without understanding tragedy's particularity – the many ways in which the worst not only might be but *has been* brought to us – we're left defenseless against the numerous ways in which the space of the essence, the very essence, of human life might be narrowed: again, the chance to act ethically that only life with others can provide. We thus need to be able to see every deleterious event for the narrowing-down of life that it is – every internment and denial of basic sustenance in addition, of course, to every act of bare, explicit murder. That's so that we can hear *all* caught in the maelstrom: the calling of the sound of the many that we are as well as the singular humanity that each of us has. That's the sound of many and one: the universal humanity we maintain, yet which gains body only through singular eperience and voice.

---

53 The phraseology of "promotion" is borrowed from ibid., 199–200.

List of Illustrations

Cover: "Closeup of People Holding Candle Vigil in Darkness Seeking Hope." © ThamKC / Fotolia.com

Political and Social Change

Edited by Martin Bak Jørgensen and Óscar García Agustín

www.peterlang.com